Regional Economic Institutions and Conflict Mitigation

In addition to the explicit goal of advancing mutual economic interests, regional economic organizations (REOs) are intended to foster regional cohesion and peace. Drawing on a data set detailing the institutional features of 25 REOs established during the 1980s and 1990s, complemented by a case study of the Association of Southeast Asian Nations, Yoram Haftel investigates the factors that affect REOs' ability to mitigate interstate military conflict. Haftel finds fewer interstate conflicts among REO members who have developed high levels of economic integration and who cultivate regular interaction among member states' top government officials. Haftel concludes that with an appropriate institutional design and fully implemented agreements, an REO can indeed play a role in mitigating interstate conflict and make a meaningful contribution to regional peace.

Yoram Z. Haftel is Associate Professor of Political Science at the University of Illinois at Chicago and the Hebrew University of Jerusalem.

Michigan Studies in International Political Economy

SERIES EDITORS: Edward Mansfield, Lisa Martin, and William Clark

Michael J. Gilligan
Empowering Exporters: Reciprocity, Delegation, and Collective Action in American Trade Policy

Barry Eichengreen and Jeffry Frieden, Editors
Forging an Integrated Europe

Thomas H. Oatley
Monetary Politics: Exchange Rate Cooperation in the European Union

Robert Pahre
Leading Questions: How Hegemony Affects the International Political Economy

Andrew C. Sobel
State Institutions, Private Incentives, Global Capital

Roland Stephen
Vehicle of Influence: Building a European Car Market

William Bernhard
Banking on Reform: Political Parties and Central Bank Independence in the Industrial Democracies

William Roberts Clark
Capitalism, Not Globalism: Capital Mobility, Central Bank Independence, and the Political Control of the Economy

Edward D. Mansfield and Brian M. Pollins, Editors
Economic Interdependence and International Conflict: New Perspectives on an Enduring Debate

Kerry A. Chase
Trading Blocs: States, Firms, and Regions in the World Economy

David H. Bearce
Monetary Divergence: Domestic Policy Autonomy in the Post–Bretton Woods Era

Ka Zeng and Joshua Eastin
Greening China: The Benefits of Trade and Foreign Direct Investment

Yoram Z. Haftel
Regional Economic Institutions and Conflict Mitigation: Design, Implementation, and the Promise of Peace

Nathan M. Jensen, Glen Biglaiser, Quan Li, Edmund Malesky, Pablo M. Pinto, Santiago M. Pinto, and Joseph L. Staats
Politics and Foreign Direct Investment

Yu Zheng
Governance and Foreign Investment in China, India, and Taiwan: Credibility, Flexibility, and International Business

Regional Economic Institutions and Conflict Mitigation

*Design, Implementation, and
the Promise of Peace*

YORAM Z. HAFTEL

The University of Michigan Press
Ann Arbor

Published in the United States of America by
The University of Michigan Press
Printed and bound by CPI Group (UK) Ltd, Croydon, CR0 4YY

2017   2016   2015   2014   5   4   3   2

A CIP catalog record for this book is available from the British Library.

Library of Congress Cataloging-in-Publication Data

Haftel, Yoram Z., 1968–
    Regional economic institutions and conflict mitigation : design,
  implementation, and the promise of peace / Yoram Z. Haftel.
        p.   cm. — (Michigan studies in international political economy)
    Includes bibliographical references and index.
    ISBN 978-0-472-11834-2 (cloth : alk. paper) — ISBN 978-0-472-02844-3
  (e-book)
    1. Interregionalism.   2. International relations.   3. International
  economic integration.   4. Regional economics.   5. International
  organizations.   6. Peace.   I. Title.

JZ1320.7.H34   2012
337.1—dc23

                                                                2012005003

ISBN 978-0-472-03584-7 (pbk. : alk. paper)

To Einat

CONTENTS

CONTENTS

ACKNOWLEDGMENTS

Much like the implementation of ambitious regional economic agreements, the process of writing this book was long and occasionally frustrating but, in the end, rewarding. I have incurred intellectual and personal debts to many people and a number of institutions along the way.

I have benefited from a number of remarkable advisors who shaped my thinking as a scholar and my understanding of the issues at the core of this project. While in graduate school, Brian Pollins gave me a much-needed sense of direction. His guidance and comments greatly improved the quality of my work. Don Sylvan was never too busy to have a conversation or to give me helpful advice on academic or personal matters. David Rowe expanded my intellectual horizons and taught me how to think critically on international political economy and beyond. Alex Thompson thoroughly read everything I sent his way and offered priceless substantive and editorial comments on numerous drafts and proposals. Alex remains an indispensable source of unconditional support, sound advice, and friendship. Ed Mansfield sparked my interest in economic regionalism. His scholarly work inspired, served as a springboard for, and provided a benchmark to the research presented in the following pages. Over the years, Ed continued to offer me very useful feedback on my work, words of encouragement, and invaluable guidance.

I was also lucky to study, work, and form enduring friendships with several students, who made my graduate experience very exciting and enjoyable. My "grad school buddies" Paul Fritz and Yoav Gortzak engaged me with endless conversations that greatly enriched my thinking on and understanding of international relations. They also commented tirelessly on my work and always provided me with valuable feedback. I owe a great deal to David Bearce, Pat McDonald, and Jon Pevehouse. All three generously shared with me their knowledge and expertise on international political economy, offered numerous insights on various drafts, and on much else. They remain a source of inspiration, helpful advice, and camaraderie.

At the University of Illinois at Chicago, Doris Graber helped me improve the book proposal and navigate the publishing process. Dick Simpson provided me with encouragement, support, and much-needed time. For useful comments and advice on parts or the entirety of this book, I thank participants of Chicago's North-South Seminar, Dan Drezner, Lilach Gilady, Tim McKeown, Jennifer Mitzen, Peter Rosendorff, Duncan Snidal, Peter Trumbore, and the anonymous reviewers. I also thank Melody Herr at the University of Michigan Press for her useful suggestions and very effective management of the publication process.

Parts of chapter 2 and an earlier version of portions of chapter 5 previously appeared in "Designing for Peace: Regional Integration Arrangements, Institutional Variation, and Militarized Interstate Disputes," *International Organization* 61 (2007): 217–37. I thank Cambridge University Press for the permission to reprint parts of this article. The discussion of institutional independence in chapters 2 and 3 draws on portions of "The Independence of International Organizations: Concept and Applications," *Journal of Conflict Resolution* 50 (2006): 253–75. I thank my coauthor Alexander Thompson and Sage Publications for their permission to reprint parts of this article. I also thank the Department of Political Science and the Mershon Center at the Ohio State University and the Department of Political Science at the University of Illinois at Chicago for financial support.

Finally, I am grateful to my parents, who raised me and always stood by me. I also thank my siblings, my childhood classmates, and the greater community of Kibbutz Ze'elim for their continuous support and friendship, notwithstanding an ocean between us. My deepest gratitude goes to Einat, my wife, and to my two sons, Gillad and Ehud. Both Gillad and Ehud were born and turned from toddlers to young boys as I was writing this book. While their appearance was hardly conducive for its speedy completion, it is impossible for me to envision my life without them. The excitement and the pleasure they brought into my life made it all worthwhile. Einat left a family, a successful career, and pretty much everything else and moved with me to the American Midwest. She was then and still is a constant source of love, encouragement, and unconditional support.

CHAPTER 1

Introduction: How Regional Institutions Promote Peace

Regional conflict and war continue to plague our world. While the total number of interstate wars worldwide has fallen and while great-power war is seemingly obsolete, regional tensions remain high in many parts of the world, including sub-Saharan Africa, Southeastern Europe, and the Indian subcontinent. The wars that revolved around the Democratic Republic of Congo, recurrent violence between Israel and its Arab neighbors, and ongoing clashes between India and Pakistan illustrate this troubling development. Compounding these growing regional frictions, diminished global rivalries have reduced the willingness and ability of great powers to intervene and manage disputes that have no direct consequences for their immediate interests. In contrast, in some regions, such as Western Europe, Southeast Asia, and parts of Latin America, cross-border violent conflict has all but disappeared. These so-called zones of peace, it seems, handle regional disagreements much more effectively.

At the same time, the end of the Cold War ushered in an era of unparalleled economic interaction across national borders. The rising prominence of regional economic cooperation is one of the hallmarks of this increasingly globalized world. In particular, the proliferation of regional economic organizations (REOs) reflects the efforts of neighboring countries to regulate and institutionalize the growth of regional economic interdependence. The expansion and deepening of such organizations as the European Union (EU) and the Economic Community of West African States (ECOWAS) and the formation of new organizations, such as the North American Free Trade Agreement (NAFTA) and the Common Market of the South (Mercosur), reflect the pervasiveness of this phenomenon. Today, almost all countries are members of at least one REO, and many have multiple memberships.

While they commonly do not address security concerns directly, many of these institutions aspire to promote peace and understanding among their members. The treaty of the Common Market for Eastern and Southern Africa (COMESA), for example, states that one primary objective of the organization is "to co-operate in the promotion of peace, security and stability among the Member States in order to enhance economic development in the region."[1] Indeed, the rise of REOs is accompanied by a widespread perception that they are indispensable in reducing frictions between their members. As such, they have the potential to address regional conflict and fill the void left by the disengagement of global powers.

The view that regional institutions can promote peace is, of course, not new. It gained particular prominence with the launch of the European integration project in the wake of World War II (Mansfield 2003; Nye 1971). Six decades on, the potentially stabilizing effect of REOs is equally and perhaps even more pertinent to matters of international security. The rapid emergence of several large but still developing countries, such as Brazil, China, India, Russia, and South Africa, is transforming regional and global geopolitics. From a global perspective, these shifts reduce the ability and willingness of global powers, especially the United States, to preserve previously established orders. At the local level, the urge of newly powerful regional actors to flex their muscles leads to frictions and sometimes open conflict between them and their neighbors. Russia's attempt to affirm its influence in the "near abroad" (expressed most visibly with its 2008 assault on Georgia) and China's growing assertiveness in the South China Sea are prominent examples of this phenomenon. In both regions, these broader developments are accompanied by more localized squabbles, such as the rivalry between Armenia and Azerbaijan and an ongoing territorial dispute between Thailand and Cambodia.

Regional economic institutions are well positioned to constructively engage emerging powers in their regions and alleviate some of the negative repercussions of their ascendance. They may also be instrumental in managing potential discord between dominant and less powerful neighbors and other regional wrangles. In the prominent case of East Asia, many analysts believe that effective institutions are essential to the region's stability. The *Economist*, for example, argues that China's territorial claims and disputes between Indonesia and Malaysia and between Thailand and Cambodia are best tackled by multilateral regional forums. It adds, "The American umbrella still keeps the region safe. But it will not be rainproof forever" (Simon

Long 2010). In short, REOs can play a major role in the management of regional security in this increasingly multipolar and multilayered world.

The track record of regional institutions on tackling matters of stability and peace is decidedly mixed, however. Some REOs, such as the EU and the Association of Southeast Asian Nations (ASEAN), are credited with averting armed conflict in their regions. By contrast, the South Asian Association for Regional Cooperation (SAARC) and COMESA appear to have had little success in curbing violence. Why, then, do only some of these organizations facilitate peace? And how, specifically, do REOs that effectively mitigate conflict realize this objective? The purpose of this book is to answer these important and poorly understood questions. To do so, it explores the relationships between REOs and their design, on the one hand, and regional conflict, on the other, using original data and a combination of quantitative and qualitative methods. The key conclusion drawn from this study is that thoughtful design and, importantly, implementation thereof render REOs an effective vehicle of regional peace and security.

By shedding light on this nexus, the book offers some valuable lessons for policymakers. If the past 20 years are indicative of the foreseeable future, regional politics are likely to remain a prominent aspect of international relations. REOs can therefore expect to play a growing role in the management of regional conflict and cooperation. This study provides guidance on how to design regional institutions in order to improve their effectiveness as vehicles of peace and stability. It also identifies a number of conditions under which regional organizations are most likely to meet their goals, as well as when they are more likely to fall short of their members' aspirations. Consulting this book will allow governments, their advisors, and international agencies that promote regional cooperation to make the most of the resources devoted to these schemes. This is especially important in developing regions, where human and physical resources are in short supply.

The book also has implications for those interested in International Relations (IR) theory. The relationship between institutions and conflict has been central to debates between institutionalists and realists, with the former stressing the pacific benefits of international organizations (Keohane 1984; Russett and Oneal 2001) and with the latter doubting that they have any independent effect (Grieco 1993; Mearsheimer 1994/95; Waltz 1979). The literature on institutions has evolved substantially, and scholars today are more interested in precisely how institutions shape behavior and in how variation in institutional design matters (Acharya and Johnston 2007; Aggarwal and Koo 2008; Fortna 2004; Koremenos, Lipson, and Snidal 2001). This study incorporates these newer theoretical concerns over institutional variation and design into the age-old debate over the relationship between institutions and conflict. It also brings systematic evidence to bear on this question in the regional context. The result is a more nuanced understanding of their relationship.

The Argument: How Regional Organizations Promote Peace

REOs are a type of international governmental organization (IGO) whose membership is confined to geographically proximate states and whose core missions include economic cooperation and integration. Thus, many of these organizations endeavor to reduce barriers to the movement of goods, services, labor, and capital and to promote sectoral, financial, and industrial cooperation.[2] This book begins with the observation that despite sharing several common characteristics, REOs come in many shapes, and their ability to meet their objectives varies greatly. Some REOs, such as the European Free Trade Association (EFTA), have rather limited aims and focus almost exclusively on trade liberalization. Other organizations, such as the Gulf Cooperation Council (GCC), cover a wide range of issue areas that go well beyond trade liberalization. Similarly, the members of some REOs, such as ASEAN, largely realize their signed agreements. In other cases, such as the Economic Community of Central African States (ECCAS), members sign many more agreements than they carry out.

Like other international organizations, REOs are not merely agreements but have a permanent organizational structure. This structure often includes regular meetings among government officials, bureaucracy, working committees, and the like. Here, too, the institutional makeup of these arrangements is very diverse. Many organizations institute annual meetings of top-level policymakers. Other REOs, such as Central Asia's Economic Cooperation Organization (ECO), are managed by lower-ranked diplomats. Some REOs, such as the Andean Community (ANCOM), have an independent regional bureaucracy and judiciary. Others, such as the Southern African Customs Union (SACU), have a weak secretariat and a nonbinding dispute settlement mechanism (DSM), if they have a DSM at all.

In this book, I argue that this variation has important implications for the effectiveness of these organizations in reducing armed conflict. I develop this argument within a broader theory of conflict, commonly referred to as the rationalist theory of war (Fearon 1995; Powell 2006). This theory begins with the assumption that armed conflict is costly and that states are better off resolving their disagreements peacefully. Thus, violent disputes stem from a failed bargaining process, which may result from the parties' uncertainty regarding the interests and power of their opponents, their inability to credibly commit to peace, or issue indivisibility. As will be discussed in chapter 2, because regional organizations rarely have the capacity to commit their members not to fight, the theoretical framework emphasizes issues of information and indivisibility.

Using this approach as a springboard to explore the relationships between REOs and armed conflict offers a number of advantages. Thinking about violent conflict as one step in an interstate bargaining dynamic calls attention to the factors that lead to escalation and war (or not). In particular, this theory highlights the difficulties involved in sharing believable information, striking a mutually acceptable bargain, and making a credible commitment under conditions of anarchy, which is endemic to world politics. It thus shows that even if states do not intend to resort to arms, they may find themselves fighting. Making a handful of reasonable assumptions, this approach provides a logical and coherent framework to contemplate the causes of violent conflict and, in turn, to identify potential solutions to these problems.

Building on these foundations, I identify three specific mechanisms by which REOs can reduce uncertainty, widen the bargaining range, and thus improve the prospects of peace. First, these organizations facilitate long-term economic cooperation to the benefit of their members, thus raising the cost of any conflict that could jeopardize these joint gains and opening up room for otherwise unfeasible compromise. Second, REOs foster communication and exchange of reliable information between member states. This, in turn, reduces the risk of miscalculation of the opponent's strength or its willingness to fight and helps disputants build mutual trust. Third, REOs serve as a medium for negotiations, especially through third-party mediation or adjudication. Third parties associated with the organization can be instrumental in identifying an acceptable middle ground, in introducing creative solutions to difficult problems, and in pressuring both sides to resolve their conflict amicably.

These causal mechanisms are linked to three institutional features typical to regional economic organizations. The *scope of economic activity*, which refers to the breadth and depth of economic cooperation, advances peace by increasing the opportunity cost of conflict, smoothing tough bargaining through issue linkage, and providing member states with more ways to interact peacefully. Recurrent regional diplomatic summits, labeled *regular meetings of high-level officials,* are instrumental in improving communication between member states and providing an effective forum for third-party mediation. *Institutional independence*—embodied in the *corporate bureaucracy* and *dispute settlement mechanism*—fosters peace through mediation, adjudication, and the provision of information. Here, however, a number of convincing counterpoints indicate that the relations between the independence of REOs and violent disputes may be weak. It especially appears that greater neutrality and strong preference for regional peace, which are associated with greater independence, actually undermine the effectiveness of would-be mediators or adjudicators.

I also consider the cumulative effect of the individual design features when bundled under one institutional umbrella, which I label *regional institutionalization.* I argue that greater opportunities for issue linkage amplify the pacifying role of the separate components it subsumes. Taken as a whole, the theoretical discussion indicates that to grasp the relationships between REOs and violent conflict, one has to take into account both the type and degree of institutionalization. Finally, the theoretical framework highlights the need to go beyond institutional design and account for the extent of *implementation* of agreements on which such regional organizations are founded. Specifically, I contend that in order for REOs to promote peace, member states have to follow up on their promises and put them into practice.

By the term *implementation,* I refer to the "adoption of domestic rules or regulations that are meant to facilitate, but do not in themselves constitute, compliance with international agreements" (Simmons 1998, 77–78).[3] Integrating implementation into the analysis is essential, because implementation is neither automatic nor mechanical. Rather, it is often a politically charged process, in which governments may attempt to evade their commitments or be slow to honor their pledges. Given the wide gap between words and action in many regional organizations, especially in the developing world, this issue is of great significance. Notably, despite broad scholarly recognition of this reality, almost no study examines the implementation of international institutions in a rigorous manner. By accounting for REOs as they exist both on paper and on the ground, this book takes a first step to address this oversight.

This book, like any other work that makes claims about the effect of international institutions, must consider their endogenous nature; that is, international institutions, REOs among them, are created and utilized by states in order to serve their common interests. Subject to human manipulation, they are therefore designed by and operate in accordance with the goals and expectations of their members (Koremenos, Lipson, and Snidal 2001). Thus, to the extent that one observes a positive association between regional institutionalization or particular institutional features, on the one hand, and peace, on the other, one should proceed with caution to assert that the former causes the latter. It may be the case that some underlying conditions, such as a shared political orientation, foster both high levels of institutionalized cooperation and peaceful coexistence. Here, both phenomena are caused by a third factor, making them spurious. It is also possible that only states that already enjoy durable peace would engage in meaningful cooperation—in other words, that cause and effect are reversed. Perhaps REOs are likely to flourish where peace is already ingrained, and perhaps they have little prospect in war-prone regions, where they are most needed.

I tackle this issue head-on by pointing out that states simultaneously shape international institutions—through their creation and design—and are constrained by them in their behavior and interactions. The reason governments form and implement international organizations and bargain hard over their design is precisely because they believe that they have lasting consequences. This perspective indicates that the relationships between REOs and conflict hinge on their members' wants and expectations.

It is conceivable that states will hesitate to engage in long-term cooperation with their adversaries. It is also possible, however, that neighboring states that face a greater risk of conflict will invest in regional institutions exactly because they anticipate their pacifying effects. The formation of the European Coal and Steel Community (ECSC) shortly after World War II and the membership of both India and Pakistan in SAARC are two examples of states with a long and bitter history of conflict that nonetheless engage in economic cooperation through regional institutions. Given these indeterminate theoretical expectations, I argue that this issue is best tackled empirically by accounting for factors that can potentially explain both regional institutionalization and peace, as well as by investigating the effect of militarized disputes on institutionalized cooperation.

Methodology and Findings

This book's arguments are evaluated with a combination of quantitative and qualitative methods. Specifically, I employ a mixed-method strategy in which an in-depth case study is nested in and complements the statistical analysis (Lieberman 2005; also see Tarrow 1995).

The quantitative analysis employs an original data set that contains detailed information on the planned activities, their implementation, and the institutional structure of 25 REOs in the 1980s and 1990s.[4] This set of organizations spans five continents and a large number of developed and developing countries. It provides a panoramic view of regional economic institutions before and after the end of Cold War. With this data set, I generate a number of variables that correspond to the theoretical institutional dimensions discussed in chapter 2. I then employ regression techniques to assess the effect of regional institutionalization and specific features (designed and implemented) on regional armed disputes.

The setup of the data set used in the statistical analysis is unconventional with respect to two features. First, because the focus of the analysis shifts from mere membership in any international organization to the characteristics of the organizations themselves, the REO serves as the unit of analysis. This setup diverges from the setups of most extant studies of interstate conflict, which focus on either a country pair (dyadic) or an individual country (monadic). My approach glosses over some of the differences among REO members and their bilateral relationships. At the same time, it captures some important regional dynamics that cannot be easily reduced to domestic factors or bilateral interaction. The trade-offs between the regional setup used here and more conventional setups suggest that we treat these alternative approaches as complementary rather than competing.

From a broader perspective, the emphasis on the regional level of analysis meshes well with a number of recent studies that bring the region back to the center of IR scholarship (Buzan and Wæver 2003; Gleditsch 2002; Kacowicz 1998; Katzenstein 2005; Lake and Morgan 1997; Solingen 1998). Like these works, this book takes the position that all states are simultaneously part of one global system and of subglobal, geographically circumscribed systems. These regional systems, or complexes, are affected by the interplay of global and local forces (Acharya 2007; Buzan and Wæver 2003, 45). Thus, while global power politics always lurk in the background, geographical proximity remains a powerful source of international interaction, both positive and negative. This book sheds new light on these often overlooked dynamics.

The second distinctive aspect of the setup is that data on the institutionalization of REOs is collected every five years. As a consequence, other variables are aggregated over five-year periods. This arrangement differs from most current statistical studies, in which data is commonly aggregated annually. As discussed in chapter 3 in greater detail, I collected data on 29 indicators related to the design of REOs for 25 organizations at up to four time points, resulting in over 2,600 data points. Moreover, for the 24 indicators that pertain to actual policies, I also assessed their degree of implementation, which is often gradual and uneven.[5]

The fine-grained depiction of activities and institutional structure that this effort provides goes well beyond extant efforts to describe and analyze either differences across REOs or international institutions more generally, which only look at their design on paper and at one point in time (Boehmer, Gartzke, and Nordstrom 2004; Koremenos 2005; Smith 2000). Facing the trade-off between many observations that provide an incomplete picture of existing REOs and fewer observations that offer a much richer description of current regional economic institutions, this book adopts the latter approach. Here, again, it complements studies that employ less granular data in tandem with annual setups. Furthermore, to make the most of this data collection effort, I build on the statistical results to carry a large-N qualitative analysis. Here, I contrast regions with similar levels of risk for armed conflict but different levels of institutionalization. This comparison points to some of the conditions under which REOs promote peace.

As pointed out in the previous section, REOs are formed by their members in order to achieve some specific goals. To the extent that one finds a positive association between these institutions and peace, one should consider the endogenous nature of the former before making claims regarding their causal effect. I take several steps to increase confidence that the statistical correlations reported in this study are not artifacts of other dynamics. First, the statistical models include several control variables that might account for both institutionalized cooperation and violent conflict, such as the distribution power, regime type, and commercial interdependence. Insofar as these factors drive economic and security relations, the effect of regional institutionalization ought to fade away. To address concerns of reversed causality, I first measure institutional variables prior to the eruption of violent conflict. Second, I conduct statistical tests to identify the determinants of regional institutionalization and its components. This analysis pays particular attention to the potential impact of militarized disputes on economic cooperation, but it also sheds light on the sources of variation across current REOs. It thus provides a more complete account of regional interstate political processes.

One more way to cast light on this complex matter is through an in-depth case study. The qualitative analysis in this book provides an evaluation of cooperation and conflict in the ASEAN region. The primary objective of this investigation is to further test the effect of variation in REOs on interstate violent conflict and to put a magnifying glass on the causal processes by which their functions and structure bring peace (or not). Given the limitations of the statistical analysis and the risks of endogeneity, spuriousness, and selection effects, additional evidence on the robustness of the results can increase confidence in the causal claims made in this study (George and Bennett 2005; Gerring 2004). The recent history of Southeast Asia provides an excellent testing ground in this respect.

Lieberman (2005) identifies two primary criteria for selecting cases for purposes of theory testing. First, one ought to select a case that the quantitative models predict well. The case can either substantiate or challenge causal assertions that are made based on correlational evidence. As shown in chapter 4, the ASEAN case fits the regression model quite well. The historical narrative also traces the causal processes by which institutional variables affect conflict. For example, the statistical results find a strong association between regular meetings of high-level officials and peace. The willingness of top officials to meet is likely to be contingent on the political relations in the region, however. In addition, such regular meetings may promote peace through a number of mechanisms, such as the provision of information, mediation, and socialization. ASEAN provides ample support for the claim that regular meetings among foreign ministers and heads of state indeed mitigated violent conflict, and it casts light on the manner by which they did so.

Second, the case should display as much variation as possible on the explanatory variables. This variation allows the researcher "to demonstrate the nature of the predicted causal effect associated with the model in contrasting contexts" (Lieberman 2005, 444). ASEAN meets this demand remarkably well. Attempts to promote regional economic cooperation through international organizations in the region date back to the early 1960s and continue to this day. The evolution of this cooperation, mainly through ASEAN, has been bumpy and uneven. Some time periods were marked by institutional growth and development, while others were typified by stagnation and declining effectiveness. Moreover, during the same period, tensions between Southeast Asian countries have persisted. In some instances, such disagreements were resolved peacefully, but they occasionally resulted in violent clashes. The qualitative analysis therefore complements the statistical findings by fostering a comparison of regional security relations before and after the formation of ASEAN and during times of institutional change. In addition, the case analysis is extended into the 2000s, a time period not covered in the statistical part of this study.

The findings reported in subsequent chapters offer strong empirical support for the theoretical framework and underscore the benefits of a nuanced institutional analysis. Accounting for a host of alternative explanations, the quantitative analysis indicates that a wider scope of economic activity, regular meetings among high-level officials, and the aggregate level of regional institutionalization, *when implemented,* mitigate violent conflict. The pacifying effect of regional bureaucracy, adjudication, and unrealized agreements, however, appears weak. The ASEAN case further substantiates these findings and casts additional light on the complex relationships between international organizations and peace. It shows that the evolution of the organization reflected regional political realities and, at the same time, shaped security relations among its members. Despite a widely held view of ASEAN as a political organization, the features that address security matters directly did little to mitigate conflict. Regular meetings among high-level officials and institutionalized economic cooperation, it appears, were more instrumental in fostering peace.

If we pay close attention to endogeneity and reversed causality in the quantitative and qualitative analyses, the findings indicate that such concerns should not be exaggerated. In most instances, militarized disputes do not systemically affect the design and implementation of REOs. In a notable exception, armed conflicts are associated with more, rather than less, institutional independence and legalization. This finding corroborates the view that conflict creates demand for institutions. In addition, while regional institutions are driven by the interests of and interaction among their members, their impact is real and considerable. Thus, the ability of REOs to shape security relations among their members is genuine.

The Study of Regional Institutions and Peace

The study of international organizations, regional integration, and conflict provides the theoretical underpinning for this book. Disagreements regarding the consequences of cooperation through international organizations for questions of war and peace are at the heart of theoretical debates in IR. At one end, some realists dismiss international institutions as no more than window dressing for the interests of their most powerful members. They thus reject the notion that institutions, regardless of their type, structure, or purpose, can inhibit violent conflict (Mearsheimer 1994/95; Waltz 1979). More moderate—sometimes dubbed "defensive"—realists have a more nuanced view of international institutions. They believe that institutions can promote cooperation but that their contribution is modest, conditional, and hinges on the willingness of states to cooperate in the first place (Glaser 1994/95, 84–85; Jervis 1999). Despite having some limited faith in the ability of institutions to improve security relations, defensive realists rarely pay attention to different institutional features and how they affect conflict and cooperation.

At the other end of the debate, institutionalists of different stripes have a much greater faith in the power of international institutions to leave their mark on world politics. Early institutional analyses, most notably those applying functionalism and neofunctionalism, advanced the notion that technical cooperation through international organizations can potentially spill over to political cooperation and eventually restrain aggression and war (Haas 1964; Mitrany 1946).[6] Indeed, this line of reasoning spurred the formation of the ECSC in the early 1950s. Despite the initial appeal of this logic, it suffered from a number of weaknesses. It offered little guidance on the specific manners by which cooperation on technical problems may spill over to politically sensitive matters, such as international security. It also overestimated the power of supranational and subnational actors and failed to appreciate the lasting influence of the nation-state (Moravcsik 1998). As the political impediments faced by regional projects in Europe and around the world during the 1960s and 1970s exposed these limitations, this approach was largely discarded.

Following the pathbreaking work of Karl Deutsch and his collaborators (1957), constructivists argue that regional organizations play an important role in the creation of pluralist security communities. According to them, these communities shape the identities of their members, facilitate mutual trust and shared norms, and render armed conflict inconceivable (Acharya 2001; Adler and Barnett 1998). This research program has yet to offer a detailed account of the ways by which international institutions socialize their members and to identify the institutional facets that matter.[7] Empirically, evidence of socialization is scant even in the context of the highly institutionalized EU (Checkel 2007; Hooghe 2005).

The "regime theory" of the 1980s brought international institutions back to the center of IR analysis. Not losing sight of the enduring relevance of power, politics, and states, this approach promotes the idea that international institutions do make a difference by facilitating cooperation and communication among their self-interested members (Keohane 1984). But the application of this theory was largely confined to cooperation on economic, rather than security, issues. It also paid insufficient attention to the structure and functions of different institutions and regimes. More recent research has begun to correct this shortcoming by investigating the sources and consequences of institutional design (Acharya and Johnston 2007; Koremenos, Lipson, and Snidal 2001; Smith 2000). These studies, too, examine a variety of issue areas but overlook the implications of institutional differences for questions of war and peace. Nonetheless, the insights offered by this body of work provide some key elements in the theoretical edifice of this study.

In the liberal tradition, the research program based on the three Kantian foundations of world peace offers the most systematic inquiry into the links between international institutions and conflict. Building on Immanuel Kant's proposition that international law is an important building block of a lasting world peace, some scholars argue that international institutions mitigate violent conflict (Mansfield and Pevehouse 2000; Mansfield, Pevehouse, and Bearce 1999/2000; Russett and Oneal 2001; Russett, Oneal, and Davis 1998).[8] The main contribution of these studies is to empirically assess the effect of international organizations and trade agreements on armed conflict in a rigorous manner. This research points to several potential mechanisms by which these arrangements facilitate peace, but it stops short of developing a thorough theoretical framework and of linking these mechanisms to specific institutional features.

The empirical relationships between international institutions and conflict are not well understood. Early attempts to evaluate this link are inconclusive. One sophisticated qualitative study concludes that regional organizations do mitigate conflict but that their effect is probably small (Nye 1971). Preliminary quantitative analyses found little empirical support for the pacifying effect of international organizations (Domke 1988; Singer and Wallace 1970). More recent studies, which employ more advanced methods and more comprehensive data sets but treat international organizations as homogenous, have produced mixed results. Some studies find that international institutions reduce conflict (Dorussen and Ward 2008; Mansfield, Pevehouse, and Bearce 1999/2000; Russett and Oneal 2001; and Russett, Oneal, and Davis 1998), others find that their pacifying effect is conditional on other factors (Mansfield and Pevehouse 2000; Pevehouse and Russett 2006), and still others find no such effect (Gartzke, Li, and Boehmer 2001; Oneal and Russett 1999). These inconsistencies point to the limits of empirical analyses—even highly sophisticated ones—that overlook the diverse landscape of current international institutions.

A handful of recent studies have begun to unpack this variation and look inside these institutions to draw out specific features that make a difference. Boehmer, Gartzke, and Nordstrom (2004) classify international organizations according to their mandate and three levels of institutionalization. They find that organizations that are highly structured or have a security mandate are instrumental in promoting peace. A few studies build on the classification of Boehmer and his colleagues, as well as on a distinction between passive and active organizations, to explore the contingent effect of IGOs on the peaceful settlement of territorial disputes (Hansen, Mitchell, and Nemeth 2008; Mitchell and Hensel 2007; Shannon 2009). They, too, indicate that active and highly institutionalized IGOs are more effective in promoting peace than passive and weakly institutionalized ones. Finally, Bearce and Omori (2005) take a first-cut look at the relationship between the design of regional integration arrangements and conflict. Their findings indicate that regular meetings of high-level officials are the only feature that mitigates conflict. These studies greatly improve on previous analyses, but they, too, pay insufficient attention to specific institutional characteristics and their implementation. This book joins and expands on this growing body of research.

The purpose of this book is not to rehash worn-out debates between realists, liberals, and constructivists with respect to the general significance of international institutions. With few exceptions, most students of international institutions agree that they are a product of their members' preferences and existing constraints and opportunists and, at the same time, that they can have a genuine and sometimes noticeable impact on international politics. The challenge is therefore not to show that international institutions matter but, rather, to illuminate the manner and conditions under which they do so (Martin and Simmons 1998). Building on some of the latest theoretical and empirical advancements in the field, this book takes on this challenge by bringing considerations of institutional design and implementation to the center of the analysis. It is perhaps the first scholarly work to integrate a broad comparative perspective and a detailed institutional analysis to the study of the link between regional cooperation and violent conflict.

Organization of the Book

Chapter 2 presents the theoretical framework. Using the rationalist theory of war as a springboard, it identifies three causal paths by which regional integration arrangements reduce conflict, labeled the *opportunity cost mechanism,* the *information mechanism,* and the *conflict management mechanism.* It also considers one causal path that goes beyond rationalist explanations, labeled the *socialization mechanism.* It then links peace to a number of important REO features through some or all of these mechanisms. The discussion draws attention to the different ways by which specific institutional elements may or may not reduce conflict. It also highlights the benefit of synergy between the separate design features and the essential role of implementation in promoting regional peace. The theoretical development of these links builds on several research areas, some of which, such as the study of diplomacy and mediation, have not been considered before in this context. Taking into account issues of endogeneity and reversed causality, this chapter indicates that the link between regional institutionalization and intraregional peace has firm theoretical foundations.

Chapter 3 takes a closer look at the empirical landscape of regional economic organizations. It provides a framework to systematically compare these institutions with respect to their design, level of institutionalization, and degree of implementation. This conceptualization facilitates operational definition and measurement of the features theorized to mitigate conflict. The chapter then describes the original data set coded according to these guidelines. This description underscores the significant institutional variation across the organizations included in the data set.

Chapter 4 presents the first part of the quantitative analysis. It is concerned with aggregate levels of regional institutionalization and pays particular attention to the distinction between agreements on paper and their realization. It explains and justifies the research design used to assess the effect of REOs, taken as a whole, on militarized disputes. The results indicate that more institutionalized organizations mitigate intraregional violence, but only to the extent that they are implemented. Agreements that remain "dead letters" are of little value. These findings are used as a springboard for a more fine-grained analysis of the link between regional institutionalization and conflict. It offers additional support for the initial findings and points to the conditions under which implemented regional institutionalization reduces violent conflict.

Chapter 5 contains the second part of the quantitative analysis. It evaluates the pacifying effect of separate design features and empirically addresses concerns of reversed causality. The findings reveal a robust pacifying effect for greater economic scope and more frequent meetings at the highest levels, when implemented. However, the effects of regional bureaucracies and DSMs appear weak. These results highlight the analytical advantage afforded by the appreciation of institutional design. The chapter then examines the sources of variation across REOs. This analysis sheds light on the factors that lead to the establishment of specific design features and the level of regional institutionalization. In so doing, it provides a more complete picture of the relationships between interests, institutions, and conflict. The findings indicate that while the functions and structure of REOs are affected by a number of international and domestic factors, prior violent conflict is, for the most part, not one of them. From this perspective, the results indicate that REOs are not mere reflections of preexisting peaceful relationships. In fact, armed disputes tend to spur greater legalization of regional DSMs.

Chapter 6 examines the Southeast Asian history of violent conflict and regional integration over the last five decades in light of the theoretical framework. It is centered on the role of ASEAN in mitigating conflict among its members. This case study casts light on the pacifying role of REOs in conflict-prone regions and on the specific mechanisms by which they advance tranquility. It underlines the constructive role played by top-level face-to-face meetings and by the growing economic interdependence among the members of ASEAN. Given lingering frictions in the region, exposed most recently by the Thai-Cambodian border dispute, these findings indicate that the organization should manage such disagreements by further deepening economic cooperation among its members and by maintaining its commitment to frequent and informal high-level meetings. Echoing the quantitative analysis and the mixed theoretical expectations, the organization's bureaucracy and dispute settlement bodies appeared to play a secondary role in this respect. Keeping in mind that ASEAN has an important security component, chapter 6 considers this institutional aspect as well. It finds that formal security cooperation played only a secondary role in regional politics. The examination of reversed causality and alternative explanations reveals that the effect of conflict on regional institutions varied across time and context and that both phenomena interact with additional factors in an intricate manner. Finally, this narrative points to some empirical complexities that call for further refinement of the theoretical framework, and it offers a fresh angle on the hotly debated role of ASEAN in the region's security relations.

Chapter 7 presents conclusions regarding the overall argument and the specific hypotheses presented in chapter 2. It highlights the manners by which regional institutions mitigate armed disputes and underscores the need to account for the diverse institutional configuration of these organizations. It also draws policy implications for how regional peace can be crafted through economic and political organizations. In particular, it argues that the implementation of signed agreements is essential for the promotion of regional peace.

CHAPTER 2
Theorizing Institutional Design and Conflict

Geographical proximity commonly gives rise to recurrent interaction that can be either amicable or antagonistic. Neighboring countries have an interest in mutually beneficial cooperation, and in an anarchical international system, they also have to worry about the potential harmful implications of disagreement and conflict. What can adjacent countries do to reduce the risk of violent conflict and war? This chapter advances the argument that economic cooperation through regional institutions can facilitate peaceful coexistence in several ways: it increases the opportunity cost of violent conflict, reduces uncertainty with respect to intentions and resolve, builds trust between governmental officials, and offers a channel for a peaceful management of outstanding disagreements. Importantly, the deeper and wider the cooperation—here labeled *regional institutionalization*—the greater the contribution to regional peace and stability. The first and main part of this chapter elaborates on the specific ways by which regional institutionalization mitigates violent conflict. Table 2.1 summarizes the hypotheses developed in this part.

The second part of this chapter is devoted to the issue of endogeneity. Like other international institutions and organizations, REOs are created and designed by states in order to advance some specific objectives. It is therefore important to separate the effects of REOs from the circumstances that led to their creation in the first place. In particular, because international institutions reflect the preferences of their members over a desired outcome, association between institutionalization and peace may emanate from preexisting mutual trust and common interests. As a consequence, institutionalized cooperation is likely to bloom where peace already flourishes, but such cooperation has little prospect in war-prone regions, where it is most needed. A counterargument can be made, however. Adjacent countries that face greater risk of conflict may make greater efforts to forge regional institutions exactly because they anticipate their pacifying effect. The statement that institutions reflect preferences over outcome is thus true but of limited theoretical utility. The more important task, I argue, is to identify the interests, opportunities, and constraints that shape regional institutions and to incorporate them into the theoretical and empirical analyses.

Regional Institutionalization and the Risk of Conflict

A study that aspires to uncover the causes of peaceful coexistence has to begin with a theory of conflict. Neighboring countries sometimes disagree on various issues that may include control over territory, natural resources, population, and the like. Only occasionally, however, do these disagreements escalate into an armed dispute. Why do governments resort to violence in some instances but not in others? I employ the widely used bargaining framework to answer this question.[1] In a very influential study, James Fearon (1995) argues that war erupts only when governments fail to strike a deal by other means.[2] This assertion is rooted in a number of important assumptions. First, interstate violence is a very costly endeavor. Regardless of their outcome, military confrontations commonly require substantial material and human sacrifice from the battling parties involved.

TABLE 2.1. Summary of Hypotheses with Respect to the Effect of Regional Institutionalization on Violent Conflict

	Hypothesis	Mechanisms	Expected Effect on Violent Conflict
H0	International institutions and/or their specific features		None
H1	Scope of economic activity	Opportunity cost information	Decrease
H2	Regular meetings of high-level officials	Conflict management information (socialization)	Decrease
H3	Institutional independence—corporate bureaucracy	Conflict management information	Decrease
H4	Institutional independence—dispute settlement mechanism	Conflict management information	Decrease
H5	Regional institutionalization	Opportunity cost conflict management information (socialization)	Decrease

Second, states are rational; that is, they engage in a cost-benefit analysis and prefer alternatives that are less costly, as well as risk averse.[3] Finally, there is a bargaining range that allows for a peaceful settlement of the dispute. Taken together, these assumptions indicate that states are better off using nonviolent means to negotiate the same bargain arrived at militarily. In other words, war is inefficient in the sense that both sides could use alternative and less costly policies to reach the war outcome. Fearon points to three general reasons that may lead to armed conflict nevertheless.

First and foremost, states lack complete information on the power and intentions of their potential rivals. Because states have an incentive to conceal their true capabilities and resolve, other states sometimes miscalculate the costs and benefits of violent conflict. Too rosy expectations or too gloomy fears may, in turn, lead to escalation and violence that both parties would rather avoid. Second, disputes over indivisible issues result in an all-or-nothing outcome and thus violate the assumption that states can split their differences (not necessarily equally). Proponents of the bargaining framework tend to discount the significance of indivisibility, however. They contend that very few issues, if any, are inherently indivisible and that a bargaining range can almost always be devised—for example, through issue linkage (Fearon 1995; Powell 2006). Third, even if states are well informed and a peaceful settlement can be reached, states may fail to credibly commit to this agreement. If states do not trust their counterparts to abide by the agreement, they will prefer to fight rather than strike a deal. Problems of commitment arise when there is a clear advantage for a first strike, when the balance of power (rapidly) shifts over time, and when the contested issue affects the future bargaining position of the parties.

These three sources of conflict call for different solutions. The risk of miscalculation is best mitigated by the exchange of credible information regarding capabilities and resolve. The problem of indivisibility can be rectified by the creation and expansion of a bargaining range that is conducive to deal making and compromise. Key strategies involve issue linkage, which increases the cost of armed conflicts or the benefits of peaceful settlements. While proponents of the rationalist framework view the making of a bargaining space as unproblematic, this undertaking often requires careful and creative conflict management (Gilady and Russett 2002). The inability to credibly commit to peace can be addressed by calling on a third-party to enforce the agreement or by devising a mechanism that transfers resources from one party to the other. I argue that regional institutionalization reduces the peril of violent conflict in three specific manners that address challenges related to information and indivisibility but not credible commitments.

First, institutionalized cooperation confers member states with economic and political benefits that they have to forgo if their relationships deteriorate. Thus, more intense cooperation increases the cost of conflict and decreases its net benefits (if we hold the expected gains from aggression fixed). These growing costs, in turn, broaden the range of possible settlements, render the dispute more tractable, and make a peaceful solution more likely (Polachek and Xiang 2010). I refer to this factor as the *opportunity cost mechanism*. Second, greater institutionalization provides believable information on the interests and resolve of other member states. As a consequence, it lowers the risk of misperceptions and miscalculations that may lead to mutually undesirable hostilities. I refer to this factor as the *information mechanism*. Third, greater institutionalization is conducive to bilateral negotiations as well as third-party mediation and adjudication. These strategies expand the menu of feasible solutions and thus make the disputed issue more divisible and workable. I refer to this factor as the *conflict management mechanism*.

Before proceeding to a more detailed discussion of these mechanisms, it is worth noting that they are not grounded in the logic of credible commitments. As pointed out already, solutions to this problem are very demanding and require "some third party capable of guaranteeing agreements" (Fearon 1995, 405). Most, if not all, regional organizations lack the authority and do not marshal the capabilities necessary to transfer resources from one member to its counterparts or to compel their members to abide by peace agreements. As Gilady and Russett (2002, 404) point out, conflicts where problems of credible commitments are present call for "a high level of commitment by the mediator, a level usually more appealing to great powers who can afford it."

European integration is perhaps the only contemporary exception to this general rule. Eilstrup-Sangiovanni and Verdier (2005; see also Eilstrup-Sangiovanni 2008) argue that, indeed, the ECSC and subsequent economic arrangements facilitated a solution to the "German problem." Specifically, they contend that these institutions were designed to constrain German economic and military growth by freezing the postwar balance of power. Even they conclude, however, that "the coal and steel pool was less efficient in terms of equalizing industrial growth than expected" (Eilstrup-Sangiovanni and Verdier 2005, 120).[4] There can be little doubt that other, less institutionalized REOs have the capacity and authority to commit their members to regional peace in a credible manner.

With this caveat in mind, the remainder of this section examines the manners by which three fundamental components of regional institutionalization—namely, economic scope, regular meetings of high-level officials, and institutional independence—foster peace between members of regional economic organizations. It also considers the additional benefits of incorporating these three aspects together. Each individual component is loosely linked to some of the causal mechanisms previously mentioned. Specifically, economic scope fosters peace mainly through the opportunity cost mechanism but also has an informational effect; regular meetings of high-level officials reduce conflict through the information mechanism as well as the conflict management mechanism; and institutional independence fosters dispute resolution primarily through conflict management and secondarily through the provision of information. Regional institutionalization, which subsumes the three design features, operates through all the causal mechanisms (see table 2.1).

The Scope of Economic Activity

Regional cooperation and integration are commonly associated with the liberalization of international trade. Most REOs, however, address a number of economic issues that go above and beyond international commerce. These organizations may promote the free movement of labor and capital, monetary integration, and economic development. They may also increase the collective bargaining power of the group members vis-à-vis other economic powers. The scope of economic activity refers to the breadth and depth of the issue areas covered by the REO (this concept and its components are described in much greater detail in chapter 3). The pacifying role of the scope of economic activity can be best understood within the context of the broader debate on the link between economic interdependence and conflict.

Economic Interdependence and Peace

The claim that economic relations promote peace can be dated to such eighteenth- and nineteenth-century liberal intellectuals as Immanuel Kant, John Stuart Mill, Thomas Paine, and Richard Cobden (McDonald 2009,

36–39; Russett and Oneal 2001, 127–29). The thesis put forward by these thinkers is straightforward: international commerce benefits all parties involved; violent conflict interrupts international commerce; hence, the stronger the economic ties between two countries are, the higher the opportunity costs of conflict are, and the less likely it is that leaders would be willing to assume these costs. Cobden (1868, 294) nicely illustrates this line of reasoning.

> This commerce, unparalleled in magnitude, between two remote nations [England and America], demands no armament as its guide or safeguard: nature itself is both. And will one rational mind recognise the possibility of these two communities putting a sudden stop to such friendly traffic, and, contrary to every motive of self-interest, encountering each other as enemies? Such a rupture would be more calamitous to England than the sudden drying up of the Thames; and more intolerable to America than the cessation of sunshine and rain over the entire surface of one of her maritime states.

This logic is echoed by more recent scholars (Crescenzi 2005; Polachek 1980; Russett and Oneal 2001). Summing up the significance of this argument, a recent review states that it "has been a centerpiece of liberal views on war for centuries" (Mansfield and Pollins 2003, 3).[5] The potential pacifying effect of interdependence on conflict was not lost on practitioners, as two examples illustrate. The U.S. efforts to "engage" China—a cornerstone of American foreign policy in the 1990s and 2000s—are grounded in the belief that integrating China into the global economy will have a moderating effect on this rising power. As President Clinton pointed out, it is "in our interest to bring the Chinese people more and more fully into the global trading system to get the benefits and share the responsibilities of emerging economic prosperity."[6] Similarly, the initial rationale for European economic integration was firmly rooted in the belief that economic interaction will constrain aggressive instincts in continental Europe (Diez, Albert, and Stetter 2008; Eilstrup-Sangiovanni 2008; Mattli 1999, 69). The objectives of the founders of European integration—like Jean Monnet and Robert Schuman—are especially relevant here, as they inspired and were emulated by many regional institutions around the world.

Building on these theoretical foundations, I argue that, indeed, economic regionalism promotes economic interdependence and increases the opportunity cost of violent conflict. REOs commonly commit their members to the liberalization of trade in goods and services as well as of labor and capital markets. Presumably, these liberalization efforts result in greater economic specialization and higher levels of cross-border trade, investment, and labor movements (Baier and Bergstrand 2007; Büthe and Milner 2008). Some REOs go beyond the elimination of cross-border barriers and allow for the pooling of national resources. These may involve a common external tariff, monetary coordination, collective bargaining power, joint industrial projects, and other forms of cooperation. These schemes provide member states with benefits that they cannot obtain separately, thus promoting mutual dependence.

Since belligerents commonly suspend normal economic relations, seal off their borders, and impose economic sanctions, they are likely to forgo the gains that international trade (Polachek 1980, 60; Polachek and Xiang 2010), foreign investment (Gartzke, Li, and Boehmer 2001; Rosecrance and Thompson 2003), and other areas of functional cooperation accrue. One recent study concludes that territorial disputes—which are common between proximate countries—result in substantial economic losses to the combating parties (Simmons 2005b). From this perspective, REO members that benefit from their cooperation have an incentive to resolve their differences peacefully (Mansfield, Pevehouse, and Bearce 1999/2000; Mansfield and Pevehouse 2000). As Joseph Nye (1971, 110) points out, "The higher each disputant's level of interest in the other disputant's welfare, the greater the incentives to resort to non-violent forms of settlement of dispute." In the language of the bargaining framework, greater economic interdependence expands the negotiation space and the prospects of a diplomatic solution to conflict.

REOs and Future Gains

Economic cooperation and integration through regional institutions not only confers immediate benefits but also increases the members' confidence that they will continue to reap these gains in the future. REOs provide an institutional framework that helps to ensure that economic exchange between their members will be steady, predictable, and less volatile (Mansfield and Reinhardt 2008). Such a framework is likely to boost the confidence of private businesses in the stability of access to markets in neighboring member states (Mansfield and Pevehouse 2000, 780). Therefore, institutionalized economic interdependence will lead policymakers to expect an increasing stream of benefits in the future. This is not a trivial matter, as the future expectations of benefits may well determine policymakers' willingness to go to war (Bearce 2003; Copeland 1996; Mansfield 2003). For example, in the aftermath of a 1995 clash between Peru and Ecuador, the two parties, with the assistance of their neighbors, signed several agreements that were expected to generate substantial gains. Simmons (2005a, 244) argues that the current amity between the two countries is a consequence of "forward-looking institutional arrangements that hold out some hope of future stream of benefits to continued cooperation." More generally, Copeland (1996, 41) points out that "international institutions may help reinforce the chances for peace: insofar as these institutions solidify future expectations about the future, they reduce the incentive for aggression." In short, the shadow of the future increases the opportunity cost of violent conflict and the incentive to locate a peaceful solution to contested issues.

Importantly, the scope of economic activity can be substantial in some cases but rather limited in others. Some REOs, like the EU and the Gulf Cooperation Council (GCC), tackle a large number of economic issues. Others, like ECO and the Arab Maghreb Union (AMU), address fewer issues or fail to implement their stated objectives (Page 2000b). In addition, on the whole, greater cooperation provides greater benefits to participating members (I discuss distributional concerns shortly). In the area of trade—the most studied element of REOs—empirical research indicates that greater liberalization is associated with higher trade flows. Those REOs that embraced ambitious reductions of trade barriers (e.g., ASEAN) and those REOs that went beyond cutting tariffs and eliminated nontariff barriers or established a common external tariff (e.g., the EU, Mercosur, and ANCOM) were more effective than other REOs in boosting international commerce (Foroutan 1998; Frankel 1997; World Bank 2000). The implications of the argument based on opportunity costs are thus straightforward for the variation in the scope of economic activity. The wider the scope of an REO and the more intense the cooperation in any particular issue area are, the greater are the gains member states have to forgo if they choose to engage in violent conflict. Thus, REOs that offer more economic advantages for their members are more likely to restrain aggression.

Economic Scope and Issue Linkage

The scope of economic activity has another important implication. Linking more issue areas under one institutional umbrella offers more opportunities for side payments that address distributional concerns. While all members benefit from regional cooperation—otherwise, they would not join (or they would pull out of) the REO—some members gain more than others (World Bank 2000, 21).[7] For example, it is often asserted that larger or more developed economies benefit more than their smaller or less developed partners (Foroutan 1993, 256–60; Mytelka 1973). If distributional concerns are not adequately addressed, they can paralyze or even lead to the collapse of REOs (Mytelka 1973, 240; Nye 1971, 78). The primary source of the tensions and eventual breakup of the East African Community, for example, was the disproportional benefits Kenya obtained at the expense of its poorer partners, Tanzania and Uganda (Goldstein and Ndung'u 2001, 11).[8] Recent research demonstrates that another cause of friction emanates from differences in the comparative advantage of different members. Regional integration tends to reward members whose regional competitiveness is compatible with their global competitiveness and to penalize members with opposite regional and global competitive pressures. REOs that include members with divergent comparative advantage may lead to inequitable share of benefits and, unless tackled, conflict with respect to intraregional and common external tariffs (Kono 2007b, 179).

Linking several issues in one agreement provides a valuable way to overcome distributional concerns and to promote economic liberalization (Aggarwal 1998; Axelrod and Keohane 1986, 239–40; Davis 2004; Tollison and Willet 1979). Members that lose (either relatively or absolutely) in one issue area may gain in another. As the World Bank (2000, 22) asserts, REOs "help by putting more issues on the table and embedding them in a wider agreement, both of which lower the size of compensatory transfers required and make it easier to reach an agreement." Of course, the wider the scope of an agreement, the higher the prospects for constructive issue linkage. The conclusion of NAFTA, for example, was secured after labor and environmental issues were incorporated into the treaty (Kahler 1995, 106).

Embedding many issues in one agreement not only facilitates the conclusion of a bargain but also makes defection less likely. Members that may be dissatisfied with some dimensions of the agreement have to consider the benefits they obtain in other dimensions before pulling out. Miles Kahler (1995, 85–86) argues that the ever-expanding bargains and issues linked by the EU greatly contributed to the strength of European integration and that, in turn, "the effects of reneging in one sphere on valuable bargains in another have served to keep European institutions intact." Similarly, although Mercosur went through a serious crisis in the early 2000s, the wide range of topics addressed by this organization prevented members from leaving it (Hurrell 2001, 203). Hence, REOs that encompass a large number of issues provide more benefits to their members and increase the opportunity cost of armed conflict. Wider scope of economic activity should therefore induce a peaceful resolution of interstate disputes.

Economic Scope, Vulnerability, and Society

Linking economic scope and peace through the opportunity cost mechanism warrants a consideration of a number of critiques leveled against this line of argument. One critique draws attention to the key assumption that the interruption of commercial relations is, indeed, very costly to the states involved. According to the opportunity cost logic, states are assumed to be *vulnerable*—rather than merely *sensitive*—to the disruption of commerce, in the sense that they may find it difficult to substitute it.[9] As several recent works point out, however, the sheer size of commercial flows does not capture this vulnerability in a convincing manner. If the goods exchanged between the two countries are not essential or are easy to obtain from other countries, the potential suspension of trade is unlikely to deter policymakers from engaging in a militarized conflict (Crescenzi 2005; Mansfield and Pollins 2003; Ripsman and Blanchard 1996/97). While this critique is not unreasonable, it is less damaging to my argument based on the scope of economic activity than to an argument based more narrowly on trade flows. As indicated earlier, the institutionalization of a trading relationship suggests that REO members expect an enduring partnership that will yield long-lasting benefits. Presumably, it ought to be quite difficult to supplant such long-term partnerships (Eilstrup-Sangiovanni and Verdier 2005; Mansfield and Pollins 2003, 14–15).

Moreover, the scope of economic activity includes integration and cooperation in several issue areas that may render states vulnerable to their disruption. This is largely because these activities are contingent on the geographical proximity of the REO members. While this factor is an important determinant of international trade, low transportation costs permit trade between distant states as well. Cooperation on several other issue areas, however, is likely to thrive only between neighboring states. Thus, states will find it very difficult to substitute a defecting partner and will be more vulnerable to such defection. For example, the Southern African Development Community (SADC) sponsored the Southern African Power Pool, a project that provided for regional exchanges of electricity in southern Africa. According to the World Bank (2000, 22), "The gains [from this project] over the period are estimated at an astonishing $785 million, a 20% saving." ANCOM's border integration zones, AMU's oil pipeline, and Air L'afrique, the regional airline of the Western African Economic and Monetary Union (WAEMU), offer additional illustrations of regional cooperation.[10] It is difficult to imagine such projects among states that are not adjacent. States are thus quite vulnerable to the disruption of such cooperation.

Finally, cooperation in some issue areas has characteristics of collective goods (regardless of the need for proximity) that require enduring obligations. Regional institutions are very instrumental in sustaining these kinds of agreements, which can be very costly to end. For example, several REOs have agreements on the treatment of foreign investors from third parties. Because such agreements provide a common ground for neighboring states that compete for similar sources of capital, they may prevent a "race to the bottom" for this capital between the member states (Büthe and Milner 2008). The Mercosur agreement, for instance, "[leaves] little room for asymmetrical treatment of non-party investments by individual MERCOSUR countries" (United Nations Conference on Trade and Development 2006, 50). Thus, a defection of one member from this agreement may render all member states worse off. Several issue areas—like a common bargaining position, a common external tariff, and monetary cooperation—have similar attributes. In the monetary area, WAEMU's monetary union provides its members with "an important set of common interests, additional to any that might be expected in a geographical and historical region, and thus clearly an additional force in support of regional integration" (Page and Bilal 2001, 12). These kinds of cooperative endeavors, like most international institutions, are not easy to craft and, if abandoned, are difficult to re-create or replace (Keohane 1984). Additionally, keeping in mind that issue linkage reinforces interdependence, REOs that facilitate cooperation in several issue areas compel leaders to consider the substitutability of the organization as a whole and its accompanied benefits. From this perspective, it is apparent that the wider the scope of economic activity is, the greater is the vulnerability of the member states to the secession of regional integration, and the higher will be the opportunity cost of conflict.

A second challenge to the opportunity cost argument stresses that the interruption of international commerce usually damages private actors, like exporters, importers, bankers, and investors (Stein 1993, 254). Researchers have yet to convincingly demonstrate, it is argued, that the former influences the latter with respect to matters of "high politics" (Bearce 2003; Mansfield and Pollins 2003; McDonald 2009; Stein 2003, 121–22). This is especially so if one assumes that the state is autonomous and possesses a broad national interest (Simmons 2003).[11] This critique carries certain weight with respect to the aggregate level of trade but appears to be on shakier ground when considering the broader scope of economic activity. Cooperation in some of the issue areas subsumed by the scope of economic activity provides benefits not only to organized interest groups but also to the country as a whole. For example, a monetary union has important implications for the stability of the currency and for monetary reserves. Thus, governments that choose to abandon a monetary union risk losing monetary assets as well as damaging the credibility of their monetary policy (Cohen 1997; Gartzke 2003). Similarly, the enhanced bargaining power that REOs may provide for their members is an important function of many such organizations. Collective bargaining negotiations that result in favorable outcomes enhance the prestige of policymakers and their countries, as demonstrated by REOs like the EU, the Caribbean Community (CARICOM), and ASEAN (Jorgensen-Dahl 1982, 48; Mattli 1999, 71; World Bank 2000, 20). In sum, it appears that a wide scope of economic activity advances a broad array of economic and political interests. The wider this scope is, the less likely it is that leaders will sacrifice these interests for the benefits they may obtain from aggression.

Economic Scope, Bargaining, and Information

A third important criticism emphasizes the bargaining process that may lead to the escalation of conflict. Building on Fearon's rationalist theory of war, several scholars call attention to the role that economic interdependence plays in this process. They argue that while the opportunity cost associated with higher dependence is likely to restrain a dependent state, potential opponents may be tempted to take advantage of this dependence and escalate the conflict. From this perspective, the effect of economic interdependence on conflict is indeterminate (Gartzke 2003; Gartzke, Li, and Boehmer 2001; Levy 2002, 356; Morrow 1999, 2003; Stein 2003; cf. Crescenzi 2005, 17–18; Polachek and Xiang 2010).

This critique, while very powerful, does not undermine the argument thus far advanced, for two reasons. First, advocates of this critique admit that sufficiently high levels of interdependence will deter violent conflict (Gartzke, Li, and Boehmer 2001, 401; Morrow 1999, 486). Second, as the proponents of the rationalist argument point out, economic interdependence can still be used as an effective instrument to mitigate violent conflict. As discussed earlier, conflicts sometimes escalate because governments have incomplete information on the intentions and resolve of their opponents. Economic interdependence can be very instrumental in this respect. To the extent that political disagreements arise, states can sever or threaten to cut off their beneficial economic ties in order to signal their resolve in a particular dispute. Greater benefits reflect higher opportunity costs of such economic sanctions and thus a more efficient signal (Bearce 2003; Gartzke 2003; Gartzke, Li, and Boehmer 2001; Morrow 1999, 2003). In particular, more intensive economic cooperation through regional international institutions provides states with a valuable informational tool regarding their national interest and resolve (Aydin 2010; Dorussen and Ward 2008). This additional information is conducive to a more peaceful bargaining process and thus to less violence. In terms of the different causal mechanisms previously presented, this line of reasoning suggests that economic scope alleviates conflict not only through the opportunity cost mechanism but also through the information mechanism.[12]

The signaling logic offers one distinctive empirical expectation: member states can use or threaten to use economic sanctions as a substitute for aggression (Morrow 2003; Stein 2003). It may be difficult to observe such incidents, because the threat of economic sanctions is often implicit or made off the record. Nonetheless, an example involving Suriname and Guyana illustrates this mechanism (chapter 6 provides a second example). In 2000, Suriname used force against Guyana in the context of an enduring maritime border dispute between these two CARICOM members. Guyana chose not to respond militarily and instead asked CARICOM to impose sanctions against Suriname (BBC, June 21, 2000). Thus, the joint membership allowed Guyana to demonstrate its resolve without resorting to violent measures that could have prolonged the cycle of violence.

In summary, using the commercial liberal thesis as a springboard, I argue that economic cooperation through regional institutions increases the opportunity cost of conflict, expands the bargaining range, and fosters peace between the members of an organization. Importantly, the pacifying effect of regional integration varies with the breadth and depth of the cooperation such organizations support. A consideration of a number of critiques leveled against this argument fails to seriously dent it and indicates that it stands on firm theoretical grounds. It also suggests that economic scope may foster peace through the information mechanism. I thus make the following hypothesis:

> *H1: A wider scope of economic activity results in lower levels of intraregional violent conflict.*

Regular Meetings of High-Level Officials

Many REOs institute regular meetings of top-level officials, which usually operate as the highest body of decision making. While the formal agendas of these meetings often emphasize economic cooperation, they allow senior policymakers the opportunity to discuss outstanding issues directly and openly. I argue that these face-to-face interactions are conducive to peaceful management of disputes between member states. This argument rests on three building blocks. First, these sequential conferences should be understood as diplomacy that promotes the exchange of important information about interests and resolve.[13] Second, face-to-face meetings amplify the pacifying effect of diplomacy at the highest levels. Third, regional forums have unique characteristics—compared to bilateral diplomacy—that render them effective instruments of conflict management and resolution. In the discussion that follows, these assertions are developed in turn, and then potential challenges to this argument are considered. This discussion indicates that top-level diplomacy promotes regional peace through both the information mechanism and the conflict management mechanism.

Diplomacy and Peace

Diplomacy is a widely used form of statecraft practiced by states in their daily interaction with other states. Governments use diplomacy to communicate, exchange information, and negotiate with each other peacefully. Thus, when states have disagreements, diplomacy and the use of force offer two alternative techniques to resolve their differences. The effect of diplomacy on conflict is not straightforward, however. Many scholars and practitioners dismiss diplomacy as ineffective. In particular, some studies that adopt the rationalist framework dismiss diplomacy as "cheap talk." According to them, talk is inexpensive, so policymakers may bluff in order to improve their bargaining position. Because other states understand this, they are suspicious of diplomatic statements, do not incorporate this information into the bargaining process, and fail to build trusting relationships (Fearon 1995, 396; Kydd 2005, 198; Morrow 1994).

Nonetheless, other recent studies that employ the same rationalist framework demonstrate that diplomacy can mitigate violent conflict. Fortna (2004, 27–28) argues that negotiation and mediation can indeed substitute military clashes in the aftermath of war. Anne Sartori (2002, 2005) shows that states that continuously interact during more peaceful times and share some common interests have a strong incentive to acquire a reputation of honesty. This motivation renders diplomacy informative and thus an effective tool of conflict mitigation.[14] Although the assumptions that states have common interests and that they can develop a reputation for honesty may not always hold, adjacent states are more likely to satisfy these conditions: they interact frequently and often have convergent interests. In addition, empirical research shows that reputation is a particularly important consideration in bargaining between neighboring states (Huth 1997). It appears, then, that diplomacy can provide valuable information and prevent the escalation of regional disputes.

The Role of Face-to-Face Interaction

States can, of course, practice diplomacy indirectly, through ambassadors, letters, phone conversations, and the like. Some benefits to face-to-face meetings among leaders cannot be obtained through indirect interaction, however. Experimental research demonstrates that communication in person provides the opportunity for individuals to offer and extract promises of cooperation, which, in turn, widens the bargaining range and improves the prospects of compromise (Ostrom and Walker 1991, 287). Moreover, recurrent face-to-face meetings foster interpersonal familiarity, trust, and mutual confidence (Bearce 2003; Dunn 1996; Melissen 2003; Russett, Oneal, and Davis 1998; Weilemann 2000). According to Barnett and Gause (1998, 177), for example, "The shell of the GCC was providing the home for increased inter-state contacts, consultations, and modest moves toward cooperation. The successful discussions and decisions on items of shared interests were having a snowball effect gathering greater speed, leading to institutionalized norms of consultation and coordination, and offering a glimmer of greater trust."[15] Thus, direct communication between high-level officials operates as a confidence-building measure that enhances the exchange of believable information among these officials (Berridge 2002, 176).

The Advantage of the Regional Arena

Policymakers can conduct interpersonal diplomacy bilaterally rather than regionally, in which case one should still observe their pacifying effects thus far discussed. What, then, is the added value of a regional—as opposed to a bilateral or a multilateral—forum? Regional meetings of high-level officials have some distinct benefits. For instance, with respect to the information mechanism, leaders who offer details on their intentions and resolve do so in the presence of several peers, not just one. This amplifies the reputational effects of integrity (Johnston 2001).

Even more important are the dynamics related to the conflict management mechanism. First, a regional setting allows top officials to negotiate outstanding issues in an informal, quiet, less demanding atmosphere, compared to bilateral negotiations or formal arbitration by extraregional bodies. Discussion of such issues in the framework of a regional summit that deals with other, mostly functional and economic issues provides the different parties with valuable flexibility. A peace deal between India and Pakistan, for example, was secured after an informal discussion between the leaders of these two countries during a 2003 SAARC summit.[16] The utility of such informal negotiations may actually be underappreciated because they commonly take place off the record and because their achievements are not publicized (Fawn 2009, 23). Second, the regional setting provides an opportunity for members that are not directly involved in a conflict to act as third-party mediators or honest brokers (Dunn 1996, 252). Regional forums are especially well suited to offer such services, because member states frequently have a stake in the peaceful management of the dispute and are likely to be familiar with the situation and the actors, to have a similar cultural and value system as the actors, and to enjoy greater legitimacy with them than do multilateral bodies (Bercovitch 1997, 143; Bercovitch and Houston 1996, 27; Dorussen and Ward 2010; Peck 2001, 578). Moreover, these policymakers can provide additional information to the two parties and expand the bargaining range by introducing creative solutions to outstanding regional problems (Dorussen and Ward 2008; Press-Barnathan 2009). The latter activity, in particular, renders seemingly indivisible issues more tractable (Gilady and Russett 2002; Nye 1971, 17).

Notably, extant research indicates that high-ranking officials are more successful mediators than middle-ranking officials. As Bercovitch and Houston (1996, 26) explain, "Leaders of states and high-level officials such as foreign and prime ministers have legitimacy and can bring it to bear together with their status and respect." For these reasons, the mediation of regional conflict is repeatedly channeled to regional top-level meetings.[17] To offer but one typical illustration, the ministerial council of WAEMU was instrumental in defusing a 1985 border dispute between Burkina Faso and Mali. A meeting of this council allowed high-level officials from the two states to meet in a relaxed atmosphere. It also facilitated mediation between the two rivals by officials from other member states (BBC, January 1, 1986; Pondi 2000).[18]

The Practice of Meetings Matters

The argument thus far advanced requires top officials to *actually* meet. This prerequisite is as essential as it is straightforward. Only to the extent that summits are convened do they confer the benefits of face-to-face interaction and direct but unofficial mediation. A quick look at regional top-level meetings points to the significance of this issue. Many REOs provide for recurrent high-level conferences, but some of them fail to abide by the schedule initially agreed to. Delays or cancellations of scheduled meetings for technical or political reasons are not uncommon (Melissen 2003, 16). AMU summits, for example, were convened only 6 times in 9 years, instead of 18 times as planned (Mortimer 1999). Similarly, SAARC summits, intended to be held annually, met only twice from 1990 to 1997.

Additionally, there are times when top-level meetings take place even though some top officials choose not to attend them. Such interruptions not only deprive the region of the advantages previously alluded to but may actually create or intensify tensions in the region. The 2005 AMU summit, for example, was postponed after being boycotted by Morocco. This, in turn, resulted in a diplomatic row between Algeria and Morocco (BBC, May 25, 2005). From this perspective, the realization of the agreed-on meetings is crucial for their pacifying effect to materialize.

Ad Hoc versus Serial Regional Conferences

The notion that diplomacy at the highest level is conducive to peace is not uncontroversial. More than five centuries ago, Philippe de Commynes, a well-known French diplomat, remarked, "Two great princes who wish to establish good personal relations should never meet each other face to face but ought to communicate through good and wise ambassadors."[19] The failure of some high-profile summits—from the 1919 Paris Peace Conference to the 2000 Camp David Middle East Peace Summit—reinforced this perception among professional diplomats and the mass public alike (Berridge 2002, 169). According to this critical view, top government officials lack sufficient knowledge, experience, and skills to successfully handle such meetings. With little time and much publicity, it is argued, high-level officials are likely to make or accept false promises, conclude agreements that are either inconsistent with or irrelevant to their national interests, or find themselves in an embarrassing dead end (Berridge 2002, 169–70; Dunn 1996, 252–59). In addition, personal contact may not always lead to friendship and trust but, rather, could result in competition, misunderstanding, or animosity. The risk of the latter is especially pronounced when such meetings take place across cultural divides (Dunn 1996, 258–60; Melissen 2003, 2–3). From this perspective, high-level diplomacy can be counterproductive and should be discouraged.

How can one reconcile this skepticism with the previously described benefits of meetings among high-level officials? To answer this question, a more nuanced examination of this diplomatic instrument is required. A distinction between ad hoc meetings and regular meetings, in particular, sheds light on the conditions under which this instrument fosters cooperation and peace. Ad hoc conferences are convened to resolve a fairly specific issue or problem. The stakes in, expectations from, and publicity surrounding such meetings are commonly very high (Berridge 2002, 174). At the same time, ad hoc meetings are likely to convene leaders who are not adequately familiar with their counterparts, their concerns, and their interests (Weilemann 2000, 18). In addition, they frequently tackle unforeseen problems or crises, such that the parties may lack sufficient time to properly plan the conference and may lack established formats and procedures for it. The combination of high visibility and high unpredictability render ad hoc meetings a risky undertaking that is prone to failure (Berridge 2002; Dunn 1996).

Many of the pitfalls of ad hoc meetings can be averted in sequential conferences, which bring together leaders of the same states repeatedly (Dunn 1996, 265). The G8 annual summits and, more pertinent to this study, repeated REO high-level meetings exemplify this kind of diplomacy (Berridge 2002, 174–75). Their recurrence tends to reduce the expectations for concrete results from each meeting, and the meeting's agenda is commonly decided well ahead of the summit itself and includes the discussion of ongoing and anticipated concerns. To the extent that leaders attempt to tackle an unforeseen development or crisis, they can do so informally or treat it as one of several items on the agenda. From this perspective, regular meetings are well suited for earnest negotiations on sensitive issues (Berridge 2002, 174–75; Peck 2001, 565).

In addition, regular meetings foster ongoing interaction among the same group of officials. This continuous contact increases the participants' mutual familiarity and sensitivity to each other's concerns and interests. Over the long haul, the risk of misperception and misjudgment is lower, especially among leaders who share similar cultural backgrounds and norms, characteristics that many REOs share. Long-term interaction also encourages compromise and cooperation by extending the "shadow of the future." Officials may be more willing to make concessions in the present if they expect reciprocal concessions in the future (Axelrod and Keohane 1986). Alternatively, policymakers may negotiate agreements over several conferences, as EU leaders did with respect to monetary and foreign policies (Redmond 1996, 59). Thus, serial meetings approximate the conditions under which diplomacy provides believable information and builds mutual trust (Sartori 2005).

Unlike ad hoc conferences, sequential meetings tend to be institutionalized and to have accepted and predictable formats and conventions. The established rules reduce the risk of misunderstanding and potential quarrels on procedural, rather than substantive, issues (Berridge 2002, 175; Peck 2001, 565). Regular top-level meetings frequently involve advanced and detailed preparations and consultations by professional diplomats and technical experts (commonly known as "Sherpas").[20] These lower-level officials lay the groundwork, set the agenda, and negotiate many of the issues prior to the conference. This advanced planning fosters more productive discussions and negotiations at the highest level and mitigates concerns of unforeseen disagreements and rifts during the meeting (Berridge 2002, 175; Dunn 1996, 263–64; Weilemann 2000, 19). Several REOs have gone further and created a permanent body that is in charge of preparing their meetings. These bodies foster the institutionalization and predictability of meetings among high-level officials and increase the prospects of their success.

The exemplar of such a body is the Committee of Permanent Representatives (COREPER), which organizes and coordinates EU summits and ministerial conferences, known as the European Council. COREPER is a complex system that involves a large number of representatives from all EU members. These delegates meet weekly away from the limelight to consider and negotiate issues to be discussed in the Council (Berridge 2002, 177; Lewis 2000; Redmond 1996). This body is the key to smooth and productive Council meetings and to the EU more broadly (Lewis 2000). In short, sequential conferences offer the benefits of and minimize the risks associated with top-level meetings. As Dunn (1996, 265) argues,

> For serial meetings at least, as meetings have become more institutionalized many of the dangers associated with this exceptional type of diplomatic encounter have disappeared. With fixed agendas, detailed advanced planning and the ease of conversation which results from the frequency with which leaders meet in one forum or another, summits have become an established part of the dialogue between states.

Some critics object to regular conferences because, they argue, they are unjustifiably costly (Melissen 2003). Top-level meetings involve two types of (interrelated) costs: material and reputational. The preparations for and the execution of these meetings are, quite literally, very expensive. They involve a great deal of lower-level diplomacy before the meeting as well as expenses on ceremonies and security measures during it. These conferences are also rather taxing on the leaders who attend them (Dunn 1996, 261; Melissen 2003, 16–18). The potential reputational costs emanate from the attention high-level meetings attract from the mass media and the public. The high visibility and publicity of the meetings allow greater scrutiny of the statements made and agreements reached (or not) in them. From this perspective, high level officials put their reputation on the line in these meetings (Weilemann 2000, 17). Thus, the outcome of top-level conferences reflects a high level of commitment (even if the process by which the outcome has been reached is informal). The complaint about the costliness and extravagance of these meetings, especially sequential and multilateral ones, is not without merit. Nonetheless, this objection is actually consistent with the information mechanism discussed earlier. It is at odds with the dismissal of diplomacy as "cheap talk" and suggests that this policy instrument carries greater weight than is commonly assumed. Thus, the considerable material and reputational costs increase the prospects of genuine negotiations and the exchange of credible information.

In sum, regular meetings of high-level officials foster peace through the information mechanism, by building mutual trust and promoting the exchange of believable information. They also reduce the risk of violent disputes through the conflict management mechanism, by offering a forum for informal negotiations and constructive third-party mediation. While top-level conferences may, under some conditions, be counterproductive, regional sequential meetings appear to maximize the benefits of these meetings and to minimize the risks associated with them. They are instrumental in advancing regional peace and stability. I thus make the following hypothesis:

> H2: Regular meetings of high-level officials result in lower levels of intraregional violent conflict.

Regular Meetings of High-Level Officials and Socialization
H2 is derived from arguments grounded in a rationalist framework, which assumes that state interests are fixed. A growing body of work, most closely associated with the constructivist school of thought, relaxes this assumption. It purports that ongoing interstate contacts, which will alter the manner by which states understand their interests, will foster shared understanding and mutual respect. I refer to this as the *socialization mechanism.* In the context of top-level meetings (this mechanism is revisited in the broader context of security communities later in this chapter), Risse (2000) and Mitzen (2005) suggest that states can build trust through communication, argumentation, and persuasion. Over time, these ongoing personal contacts, which alter the manner by which high-level officials understand their interests, open up the possibility for greater cooperation and a peaceful resolution of disagreements. Similarly, Johnston (2001) highlights the ability of policymakers to influence their peers through social pressure, such as back tapping and shaming. According to him, constant interaction socializes policymakers into the larger community and compels them to "do the right thing."

Consistent with the argument advanced here, these works expect these dynamics to matter more in more intimate group settings with shared culture and norms, such as those offered in a regional context. Thus, moving beyond the rationalist framework, we can expect regular meetings among high-level officials to matter even more. This line of research is still in its infancy, however, and its empirical content is largely suggestive.

Institutional Independence

Institutional independence refers to the ability of an REO to operate in a manner that is insulated from the influence of other political actors—especially states. Greater independence commonly indicates greater autonomy, delegation, and neutrality.[21] Extant research on international organizations identifies independence as a key aspect of these institutions because it impinges on their ability to meet their stated objectives and the quality of their performance (Abbott and Snidal 1998; Gutner and Thompson 2010, 243). Furthermore, institutional independence alleviates concerns related to future misunderstandings or potential abuse of the agreement by some of its members. It facilitates interstate cooperation at the outset by credibly committing members to the agreements' objectives (Haftel 2011; Hawkins et al. 2006; Majone 2001; Moravcsik 1998).

As is explained in chapter 3, institutional independence is captured by the existence and power of a corporate bureaucracy as well as a DSM. These two institutional features promote peace primarily through the conflict management mechanism. The manner by which each feature does so is somewhat different. Regional bureaucrats manage disputes through mediation, while DSMs engage in more formal arbitration. The broad mission of both bodies commonly involves scrutinizing and objectively evaluating the behavior of member states with respect to the commitments made in the agreements. This may allow them to mitigate conflict through the information mechanism. At the same time, recent research on mediation and adjudication indicates, somewhat counterintuitively, that greater independence is not necessarily conducive to peaceful resolution of disputes. I here consider each regional body in turn and conclude that both have a theoretically indeterminate effect on conflict.

Corporate Bureaucracy

A permanent corporate bureaucracy—commonly labeled a "secretariat" or "commission"—is an administrative body that manages the regular operation of the REO (Jacobson 1984, 89). The staff, intended to function as management and technical experts who do not represent individual governments, are insulated from political influence in the performance of their duties. One important function of this body is to collect and disseminate objective information on the members' activities (or lack thereof) in relation to the agreement (Keohane 1984, 94). This information allows states to monitor the behavior of their partners as well as assure others of their own behavior (Abbott and Snidal 1998, 20; Feld, Jordan, and Hurwitz 1994; Pevehouse and Russett 2006; Russett, Oneal, and Davis 1998, 445–46).

Why Regional Bureaucracy Might Lead to Peace   The informational role of the secretariat hinges on the type of information it collects. To the extent that facts provided by this regional body pertain to an intraregional dispute, they can reduce this "information arbitrage" and improve the prospects of a peaceful resolution to the dispute (Boehmer, Gartzke, and Nordstrom 2004; Mitchell and Hensel 2007). Arguably, however, REO secretariats are better equipped to gather and publicize facts on trade and investment than to get information on military capabilities and other strategic variables (Bearce and Omori 2005, 672; Boehmer, Gartzke, and Nordstrom 2004). At the same time, the distinction between economic and security issues can be sometimes blurred, especially in the developing world, where many disputes have both economic and military dimensions. To the extent that these aspects intermingle, regional bureaucrats may still have an opportunity to use available information to reduce tensions or to initiate a fact-finding mission in order to collect new information in a timely manner.

In such instances, information provided and publicized by the secretariat increases the reputational consequences of members' behavior during conflict (Keohane 1984; Mitchell and Hensel 2007). In particular, the secretariat is in an ideal position to judge if the practices that pertain to the conflict are consistent with existing agreements and to "name and shame" the violators. Such delegitimization backed by objective information damages the reputation of the offending members and decreases the net gains from the potential settlement to the dispute. For example, tensions between Benin and Burkina Faso led the former to close its border with the latter, an action that further strained bilateral relationship between these two ECOWAS members. The ECOWAS secretariat was quick to point out that Benin's action was in violation of the free movement of persons enshrined by the organization. By linking the border dispute to the regional agreement, the secretariat raised Benin's reputational costs, compelled it to back down, and prevented the escalation of this crisis (Agence France Presse, January 31, 2006).

A more prominent function of regional bureaucrats is best understood in the context of conflict management, particularly mediation. When member states have disagreements that cannot be patched up through direct negotiations, they often look for an intermediary to assist them. Mediation, which refers to third-party intervention without resorting to the use of force or invoking the rule of law, is an important and common type of conflict management.[22] Mediation requires the voluntary consent of both disputing parties, and the intermediary has to be acceptable for both sides and seen as impartial, at least to a degree (I offer more on this shortly). The view that neutrality is essential to the effectiveness of the intermediary is widely held and is sometimes considered a defining characteristic of the mediator (Kydd 2006; Rauchhaus 2006; Stulberg 1987; Young 1967). As Bercovitch (1997, 141) explains, "For mediation between states to be effective, even the most highly placed decision makers must be seen as impartial, acceptable to the disputants, and deserving their trust."

A variety of actors, from individuals and nongovernmental organizations to high-level state officials, may serve as intermediaries in international disputes. It is also not uncommon for international organizations to engage in mediation efforts. This involvement is not surprising, considering that these institutions act as "'honest broker' to reduce transaction costs, improve information about preferences, transmit private offers, and overcome bargaining deadlocks" (Abbott and Snidal 1998, 22).[23] Regional organizations, including numerous REOs, have taken a growing interest in dispute mediation, especially since the end of the Cold War (Peck 2001; Touval and Zartman 2001). Some of the REOs that provided their good offices are ANCOM, ASEAN, CARICOM, ECOWAS, and the EU. But who are the particular individuals within these organizations that carry out the mediation efforts? I considered the role of high-level officials earlier. Here I examine the role of top regional bureaucrats.

To the extent that impartiality is essential to successful mediation, top regional bureaucrats, like the secretary-general, are well positioned to be intermediaries in intraregional disputes. In their capacity, they epitomize the collective regional interest rather than the concerns of any particular member. Regional bureaucrats, moreover, are not burdened by a domestic constituency, which may prefer a particular outcome. From this point of view, the disputants are likely to perceive them with a degree of legitimacy. As Young (1967, 83) argues, "A party with neither constituency nor hampering partners is likely to be relatively unfettered and free to act with considerable flexibility and dispatch." In turn, during mediation with a regional bureaucrat, disputing parties may be willing to share information and make concessions that they otherwise would not share or make. The involvement of the executive secretary of ECOWAS in the dispute between Benin and Burkina Faso referred to previously (Agence France Presse, January 31, 2006) and the involvement of the secretary-general of CARICOM in an acrimonious fishing dispute between Trinidad Tobago and Barbados (BBC Monitoring Latin America, February 13, 2004) illustrate the potential utility of regional bureaucrats as would-be mediators.

Regional Bureaucracy and the Degree of Independence   Not all corporate bureaucracies are equally independent. Some secretariats have only informational and administrative roles. Others, however, have the power to initiate policy proposals and set the REO's agenda (Acharya and Johnston 2007; Haftel and Thompson 2006). More active and independent bureaucracies can further contribute to the peaceful management of intraregional disputes. Their perceived neutrality allows top bureaucrats to initiate policies that represent a middle ground on controversial issues related to the dispute. The greater legitimacy enjoyed by regional bureaucrats enables them to expose uncooperative or inflexible parties without appearing biased. A more powerful secretariat can also utilize the organization to put pressure on the negotiating parties by calling for a resolution with respect to the dispute or by exposing members who violate established rules and agreements. This, in turn, increases the reputational costs of uncompromising or defiant members.

The secretariat of ANCOM—one of the most independent regional bureaucracies—functioned in this manner in a commercial border dispute between Venezuela and Colombia. A decision to deny Colombian trucks access to Venezuela resulted in a serious diplomatic rift between the two countries (BBC, July 20, 1999). After the secretariat examined this matter and found that Venezuela violated existing treaties, it issued a resolution that required Venezuela to lift its restrictions (BBC, July 20, 1999). While the conflict was not immediately resolved (as I shall discuss shortly), the secretariat's action put pressure on Venezuela to justify its practices, prevented escalation, and reoriented the disputants toward a more cordial interchange.

In sum, insofar as impartiality facilitates effective mediation, corporate bureaucracies and the individuals who run them can be instrumental in managing intraregional conflict. Furthermore, they "are likely to be most effective as conflict mediators when they are independent from their member-states" (Hansen, Mitchell, and Nemeth 2008). I thus make the following hypothesis:

> *H3: A more independent corporate bureaucracy results in lower levels of intraregional violent conflict.*

Why Regional Bureaucracy Might Not Bring Peace   To the extent that one accepts the potential utility of mediation as an instrument of conflict management, a countervailing logic indicates that greater independence is not necessarily conducive to effective mediation. As I have pointed out already, extracting information and concessions from the disputing parties is a central task of the intermediary. A handful of recent studies indicate that biased mediators may actually be more effective than impartial ones in performing these tasks. A partial mediator is likely to have greater leverage vis-à-vis the party it favors. It is in a better position to use sticks and carrots to pressure the disputant it is close to toward accommodating the other side (Gelpi 1999; Princen 1992; Touval and Zartman 2001).[24] From this perspective, the perceived neutrality of regional bureaucrats may hamper their ability to extract concessions from both parties.

Employing a rationalist framework, Kydd (2003) advances a somewhat different argument. He argues that impartial mediators are not the best transmitters of credible information. Ironically, the greater the mediator's interest in preserving the peace is, the less effective the mediator is in providing the parties with believable information (Kydd 2003; Rauchhaus 2006; Smith and Stam 2003). Because impartial mediators value peace more than the gains or losses of the disputants, they have an incentive to provide false information in order to convince both sides to back down. Since the disputants understand the mediator's motivation, they will mistrust and discount the information it provides. A biased intermediary that values the disputant's interests is more likely to be credible and, in turn, a successful mediator. The notion that biased parties are more effective mediators is supported by recent empirical analyses (Gelpi 1999; Savun 2008).[25]

The implications of this reasoning are that a more independent regional bureaucracy will not be an effective intermediary. Both parties will perceive an independent bureaucracy as indifferent to their concerns in the dispute and will believe that it exaggerates the power and resolve of their opponent.

Moreover, the secretariat has a powerful incentive to keep the peace. Violent conflict can be expected to hamper regional cooperation and delay regional projects. As the body that represents the interest of the region, the basic instinct of the secretariat is to secure greater cooperation among member states. The personal and organizational interests of the regional bureaucrats are also at stake. A more limited or slower cooperation through the REO is likely to weaken the authority and influence of the bureaucrats themselves. According to this logic, regional bureaucrats are expected to fail in their mediation efforts and will not be able to prevent the escalation of disputes between member states. Alternatively, disputants who recognize the motivation of the regional bureaucracy will turn to other, potentially more effective intermediaries to help them bridge their differences. For all these reasons, more independent REO bureaucracies may not reduce interstate violent conflict.

Dispute Settlement Mechanisms

Dispute settlement reflects an important dimension of institutional independence and captures elements of the autonomy, neutrality, and delegation principles (Abbott and Snidal 1998, 22–23; Haftel and Thompson 2006, 261; Smith 2000). The presence of a centralized mechanism for solving disputes facilitates exchange and cooperation among political and economic actors at the domestic level and among states (North and Weingast 1989; Yarbrough and Yarbrough 1997, 134–35). International DSMs are potentially constraining, because states must delegate important judicial powers to neutral third parties. Typically, these adjudicating bodies are designed with substantial autonomy, such that states cannot control or overturn their decisions.

Why DSMs Might Lead to Peace   DSMs are common features of existing REOs. These legal mechanisms usually address economic disputes that arise from substantive disagreements regarding the operation of the organization and other outstanding economic matters (Smith 2000; Yarbrough and Yarbrough 1997). They resolve economic conflicts that can potentially escalate into militarized disputes (Levy and Ali 1998; Mansfield 2003; Mansfield and Pevehouse 2000, 781; Pevehouse and Russett 2006; Russett and Oneal 2001; Russett, Oneal, and Davis 1998). This is especially true in the developing world, where territorial disputes are sometimes linked to economic resources like oil, fishery, and minerals.

Like the secretariat, the adjudicating body is authorized to collect objective information and to compel the disputants to justify and defend their practices (Mitchell and Hensel 2007, 724; Posner and Yoo 2005, 14–15). Unlike the secretariat, it is endowed with greater legal authority and empowered to invoke the rule of law to justify its decisions. That is why the dispute between Venezuela and Colombia mentioned earlier was eventually submitted to the Andean Court of Justice (which ruled in favor of Colombia [BBC, November 4, 2000]). In addition, the perceived neutrality of DSMs increases the domestic legitimacy of the ruling and allows policymakers to accept domestically unpopular international settlements (Boehmer, Gartzke, and Nordstrom 2004; Mitchell and Hensel 2007, 724; Simmons 1999). Finally, public DSM rulings increase the reputational costs of treaty violation and decrease the reputational costs of retaliation against violators. They improve the prospects of compliance and long-term cooperation (Kono 2007a, 749; Simmons 1999, 210; Yarbrough and Yarbrough 1997).

A dispute between Nicaragua and Honduras illustrates the potential pacifying role of DSMs. In 1999, Nicaragua slapped tariffs on Honduran exports after the latter ratified a border treaty with Colombia at the expense of the former. It was also reported that the Nicaraguan president was discussing possible military alternatives with his defense minister (Pevehouse and Russett 2006; Sequeira and Duran 1999). Because the imposition of tariffs was in violation of the Central American Common Market (CACM), the two members submitted this dispute to the Central American Court of Justice (CCJ), which has jurisdiction on this matter. The CCJ ruled to annul the treaty between Honduras and Colombia and to suspend the tariff imposed by Nicaragua. This ruling was not accepted by the two parties and was eventually submitted to the International Court of Justice (ICJ). Nevertheless, the CCJ was instrumental in defusing the initial tensions and prevented escalation of the crisis.

Not all DSMs are equally independent. Some REOs offer only a mutually agreed-on nonbinding arbitration, others provide for an automatic and binding adjudication, and still others have a permanent court (Smith 2000). A higher degree of legalization indicates a greater degree of independence (Haftel and Thompson 2006; Keohane, Moravcsik, and Slaughter 2000; Posner and Yoo 2005). More independent DSMs have greater authority and thus greater legitimacy. They also have more resources to collect and disseminate information. From this perspective, it is commonly argued that more legalized bodies are more effective instruments of dispute resolution (Keohane, Moravcsik, and Slaughter 2000). As Posner and Yoo (2005, 12) point out, "The conventional wisdom is that effectiveness of an international tribunal is correlated with its independence." The European Court of Justice and the Andean Court of Justice, for example, represent highly independent and effective tribunals. From this point of view, more independent DSMs should be more conducive to peace and stability. Like other institutional features, the pacifying effect of DSMs depends on their actual existence and operation. This is not always the case, however. Member states may agree to form a DSM but then suspend its formation or implementation, as is the case of the AMU Court of Justice. In such instances, the concept of institutional independence is hollow. Thus, to the extent that these judicial bodies are operational, I make the following hypothesis:

H4: A more independent dispute settlement mechanism results in lower levels of intraregional violent conflict.

Why DSMs Might Not Lead to Peace   Much of the case for the effect of DSMs on conflict is based on the experience of organizations that address security concerns in a direct manner, like the ICJ and the Organization of American States. A number of studies question the ability of regional economic DSMs to mitigate violent conflict in a similar manner. Boehmer, Gartzke, and Nordstrom (2004, 15) argue that organizations that have economic mandates lack the ability or willingness to settle military disputes. Similarly, Bearce (2003, 352) argues that commercial disputes rarely escalate into military ones and that "the trade dispute settlement mechanisms embedded in regional commercial institutions simply have no jurisdiction or power to resolve highly contentious territorial disagreements." The observation that commercial discord in the World Trade Organization, NAFTA, and the EU is accompanied by continued peaceful relations among the developed members of these organizations casts additional doubt on the association between commercial and militarized disputes (Haftel 2004a).

The link between judicial independence and dispute resolution can be challenged from another perspective. Even if one recognizes the constructive effect of DSMs on cooperation and peace, it is not clear that more independent bodies are more effective than less independent ones (Kono 2007a). Posner and Yoo (2005) argue that the opposite is actually true. According to them, too much legal power may lead international courts to ignore state interests and hand down biased or controversial rulings. As a result, states will be disinclined to use highly legalized international courts. Thus, they argue, "independence *prevents* international tribunals from being effective" (7). This calls attention to the issue of utilization, which is somewhat different from implementation. Even if REOs establish DSMs, these bodies may remain inactive and weak if member governments fail to use them. It is possible, then, that more independent DSMs will adjudicate fewer disputes, which will diminish their anticipated pacifying effect. An independent (and implemented) but inactive DSM will therefore contribute little to regional peace.

Recent developments in Mercosur illustrate this point. Initially, this REO provided for a formally binding but ad hoc third-party review (Bouzas and Soltz 2001). This mechanism was deemed inadequate because of its ad hoc nature and lack of supremacy over domestic laws (Beltramino 2005, 191; Bouzas and Soltz 2001, 110). Member states attempted to address these problems by creating a permanent appellate court body, labeled the Permanent Review Tribunal (PRT), which "would enhance expertise, legitimacy, independence and coherence to the extent this is aspired" (Coelho and Ferreira 2004).[26] Even so, Mercosur members—especially the more powerful ones—were very reluctant to use this new instrument and preferred diplomatic negotiations or other adjudicating bodies (Domínguez 2007, 110). In a lingering dispute between Argentina and Uruguay over the latter's installation of paper pulp mills, the two parties attempted to resolve this issue in several ways but refrained from submitting it to the PRT. One report remarked that this body "has been so dysfunctional that in October [2007] Paraguayan representative Wilfrido Fernandez resigned and said his decision was due to the four member countries 'not showing the political will' for the Tribunal to operate effectively" (Osava 2008).

This discussion underlines the potential limits of more legalized DSMs in fostering peace and stability. It calls attention to the distinct nature of economic matters, on the one hand, and military matters, on the other. It also highlights the limits of international legalization in an anarchical international system and the trade-off between independence and effectiveness. Taken as a whole, these arguments suggest that the link between the independence and autonomy of DSMs and regional conflict is weak.

Regional Institutionalization

Thus far, I have examined the pacifying effects of economic scope, regional summitry, and institutional independence separately. This section considers the interaction among these three dimensions under one institutional umbrella. It points to several linkages between these institutional features, which tend to reinforce the individual pacifying effects previously discussed. It also explores the possibility that REOs not only serve but also shape the interests of their members. In this view, international institutions may facilitate shared norms and identity that are conducive to peace. Whether one emphasizes rational calculations or ideational transformation (I offer more on this distinction shortly), this section indicates that the whole is more than the sum of its parts.

Regional Institutionalization and Issue Linkage

Previous sections underscored the constructive role of issue linkage built into a wide scope of economic activity. Two features render regional summits particularly valuable in making and cementing these linkages. First, high-level officials have the authority to strike bargains that lower-level officials usually do not have. As the ultimate decision makers, officials at the highest levels can deal across policy areas and bureaucratic boundaries. As Berridge (2002, 176) explains, "Sitting astride the apex of policy-making within their own administrations, heads of government are well placed to make trades involving bureaucratically separate issue-areas."[27] Having the power to engage in a wide-ranging give-and-take, top-level officials are in an ideal position to break existing deadlocks and move the regional agenda forward (Berridge 2002, 176; Dunn 1996, 251; Press-Barnathan 2009).

Second, high-level officials are more likely to have a more holistic view of regional cooperation and to find a middle ground on specific issues in order to advance the REO's broader goals (Berridge 2002, 176; Dunn 1996, 251). This dynamic is especially conceivable in sequential, rather than ad hoc, conferences. Repeated, institutionalized meetings allow bargaining not only across issue areas but also over time (Moravcsik 1998). As Oye (1986, 17) maintains, "By establishing a direct connection between present behavior in a single-play game and future benefits in an iterated game, tacit or explicit cross-issue linkage can lengthen the shadow of the future."

Similarly, the scope of economic activity and the independence of regional institutions are tightly linked. Simple functional logic points to a positive feedback loop between the depth of cooperation and the power of the institutions that support it. Deeper cooperation involves more complex issues, has a broader economic impact, and is more likely to result in noncompliance. Thus, greater economic cooperation calls for more intrusive regional institutions, which are capable of monitoring state behavior, collecting and disseminating information, and resolving disputes related to the agreements (Abbott and Snidal 1998; Stinnett 2007). Recent empirical work offers support for this logic (Acharya and Johnston 2007; Haftel 2011; Stinnett 2007). As Acharya and Johnston (2007, 268) observe, "Institutionalization and legalization . . . increase with expanding scope and mandate." Similarly, as regional institutions become more independent, they increase the cost and reduce the risk of defection and thus foster greater economic cooperation and integration. For example, Kono (2007a) argues that decentralized enforcement provided by DSMs facilitates regional economic interdependence. Hence, a wider scope of economic activity leads to greater institutional independence, which leads to a wider scope still. To the extent that both features are conducive to peace, this cycle ought to amplify their distinct effects.

Wider economic scope offers additional benefits in the context of dispute resolution. As I discussed already, greater benefits related to the REO increase the cost of withdrawal from the organization or the suspension of activities. Third-party mediators—either high-level officials or regional bureaucrats—can exploit this reality to persuade disputants to resolve their differences peacefully and not to undermine the regional project. In other words, greater economic scope contributes to the leverage and enhances the effectiveness of would-be intermediaries (Dorussen and Ward 2010). This is especially true if the mediator carries economic or political weight vis-à-vis the disputing parties.

In the 1985 dispute between Burkina Faso and Mali, for instance, the president of Côte d'Ivoire proved to be an effective mediator due to Burkina Faso's economic dependence on the latter. Repatriation of Burkinabê workers or suspension of trade relations (both important aspects of economic cooperation in the region) could have engendered an economic crisis in Burkina Faso. That Côte d'Ivoire "had both the means and the will to take actions to influence the behavior of Burkina Faso" (Pondi 2000, 217) compelled Ouagadougou to back down. Thus, greater economic dependence that stems from greater cooperation through REOs improves the prospects of mediation by third-party regional actors. In summary, assuming that the separate features have the hypothesized pacifying effect, linkages between them are likely to amplify their individual contribution to the mitigation of violent disputes. This synergy further advances regional peace and stability. I thus make the following hypothesis:

H5: *Greater regional institutionalization results in lower levels of intraregional violent conflict.*

Regional Institutionalization and Socialization

The prospect of peace through socialization was previously introduced in the context of top-level diplomacy. The potential effect of this mechanism has attracted greater scholarly attention in a broader institutional context, which I now consider. In a pathbreaking study, Karl Deutsch and several colleagues conceived the possibility of a community of independent states that protect and cooperate with each other (Deutsch et al. 1957). In such so-called pluralistic security communities, governments no longer act only on their own narrow self-interest but are guided by the collective interest of the community. Over time, through socialization, communication, and learning, the community transforms the identity of its members and generates "we feeling"; that is, members of this community develop mutual identification and trust as well as compatibility of core values that render interstate violent conflict illegitimate and unthinkable (Adler and Barnett 1998, 6–9; Deutsch et al. 1957).

The concept of security communities has been rehabilitated in recent years, especially by scholars identified with the constructivist school of thought (Adler and Barnett 1998; Wendt 1999). Unlike Deutsch, these recent studies pay a great deal of attention to the role of international institutions in security communities. IGOs and other institutions, they argue, establish and diffuse norms, serve as an arena of socialization, and shape national and regional identities (Adler and Barnett 1998, 40–45, 418–21; Bearce and Bondanella 2007; Checkel 2005; Risse 2000). In this context, the thickly institutional EU has attracted considerable interest (Checkel 2007; Diez, Albert, and Stettler 2008; Hooghe 2005; Wæver 1998). The concept of security communities has been applied to several REOs beyond Europe as well, including ASEAN, Mercosur, and the GCC (Acharya 2001; Barnett and Gause 1998; Hurrell 1998). In line with the argument advanced here, research on security communities indicates that socialization deepens and that ideational transformation intensifies as institutionalization increases.

Cooperation on more issues offers more opportunities for interaction and communication among both officials and private individuals; more extensive interaction among high- and low-level officials fosters the creation and diffusion of mutual trust; more independent regional institutions can more easily cultivate long-term reciprocity as well as shared norms and identity (Adler and Barnett 1998, 30; Bearce and Bondanella 2007).

Research on security communities and socialization faces a number of challenges. Theoretically, the nature of security communities, their origins, and their implications are not well understood. Adler and Barnett (1998, 49–57), who offer the most sophisticated and nuanced conceptualization of security communities to date, suggest that these communities evolve in three phases: nascent, ascendant, and mature. The initial phases involve little socialization and ideational change and fit comfortably with rationalist frameworks. Only in the mature phase do members of the community develop a shared identity, mutual trust, and self-restraint (Adler and Barnett 1998, 50–51). The conceptualization of this phase is somewhat circular, however. It is unclear whether security communities cause stable peace or a description of existing peaceful relationships caused by other factors. In addition, potential indicators of mature security communities are either consistent with alternative perspectives (e.g., changes in military planning and a common definition of threat) or ambiguous (e.g., multilateralism and discourse of community).

Empirically, the evidence is mixed. Western Europe offers a most likely case for the existence of a mature security community (Wæver 1998; Diez, Albert, and Stettler 2008). Several studies challenge the claim that European institutions facilitate socialization and promote shared identity and understanding (Checkel 2007; Hooghe 2005). As Acharya and Johnston (2007, 263) conclude, "The EU's supranationalism and the sense of European regional identity fostered by it are overstated in the face of alternative explanations focusing on intergovernmentalism and resilient national identities and interests." Scholars who entertained the possibility of security communities in the developing world have uncovered little evidence to substantiate this possibility, with the possible (but questionable) exceptions of Mercosur and ASEAN (Acharya 1998; Domínguez 2007, 111–12; Hurrell 1998).[28] Even these regions are considered to be, at best, nascent security communities. In short, the theoretical and empirical difficulties faced by extant research on security communities suggest that its utility in linking institutional variation to regional conflict and peace is currently limited.

Nevertheless, the usefulness of the research on security communities should not be dismissed too cavalierly. Further theoretical and conceptual progress of this promising research agenda may allow its incorporation into studies such as this and may foster a more thorough test of rationalist explanations (against constructivist ones) of the link between REOs and intraregional peace.

Regional Institutionalization, Conflict, and Endogeneity

The preceding part of this chapter calls attention to the ways by which variation in REOs affects interstate violent conflict. Like other international institutions, REOs are formed and maintained to perform functions that their members find desirable. Accordingly, REOs do not appear at random in different parts of the world, and their structure and functions are not arbitrary. Rather, the existence and nature of these institutions are affected by their members' interests and relationships and are predictable in this respect. This study thus faces a potential endogeneity problem: it may be that the status of relations among states—specifically, whether they are peaceful or antagonistic—influences the degree of institutionalization and institutional design, rather than vice versa. A complete theoretical discussion of the link between regional institutionalization and conflict requires a careful consideration of this matter (empirical strategies to tackle this issue are considered in subsequent chapters).

In this section, I show that, theoretically, the implications of endogeneity for the pacifying effect of REOs hinge on the specific interests that led to their creation. Here, we can identify two different views: one emphasizing reasoning from the "supply side" and one emphasizing reasoning from the "demand side." The former suggests that violent conflict inhibits cooperation through international institutions, while the latter indicates that armed conflict actually encourages the institutionalization of REOs. I argue that both perspectives are logically sound and can be at work under different circumstances and with respect to specific design features. Consequently, the key challenge is to identify, measure, and control for the underlying propensities that might make institutional design endogenous.[29] Systematic evidence on the effect of conflict and amity on the design and implementation of international institutions is scant, however. The empirical part of this book takes an important first step in filling this void.

Supply-side arguments emphasize the constraints faced by states that consider institutionalized cooperation with their neighbors. They underscore the obstacles for long-term international cooperation in the shadow of power politics, especially among governments that have diverse and incompatible interests. By the same token, cooperation is much more likely to flourish among like-minded states. This logic is best illustrated by the realist perspective on international institutions. In perhaps the most thorough discussion of this argument, Grieco (1993, 1997) contends that the inclination to cooperate on a large number of issues and delegate authority to regional institutions hinges on states' sensitivity to relative gains. This sensitivity depends, among other things, on past and present political relationships. Enmity results in greater salience of power differentials, which, in turn, inhibits the institutionalization and independence of REOs. States that have cordial relationships are less sensitive to relative gains and can therefore benefit from the fruits that international cooperation bestows. Under these conditions, members will be keener on endowing regional institutions with control over important economic matters, decision-making authority, and independence. In the case of Mercosur, for example, some observers argue that the institutionalization of this REO is "a product of the prior bilateral improvement of political and security relations and the reactivation of trade between Argentina and Brazil, not the cause of such processes" (Domínguez 2007, 109).

A number of scholars utilize this logic to challenge the purported pacifying effect of economic interdependence, already discussed in detail. Waltz (1970) argues that political considerations trump economic ones and that economic interaction between rival powers breeds animosity more than friendship. Similarly, several studies offer empirical evidence that allies trade with each other more than adversaries (Gowa 1994; Gowa and Mansfield 1993) and that states with cordial political ties engage in more commerce than states with acrimonious relationships (Pollins 1989; Keshk, Pollins, and Reuveny 2004). Extending this argument beyond trade, one should expect a scope of economic activity that is wider among friends than among foes.

Other supply-side arguments emphasize the similarity of interest and indicate that members who share a common political perspective are more likely to institutionalize their REOs and pool their sovereignty. Power-based accounts often highlight a common perception of the security environment. Waltz (1979, 70–71) and Mearsheimer (1990, 46–48), for example, cast doubt on the belief that European integration has been instrumental in bringing peace to Europe. Instead, they highlight the role of systemic forces such as bipolarity, a common external threat, and the existence of nuclear weapons. Similarly, Leifer (1989) views ASEAN as a consequence of Cold War politics. Such studies expect REOs to become less institutionalized and independent as soon as the external environment becomes less ominous. Under these conditions, distinct national interests and distributional concerns trump the gains afforded by far-reaching and powerful institutions.

Some research draws attention to domestic, rather than external, sources of political affinity. Genna (2008), Haggard (1997), and Solingen (1998), for example, conclude that regional economic cooperation is most likely to prosper among governments with similar political and economic orientations. We should therefore expect a wider scope of economic activity among like-minded governments. Similarly, governments with homogenous preferences are more likely to delegate authority to international organizations and to promote greater legalization (Hawkins et al. 2006, 20–21; Kahler 2000).

My discussion thus far underscores the conditions that may foster or inhibit the creation and institutionalization of REOs. It points to two related but distinct possibilities that bear on the argument made in this book. First, it suggests that initial peaceful relations and regional stability allow neighboring countries to benefit from highly institutionalized and independent organizations, while regional enmity and conflict result in shallow and feeble REOs. As a result, the causal arrow should be reversed; that is, an association between regional institutionalization and peace indicates that peace brings cooperation, rather than the other way around. Second, it calls attention to the possibility that both peace and regional institutionalization are artifacts of underlying shared political goals and security concerns. One ought to account for these national interests before attributing a causal effect to international institutions (Downs, Rocke, and Barsoom 1996). The null hypothesis is, therefore, that REOs have no independent effect on the level of regional violent conflict and that institutional design has little bearing on the prospect of regional peace. This hypothesis can be worded as follows:

H0: Regional institutionalization and its separate components have no effect on intraregional violent conflict.

An alternative theoretical view does not dispute the premise that international institutions are endogenous. Instead, it accepts the notion that they are created by states in order to advance their goals, but it emphasizes the rationale for creating these institutions in the first place—the demand side of the equation. The basic intuition underlying this approach is that governments institutionalize their cooperation precisely because they face difficulties that they cannot adequately tackle by other means (Keohane and Martin 1995; Martin and Simmons 1998). Thus, this perspective emphasizes the incentives for, rather than the constraints on, international cooperation.

Regarding the relationship between conflict and regional institutionalization, this approach takes exception to the claim that durable peace is an essential precondition for regional cooperation through international institutions. It points out that adversaries may deem international institutions a useful instrument to build trusting relationships and peace. According to this logic, governments are likely to invest in international institutions and to endow them with authority exactly when conflict is likely to erupt and where security challenges are frequent (Wallander and Keohane 1999, 30–32). As Fortna (2004, 31) argues with respect to cease-fire agreements, "The greater the obstacles to peace, the greater the need for mechanisms to alter incentives, reduce uncertainty, and prevent accidents." Along these lines, Lake (1997, 53–55) maintains that regions that face a greater number of security predicaments are more likely to form institutions to manage their relations. That is why, according to this approach, not only friends but also rivals—such as India and Pakistan, Indonesia and Malaysia, and Peru and Ecuador—form and sustain REOs.

This approach has specific implications for the independence of regional organizations. It indicates that member states that anticipate conflict and disagreements in the future are more likely to set up a powerful bureaucracy and a legalized DSM in the hope that these bodies will allow them to overcome their differences. Presumably, these design features reflect a commitment to settle potential wrangles by peaceful means. In particular, one should expect to see greater legalization in war-prone regions.

On the broad issues of power and interests, this approach views international institutions as instrumental in alleviating these concerns. They permit, for example, powerful states to demonstrate their benign intentions by binding themselves to an equitable international order. Although powerful states can always renege on existing agreements, the costs associated with breaking their word make their commitment more believable and credible (Genna 2008; Jervis 1999; Lake 1999). For example, some studies indicate that the thick institutional environment after World War II tied the hands of the United States and convinced its partners to support its global agenda (Goldstein and Gowa 2002; Ikenberry 2001; Thompson 2006). Similarly, greater institutionalization may help bring states with divergent interests together. Martin (1994), for example, argues that heterogeneity of capabilities and preferences induces greater institutional scope and issue linkage.[30] In short, this functionalist approach suggests that the institutionalization and design of REOs is driven by the needs of their members. These organizations are therefore expected to have a broader scope and greater independence in regions that experience high levels of conflict and divergence of interests.

As I pointed out already, the structure and functions of regional organizations is likely to be shaped by both supply-side and demand-side dynamics. In some instances, these factors may pull in opposite directions, with the net effect depending on their relative strength. In other circumstances, these factors may actually reinforce each other. In particular, realists may be right that frequent interstate violence is detrimental to regional institutionalization and that institutionalized cooperation requires a modicum of stability and trust. Nevertheless, the more nuanced treatment of this theme is open to the possibility that institutionalized cooperation can contribute to amity and peace when aggressive instincts are restrained (Glaser 1994/95; Jervis 1999; Schweller and Priess 1997). Thus, in regions where violence is tamed but stability and trust are still fragile, a thoughtful institutional design and implementation thereof may still prove useful in promoting peace. Governments that see eye to eye in the present but worry that their partners or succeeding governments in their own state will break their promises in the future can create international institutions to increase the cost of reneging (Acharya and Johnston 2007, 26; Gruber 2000; Wallander and Keohane 1999, 30–32).

Because international institutions are slow to adjust and tend to linger even when the fundamentals that led to their creation and design change, they can cement an existing but potentially reversible peace. Rather than crumbling, regional institutions formed during peacetime or under external pressure can be instrumental in working out disagreements and conflicts that arise subsequently. Thus, consistent with supply-side arguments, international cordiality may be conducive to the formation of regional institutions, which, in turn, facilitate the consolidation of peaceful relationship among member states, in line with the demand-side logic. This line of reasoning suggests that regional institutionalization and peace can produce a virtuous cycle, or, in other words, "a mutually reinforcing feedback loop" (Russett and Oneal 2001, 212).[31]

In sum, states devise REOs because they confront problems that can be dealt with through these institutions. Their design is therefore forward looking and anticipates their effects. In this respect, they are shaped by their members' preferences over outcomes but also constrain their behavior (Acharya 2007, 639). Building on these foundations, connecting regional institutionalization and violent conflict requires that we specify the interests on which governments act. As I already pointed out, emphasis on constraints, on the one hand, and emphasis on incentives, on the other, lead to different conclusions regarding states' motivations and goals. Logically, both accounts are equally plausible, and there is no a priori reason to accept one and reject the other.

In addition, that international institutions are created and designed by their member states does not preclude their subsequent effect on foreign policy and international interactions. The casual arrow may well go both ways and lead to a virtuous cycle in zones of peace and a vicious cycle in zones of war. Endogeneity is thus a multifaceted theoretical and empirical issue. This study recognizes its importance and takes several steps to tackle it. Consequent chapters elaborate on some strategies to disentangle this matter empirically and to establish casual directions. In doing so, this book takes the position that the most fruitful way to deal with endogeneity is to identify its specific sources and account for them empirically. In step with this perspective, it offers perhaps the first rigorous empirical inquiry into the reciprocal relationships between institutional design and conflict.

Conclusion

This chapter examined the relationships between regional institutionalization and intraregional violent dispute from a theoretical perspective. It moved beyond a simple dichotomous view and offered a more nuanced evaluation of this nexus. It considered the causal mechanisms by which international institutions may mitigate conflict and the role these mechanisms play in particular institutional features commonly found in REOs. It also took into account the level of institutionalization of the different features, as well as their degree of implementation. It asked which and how institutions matter, rather than if they matter.

Using the rational theory of war as a springboard, I have argued that greater economic scope leads to higher opportunity costs of conflict and provides member states with more ways to interact peacefully. I have also contended that regular meetings of high-level officials are instrumental in improving communication between member states and in the mediation of outstanding disagreements. Institutional independence—embodied in the corporate bureaucracy and DSMs—fosters peace through mediation, adjudication, and the provision of information. Here, several convincing counterarguments indicate that the relations between the independence of REOs and violent disputes may be weak.

Finally, I have considered the cumulative effect of the individual design features when bundled under one institutional umbrella. I conclude that the broader regional institutionalization ought to amplify the pacifying role of separate components it subsumes. Taking into account concerns of endogeneity, this chapter argued that international institutions are both affected by their members' interests and shape their actions. This discussion indicated that the link between regional institutionalization and intraregional peace is grounded in firm theoretical foundations. The rest of the book is devoted to the empirical evaluation of the theoretical framework developed here. The next chapter sets the stage by taking a closer look at the concept of regional institutionalization.

CHAPTER 3

The Landscape of Regional Economic Organizations

A glance at the landscape of REOs reveals a great deal of variation in the objectives and structures of these institutions. The previous chapter drew attention to the significant consequences of these differences to the ability of these organizations to promote peace among their members. This chapter takes a closer look at the functions performed by and the institutional features contained in a large number of regional economic organizations. It first describes the type of institutions considered in this study. It then discusses the design features purported to affect violent conflict. It provides a definition for each organizational characteristic and justifies it, links this feature to specific quantifiable indicators, and elaborates on the manner by which their implementation is assessed. Next, it presents an original data set of 25 REOs in the 1980s and 1990s coded according to these guidelines. This description underscores the significant institutional variation across the organizations included in the data set.

Defining Regional Economic Organizations

REOs are a class of formal IGOs. Unlike other international agreements, such IGOs have a continuous institutional framework and some kind of formal structure. In addition, the membership of IGOs is restricted to nation-states, and they have to include at least three such members (Pevehouse, Nordstrom, and Warnke 2004). Two aspects distinguish REOs from other IGOs. First, while they sometimes address noneconomic issues, the promotion of economic policy cooperation among their members is one of their primary goals (Mansfield and Milner 1999). Even though some REOs, such as ECOWAS and Mercosur, have security-related components, they are not alliances.[1] Notwithstanding the involvement of many of these communities in social and political issues, the promotion of economic cooperation and integration is one of their key missions. Second, membership in these organizations is restricted to geographically proximate states. While some REOs, like the Latin American Integration Association (LAIA), span sizable swaths of territory, they are all regional, rather than global, in nature (Mansfield and Solingen 2010; Nye 1971).

This conceptualization excludes several types of agreements that are related to economic regionalism but do not qualify as REOs. These exclusions are consistent with conventional practices.[2] Many of the PTAs that were concluded in recent decades are bilateral and almost always lack a continuous institutional framework. These agreements, as well as similar agreements between two REOs or an REO and another country, do not meet the standard criteria of international organizations. Nonreciprocal agreements, such as the U.S. Caribbean Basin Initiative and the Lomé Convention, are excluded on similar grounds. Finally, framework agreements, like the Asia-Pacific Economic Cooperation (APEC), are also excluded. While these agreements may embrace the idea of regional cooperation, they lack concrete measures to achieve this goal. Twenty-five REOs that span most continents and include the majority of the states worldwide correspond to these criteria. Table 3.1 lists these organizations, their members, and the year of their formation. To facilitate the systematic comparison of these organizations (undertaken later in this chapter), I now turn to a detailed consideration of their institutional components.

Conceptualization and Measurement of REO Variation

This section defines and operationalizes the institutional features linked to violent conflict in the preceding chapter. It begins with the scope of economic activity, continues with regular meetings of high-level officials and institutional independence, and ends with regional institutionalization. The conceptualization of these features integrates their institutional design and implementation. Table 3.2 summarizes the indicators included in these measures.

TABLE 3.1. Twenty-Five Regional Economic Organizations, Their Members, and Year of Formation

Regional Economic Organization	Members as of 1997	Year Formed
Andean Community (ANCOM)	Bolivia, Colombia, Ecuador, Peru, Venezuela	1967
Central American Common Market (CACM)	Costa Rica, El Salvador, Guatemala, Honduras (left 1970; rejoined 1990), Nicaragua	1960
Caribbean Community (CARICOM)	Antigua and Barbuda, Bahamas (joined 1983), Barbados, Belize, Dominica, Grenada, Guyana, Jamaica, St. Kitts and Nevis, St. Lucia, St. Vincent and the Grenadines, Suriname (joined 1995), Trinidad and Tobago	1973
Latin American Integration Association (LAIA)	Argentina, Bolivia, Brazil, Chile, Colombia, Ecuador, Mexico, Paraguay, Peru, Uruguay, Venezuela	1981
Mercado Común del Sur (Mercosur)	Argentina, Brazil, Paraguay, Uruguay	1991
North American Free Trade Agreement (NAFTA)	Canada, Mexico, the United States	1992
Organization of Eastern Caribbean States (OECS)	Antigua and Barbuda, Dominica, Granada, Montserrat, St. Kitts and Nevis, St. Lucia, St. Vincent and the Grenadines	1981
European Free Trade Association (EFTA)	Austria (left 1995), Finland (joined 1986; left 1995), Iceland, Liechtenstein (joined 1991), Norway, Portugal (left 1986), Sweden (left 1995), Switzerland	1960
The European Union (EU)	Austria (joined 1995), Belgium, Denmark (joined 1973), France, Finland (joined 1995), Germany, Greece (joined 1981), Ireland (joined 1973), Italy, Luxemburg, the Netherlands, Portugal (joined 1986), Spain (joined 1986), Sweden (joined 1995), the United Kingdom (joined 1973)	1957
Arab Maghreb Union (AMU)	Algeria, Libya, Mauritania, Morocco, Tunisia	1989
Association of Southeast Asian Nations (ASEAN)	Brunei (joined 1984), Indonesia, Laos (joined 1997), Malaysia, Myanmar (joined 1997), the Philippines, Singapore, Thailand, Vietnam (joined 1995)	
Bangkok Agreement (BA)	Bangladesh, India, Laos, Republic of Korea, Sri Lanka	1976
Economic Cooperation Organization (ECO)	Afghanistan (joined 1992), Azerbaijan (joined 1992), Iran, Kazakhstan (joined 1992), Kyrgyz Republic (joined 1992), Pakistan, Tajikistan (joined 1992), Turkey, Turkmenistan (joined 1992), Uzbekistan (joined 1992)	1985
Gulf Cooperation Council (GCC)	Bahrain, Kuwait, Oman, Qatar, Saudi Arabia, United Arab Emirates	1981
South Asian Association for Regional Cooperation (SAARC)	India, Pakistan, Bangladesh, Nepal, Sri Lanka, Maldives, Bhutan	1985

TABLE 3.1.—Continued

Regional Economic Organization	Members as of 1997	Year Formed
Community of the Countries of the Great Lakes (CEPGL)	Burundi, Democratic Republic of Congo (DRC), Rwanda	1976
Common Market for Eastern and Southern Africa (COMESA)	Angola (joined 1990), Burundi, Comoros, DRC (joined 1993), Djibouti, Eritrea (joined 1993), Ethiopia, Kenya, Lesotho (left 1996–97), Madagascar, Malawi, Mauritius, Mozambique (joined 1989; left 1996–97), Namibia (joined 1993), Rwanda, Seychelles (joined 1995), Somalia (left 1999), Sudan (joined 1993), Swaziland, Tanzania (joined 1985), Uganda, Zambia, Zimbabwe	1981
Indian Ocean Commission (IOC)	Comoros (joined 1986), Madagascar, Mauritius, French Reunion (joined 1986), Seychelles	1984
Economic Community of Central African States (ECCAS)	Burundi, Cameroon, Central African Republic, Chad, Congo, DRC, Equatorial Guinea, Gabon, Rwanda, Sao Tome and Principe	1983
Economic Community of West African States (ECOWAS)	Benin, Burkina Faso, Cape Verde, Côte d'Ivoire, Gambia, Ghana, Guinea, Guinea-Bissau, Liberia, Mali, Niger, Nigeria, Senegal, Sierra Leone, Togo	1975
Mano River Union (MRU)	Guinea (joined 1980), Liberia, Sierra Leone	1973
South African Customs Union (SACU)	Botswana, Lesotho, Namibia (joined 1990), South Africa, Swaziland	1969
Southern African Development Community (SADC)	Angola, Botswana, DRC (joined 1997), Lesotho, Malawi, Mauritius (joined 1995), Mozambique, Namibia (joined 1990), Seychelles (joined 1997), South Africa (joined 1994), Swaziland, Tanzania, Zambia, Zimbabwe	1980
Central African Customs and Economic Union (UDEAC)	Cameroon, Central African Republic, Chad (left 1968–84), Republic of Congo, Equatorial Guinea (joined 1983), Gabon	1964
West African Economic and Monetary Union (WAEMU)	Benin (joined 1984), Burkina Faso, Côte d'Ivoire, Guinea-Bissau (joined 1997), Mali, Mauritania (left 1994), Niger, Senegal, Togo	1973

The Scope of Economic Activity

Scope is widely recognized as an important dimension of institutional design (Koremenos, Lipson, and Snidal 2001) and regional integration (Acharya and Johnston 2007; Grieco 1997; Hicks and Kim 2010; Kahler 1995). It commonly refers to the range of issues incorporated in a given organization in order to meet its objectives. Scope therefore differs from and is subsumed by mandate, which is the broad purpose of the organization (Acharya and Johnston 2007; Boehmer, Gartzke, and Nordstrom 2004; Boehmer and Nordstrom 2008). Restricting the analysis to the economic mandate of regional organizations, one can distinguish between those that address only a handful of issues and those that touch on a variety of matters. A systematic evaluation of the scope of economic activity requires an identification and differentiation of the issues that REOs can potentially in-

TABLE 3.2. Summary of Variables and Indicators Related to the Design of Regional Economic Organizations

Component	Area	Indicator
Scope of economic activity (24 points)	1. Trade liberalization	1. Preferential trade agreement (positive list)
		2. Free trade area (negative list)
		3. All members of REO participate
		4. Nontariff barriers
	2. Customs union	5. Common external tariff (positive list)
		6. Negative list of goods
		7. All members of REO participate
	3. Movement of services	8. Free movement of services
		9. At least six service sectors
	4. Movement of capital and investment	10. Free movement of capital
		11. Intraregional investment code
		12. Extraregional investment code
	5. Movement of labor	13. Free movement of labor
		14. Facilitation of labor movement
	6. Monetary integration and macroeconomic coordination	15. Common currency
		16. Coordination of monetary policies
		17. Coordination of fiscal policies
	7. Sectoral harmonization and cooperation	18. Harmonization of business conditions (at least four issue-areas)
		19. Sectoral cooperation (at least six sectors)
	8. Development and industrialization	20. Industrial cooperation
		21. Regional development bank
		22. Compensation mechanism
	9. Bargaining power	23. Negotiation with other REOs or economic powers
		24. Negotiation in multilateral forums
Decision-making body		25. Regular meetings of high-level officials
Institutional independence	1. Regional bureaucracy	26. Permanent secretariat
		27. Recommendations and initiatives
	2. Dispute settlement mechanism	28. Third-party ruling binding
		29. Standing tribunal

clude. This task is complicated by the ambiguity of the boundaries between different subject matters (Koremenos, Lipson, and Snidal 2001, 771).

Despite their broadly similar economic mandate, issue differentiation across REOs is still a significant obstacle. For example, are fiscal coordination and monetary coordination two issues or one? Should one conceptualize trade liberalization according to the number of sectors covered in the agreement or the kind of liberalization (tariffs, quotas, nontariff barriers)? Those studies that conduct an in-depth qualitative assessment of the implications of economic scope for cooperation and integration in different regions dodge these questions (Acharya and Johnston 2007; Grieco 1997; Kahler 1995; Katzenstein 1997). They provide valuable insights into the significance of this institutional feature, but they define this concept very broadly and fail to provide guidance on how to compare economic scope across time and space in a rigorous manner. As a result, evaluation of different REOs on this aspect appears impressionistic and lacks clear metrics.

A more systematic method builds on the traditional distinction between different types of integration schemes. First developed by Bela Balassa (1961), this approach classifies REOs according to their commitment to economic integration. The four main categories, from the most limited to the broadest in scope, are free trade area, customs union, common market, and economic union. Consistent with the development of economic integration in Europe, on which this classification is founded, these categories are also conventionally used to describe the process of economic integration. In this view, REOs broaden and deepen their scope as they gradually advance from one scheme to the next. This classification is still widely used in economics (Frankel 1997; Hufbauer and Schott 1994; OECD 1993) and political science (Bearce and Omori 2005; Genna 2008; Laursen 2003; Mansfield, Milner, and Pevehouse 2008; Smith 2000). The clear and simple classification offered by this approach is very appealing. In addition, it captures some of the most important activities REOs usually cover, particularly those related to international trade.

Nonetheless, this approach suffers from three important limitations. First, these different categories fail to capture the range of activities that REOs engage in, even in the supposedly exemplary case of European integration (Nye 1971, 28–30). Indeed, many REOs deal with several important issues that do not fit easily in these traditional categories, such as foreign investment, development, and industrial cooperation. To the extent that the inclusion of these issues facilitates the expansion of linkage opportunities, side payments, and greater cooperation, this approach presents an incomplete and potentially misleading picture of the organization's scope. Second, both theory and practice show multiple paths to economic integration that diverge from this simple evolutionary model (Choi and Caporaso 2002, 483; Foroutan 1993; Page 2000b, 8). The CFA franc zones in sub-Saharan Africa, for example, have established a monetary union but not a customs union, and the GCC made considerable progress on free movement of labor and capital but not on a common external tariff. Third, this classification is formal and ignores the degree of implementation of these arrangements. As Nye (1971, 29) points out, "the popular usage of many of the terms can be misleading. The 'common market' label is more widely applied than practiced . . . A cynic might say that regional economic schemes are more common than markets." Thus, this approach overlooks the gap between intended and actual economic scope.

The conceptualization of economic scope adopted in this study begins with the traditional approach but adds some modifications to address the shortcomings I have outlined. It identifies nine broad areas of economic cooperation and integration commonly tackled by REOs. The first six areas are largely compatible with the traditional categories. These are free movement of goods, customs union, free movement of services, free movement of capital and investment, free movement of labor, and monetary and fiscal cooperation. The remaining three areas are sectoral cooperation and harmonization, economic development, and efforts to enhance collective bargaining power. These are important issues that correspond to key goals of past and present REOs (Page 2000b). Each area consists of two to four specific indicators that capture the breadth and depth of cooperation on this issue. Taken together, these 24 indicators are general enough to "travel" across different regions and detailed enough not to miss essential economic issues that REOs typically address.

Each and every indicator is measured along two dimensions. The first—labeled *designed scope*—refers to approved agreements that specify the mandate of the organization. This is a necessary and important dimension of any institution (Acharya and Johnston 2007; Koremenos, Lipson, and Snidal 2001). Each indicator can obtain a value of 1, if present, and 0 if absent. Thus, the designed scope of economic activity can range from 0 to 24. This approach does not assume a gradual process of integration but, instead, allows any indicator to score a point independent of other indicators. In addition, consistent with conventional practice, all the indicators are equally weighted (Fortna 2004; Genna 2008; Hufbauer and Schott 1994).

Implementation

The second dimension of regional institutionalization is implementation, which refers to the actual steps that member states take to realize the agreements they have reached. In most instances, it involves the process by which governments transfer their international obligations to domestic laws, regulations, and policies (Simmons 1998; Underdal 1998; Victor, Raustiala, and Skolnikoff 1998, 4). It captures the notion that international cooperation involves not only agreements and rules but also behavior according to them. It is a key component of international institutions. As Lisa Martin (2000, 18) points out, "if agreements are not implemented, and the necessary policies changed, no cooperation has taken place. So it is essential that we consider implementation of international agreements if we are to understand patterns of international cooperation." In addition, Implementation is best understood as a process and therefore a matter of degree (Underdal 1998). Member states may implement little, some, or most of their obligations under the agreement.

Notwithstanding the importance of this institutional aspect, it is widely overlooked by scholars of international politics, and cross-regional measures of this concept are not readily available.[3] Collecting comparable data on implementation is more difficult than collecting such data on institutional design and is rarely done.[4] As a first cut into this institutional dimension, I created an ordinal scale with scores from 0 to 1. If the REO members did not implement the agreement regarding a specific indicator or if implementation is low, the REO scores 0. If implementation is complete or nearly complete, the REO scores 1 on the specific indicator. If implementation is either partial or very uneven across member states, the REO scores 0.5. For example, the 1981 GCC treaty calls for the establishment of a free trade area in goods and services as well as a customs union. By 1987, GCC members largely eliminated tariffs (but not nontariff barriers) and took some modest steps to liberalize trade in services, but took no action with respect to the customs union (Peterson 1988). As a result, this REO scores 1 on indicators related to free trade in goods, 0.5 on indicators related to free trade in services, and 0 on indicators related to customs union for this year.

Implementation is commonly an incremental process. Member states first sign and ratify agreements and only then put them into practice. Especially in REOs among developing countries, the elimination of barriers to trade or labor and capital movements can stretch over several years. In the case of WAEMU, for example, tariffs were eliminated gradually from 1996 to 2000. Similarly, bringing common industrial projects, such as the South Asian Growth Quadrangle, to fruition takes several years. Thus, to the extent that member states are on track with respect to particular issue areas, the REO's score increases over several years, from 0, to 0.5, to 1. The implementation of economic scope does not always move in a positive direction, however. Some organizations may get a strong start but then suffer setbacks and delays. For example, the Mano River Union's common external tariff was implemented in the late 1970s but broke down in the early 1990s, as relationships between the organization's members deteriorated. Similarly, in the 1980s, the Communauté Économique des Pays des Grand Lacs (CEPGL), or Economic Community of the Great Lakes Countries, moved forward with sectoral cooperation in a number of areas, but these projects were abandoned in the 1990s, when this REO became moribund. Capturing the evolution of implementation therefore requires attention to its often protracted, uneven, and occasionally reversible nature.

The multiplication of institutional design and implementation thus produces a second variable, labeled *implemented scope.* Member states may implement all the planned activities; thus, this variable ranges from 0 to 24. If the agreements are not fully implemented, the value on this variable will be lower than the one on institutional design alone. For example, in 1997, CARICOM had an agreement on 19 indicators; that is, it scored 19 on designed scope. Of these, 6 indicators were fully implemented, 7 were partly implemented, and 6 remain only on paper. The value on the variable *implemented scope* is calculated as follows: $(6 \times 1) + (7 \times 0.5) + (6 \times 0) = 10.50$. I now turn to a more detailed description of the areas and indicators.

Areas and Indicators

This subsection presents the nine areas subsumed by the scope of economic activity in turn. It briefly describes the indicators included in each of these areas and justifies their selection. It also explains the manners by which these indicators were coded and builds on the design of various REOs to illustrate the coding rules.

Trade liberalization. This key area includes four indicators. The first accounts for the existence of a PTA, which indicates reciprocal concessions on a limited number of goods, also known as a "positive list." Such lists commonly include several hundred products out of many thousands of possible tariff lines (de la Torre and Kelly 1992, 34). The Bangkok Agreement, for example, contains concessions on 438 products (Kelegama 2001, 111). Thus, a PTA imposes some modest costs on the member states of the REO. The second indicator, a free trade area (FTA), commonly eliminates most trade barriers among its members. It is therefore much more comprehensive and typically includes a "negative list," which specifies the products excluded from the trade agreement. The third indicator considers the extent of participation in the trade agreement. In some REOs, such as COMESA and ANCOM, member states can and do opt out of the trade agreement. Less than full membership impedes trade liberalization and the associated benefits. The fourth indicator examines the treatment of nontariff barriers, which include such measures as import quotas and administrative and health regulations. Nontariff barriers represent a significant obstacle to free regional trade,[5] and those REOs that take steps to eliminate or reduce them score a point.

Customs union. Some FTAs apply a common external tariff (CET) vis-à-vis the rest of the world. The significance of a CET emanates from the need to agree on a regional tariff schedule and to distribute tariff revenues among the members. This arrangement thus reflects a high level of interdependence. The first of three indicators examines the existence of a customs union. Like an FTA, member states can apply a CET on a small number of products or on most of their imports. The second indicator distinguishes between using a positive or a negative list to capture such disparity. Examples of the former are the customs unions of ANCOM and the West African Economic Community (or Communauté Économique de l'Afrique l'Ouest),[6] which applied a CET on 175 and 400 products, respectively (Mace 1994, 42; Bach 1990, 58). Other REOs, such as the EU and SACU, have a negative list and a much more comprehensive customs union. Only organizations that adopt a negative list score a point. In some REOs, only some of the members participate in the CET. For example, Peru and Bolivia do not participate in ANCOM's customs union (Mendoza 1999, 91). The third indicator accounts for partial membership.

Free movement of services. Trade in services has become an important part of many economies, and free cross-border movement in these sectors is a high priority for most regional organizations (Bulmer-Thomas et al. 1992, 27–28). Some service sectors, such as communications and finance, enjoy high levels of protection (Page 2000b, 213). The first indicator accounts for an agreement with respect to the free movement of services. Some REOs, such as ANCOM and ASEAN, liberalized only a few sectors (Mendoza 1999; Tongzon 1998), while others, such as CARICOM and NAFTA, enjoy free movement of most services (Page 2000b, 247). The second indicator adds a point to REOs that liberalize at least 6 out of 11 possible sectors identified by the World Trade Organization (WTO).[7]

Free movement of capital and investment. This area examines three indicators related to the regulation of capital and foreign investment. Capital is an important factor of production, and its liberalization improves economic efficiency. At the same time, removing barriers to capital flows commonly requires change of domestic laws and institutions. It also limits the ability of governments to pursue independent macroeconomic policy (Frankel 1997, 16). REOs that provide for free movement of capital, such as the EU and WAEMU, score the first point. Governments are sometimes reluctant to allow the free movement of all types of capital. They are more enthusiastic about the liberalization of foreign direct investment (FDI), which is believed to foster economic development. The second indicator considers intraregional FDI liberalization—for example, in the form of national treatment. Many countries, particularly developing ones, attract FDI from outside the region. The third indicator considers the existence of a common investment code vis-à-vis the rest of the world. In light of the intensifying competition for FDI, the value and number of such regional frameworks continue to grow (African Development Bank 2000, 125–26).

Free movement of labor. This area includes two indicators that examine provisions related to cross-border movement of workers, service providers, and business visitors. Like movement of capital, movement of labor is considered to be an issue of deep integration that has significant economic implications as well as an impact on domestic laws and institutions (Frankel 1997, 16). In addition, movement of labor is a politically sensitive matter, due to its potential implications for immigration. The first indicator examines the existence of an agreement that facilitates the free movement of labor, like those adopted by the EU, ECOWAS, and the GCC (Peterson 1988, 149). Short of a comprehensive free movement of labor, regional organizations may facilitate the employment of citizens from other member states in several ways. They may agree on a mutual recognition of professional certificates, relax visa requirements, or offer permits in certain sectors (Page 2000b, 216–17). REOs that contain such provisions score another point.

Monetary integration and macroeconomic coordination. Three indicators account for regional cooperation in these areas. The first looks at a monetary union, which entails the adoption of a common currency, a regional central bank, and, more generally, the surrender of national autonomy in the field of monetary and exchange rate policies. Sustaining a monetary union requires a great deal of coordination and surrender of national autonomy on important policy areas. At the same time, it is conducive to exchange rate stability and reduces the costs associated with cross-border trade and investment. In addition to the well-known European and three African monetary unions, various REOs, such as CARICOM, the GCC, and ECOWAS, have considered the formation of a monetary union. To the extent that a full-blown union is not feasible, member states may agree to coordinate and consult on their monetary and exchange rate policies, by establishing a forum of central bank executives or a clearing mechanism to exchange local currencies. REOs that coordinate monetary policies in such manners score another point.[8] The coordination of fiscal and macroeconomic policies refers to harmonization of tax rules, subsidies, government spending, and the like (Page 2000b, 231–33). Such cooperation sometimes takes place through the adoption of criteria for macroeconomic convergence, which requires macroeconomic policy discipline (Economic Commission for Africa 2004). The third indicator accounts for such instances.

Sectoral harmonization and cooperation. This area includes two indicators. The first examines harmonization of business conditions in different sectors. Members may harmonize policies related to labor standards, competition, antidumping, environmental regulations, intellectual property, standards, and company law (Page 2000b, 217). Some REOs, such as the EU and Mercosur, have provisions for most of these policies. Others, such as ANCOM and ASEAN, cover only two or three policies. Only REOs that harmonize business conditions in at least four areas score a point. The second indicator looks at sectoral cooperation, which creates or strengthens economic and social links across the region. Indeed, for several REOs in the developing world (e.g., SADC, ECO, and Indian Ocean Commission [IOC]), such cooperation is a key component of the regional organization. This area includes regional working groups, exchange of people and information, common management of natural resources, regional airlines, and the like (Nye 1971, 30). This is a diverse and relatively shallow area of cooperation. To score a point, REOs have to cooperate in at least 6 of the following 10 sectors: agriculture and fisheries, energy, natural resources, transportation, communications, insurance, tourism, health, science and technology, and education and culture.

Development and industrialization. Cooperation in this area is an important component of many regional organizations, especially in the developing world (de la Torre and Kelly 1992, 25). It consists of three indicators. First, REOs may establish cross-border industrial areas (which commonly combine resources of several members and involve ongoing coordination among the participants) or common industrialization plans (Page 2000b, 228). ANCOM's border integration zones exemplify the former, and the ASEAN industrial projects illustrate the latter (Mace 1994, 43–44; Tongzon 1998, 59–63). The second indicator considers the establishment of a regional development bank, which facilitates the mobilization of financial resources toward feasibility studies and the implementation of infrastructure projects. The CACM's Central American Bank of Economic Integration (or Banco Centroamericano de Integración Económica) and the Development Bank of the Union Douanière et Économique de l'Afrique Centrale (UDEAC) are two examples of this instrument. The third indicator accounts for mechanisms that transfer benefits from some members to others. Such mechanisms mitigate thorny distributional problems that are endemic to most, if not all, REOs (Mytelka 1973; Robson 1987). Organizations that provide for direct transfers from the more developed to the less developed members (as does, e.g., SACU) or that have a compensation fund (as do, e.g., the EU and WAEMU) score a point on this indicator.

Bargaining power. The potential increase of bargaining power vis-à-vis third parties is an important motive of many regional organizations (Mansfield and Solingen 2010; World Bank 2000, 17–21). To increase such power successfully, members have to coordinate their policies and to adopt a common position in the bargaining process. The first indicator accounts for a common position in economic negotiations with other organizations, such as the EU, or with important economic powers, such as the United States or China. EFTA and CARICOM, for example, negotiated several trade agreements as unified blocs. The second indicator examines a common position in multilateral forums, such as the WTO or the IMF. Such coordination provides the members with a greater voice and more leverage in these organizations (Jenkins 2001; Mansfield and Reinhardt 2003).

Regular Meetings of High-Level Officials

Most REOs provide for regular meetings of a decision-making body, typically every six months or once a year. These bodies have the ultimate authority to make decisions with respect to the organization's policies and general direction. The rank of the representatives varies across these organizations, however.[9] Some REOs entrust this decision-making authority to a group of heads of state or foreign ministers, known as a presidential council, conference of heads of state, council of foreign ministers, and so on. Other organizations, such as the CACM before 1990 and the Bangkok Agreement, assign this responsibility to lower-level ministers or ambassadors. Regular meetings of high-level officials refer to annual regional conferences among heads of state or foreign ministers, who usually have a great deal of power with respect to issues of national security (Bearce and Omori 2005).

As discussed in chapter 2, these meetings are sometimes postponed or called off, thereby preventing top officials from congregating and dealing with regional issues. Because this body is expected to mitigate conflict through direct face-to-face meetings, only REOs in which leaders actually convene meet the benchmark. Thus, like the implemented level of economic scope, the variable *high-level officials* scores 1 if meetings take place at least once a year. If a council meets only two or three times over a five-year span, it scores 0.5; and if it does not meet at least twice, it scores 0. For example, organizations such as ECOWAS, the GCC, and CARICOM, which held meetings of high-level officials on a regular basis, score 1 for each of the four time periods. LAIA, whose Council of Foreign Ministers met only five times in the 1980s (Best 1991, 617), and SAARC, whose summit convened only biannually in the early and mid-1990s (United Nations Conference on Trade and Development 1996), score 0.5 for the corresponding five-year periods. CEPGL held its last conference of heads of state in 1994, and AMU's Supreme Council met only once since 1992. These REOs score 0 on this variable for the matching time periods.

Institutional Independence

Institutional independence includes three essential and tightly linked dimensions: autonomy, neutrality, and delegation (Haftel and Thompson 2006). Autonomy refers to the organization's ability to function in a man-

ner that is insulated from the interests of its members. Thus, greater autonomy reflects a more limited control of states over the organization and a
broader range of actions available to it (Abbott and Snidal 1998; Hawkins et
al. 2006; Thompson 2006).[10] Neutrality reflects the notion that an independent actor is not prejudiced in favor of one party over another. Instead, a
neutral actor is guided by professionalism and impartial judgment. As Keohane, Moravcsik, and Slaughter (2000, 459) propose with respect to international courts and tribunals, independence measures "the extent to which
adjudication is rendered impartially with respect to concrete state interests." Even if an organization is autonomous and neutral, its influence depends on the responsibilities and power delegated to its institutions. As institutional properties, independence and delegation are tightly intertwined
(Keohane, Moravcsik, and Slaughter 2000). International institutions with
a significant delegated authority have discretion with respect to agenda setting and dispute management (Abbott and Snidal 2000; Hawkins et al.
2006). The three elements of REO independence are captured by the existence and discretion of regional bureaucracies and the existence and legalization of third-party DSMs.

Corporate Bureaucracy. This administrative body, typically labeled a
"secretariat" or "commission," is charged with everyday operations of the
organization. The personnel is employed by the organization and thus intended to serve regional, rather than national, interests. Article 17 of the
1993 COMESA Treaty, for example, requires, "In the performance of their
duties, the Secretary-General and Assistant Secretaries-General and the
staff of the Secretariat shall not seek or receive instructions from any Member State or from any other authority external to the Common Market.
They shall refrain from any actions which may adversely reflect on their position as international officials and shall be responsible only to the Common Market."

Variation in the independence of regional bureaucracy is captured with
two indicators that examine whether an REO has a neutral bureaucracy and
the extent to which this bureaucracy is delegated meaningful discretion.
When states endow organizations with a secretariat or commission, they
are delegating to a centralized authority and generating independence in
the process. It is unsurprising, then, that governments sometimes resist the
establishment of a secretariat and that not all REOs have one.[11] SACU, for
example, was managed through the Finance Department of South Africa
until 2004, and the Bangkok Agreement is coordinated by the Economic

and Social Commission for Asia and the Pacific. Thus, one point is assigned to organizations that have a distinct permanent secretariat or its equivalent.

When there is a permanent secretariat, the degree of responsibility that the member states delegate to the organization's bureaucracy is an important sign of independence. While most secretariats perform informational and operational roles, some bureaucracies are provided with additional, much more active responsibilities.[12] In particular, some secretariats and commissions can initiate and recommend policies and thereby promote the goals of the organization, prerogatives that greatly enhance bureaucratic authority. The European Commission, with the power to initiate policies, represents the ideal type for secretariats (Majone 2001), and the bureaucracies of ANCOM and WAEMU enjoy similar powers and prestige. In contrast, as one scholar of African regionalism points out, many REOs have very weak secretariats: "Expected only to ensure the smooth functioning of the community machinery on a day-to-day basis, they are severely handicapped in doing anything else by the lack of any real decision-making power" (Ntumba 1997, 313). Without this power, secretariats such as these find it difficult to play an active role in conflict prevention and mediation. They also do not carry the kind of prestige that contributes to effective mediation. REOs whose bureaucracy can initiate policies or make recommendations score another point. Thus, the variable *bureaucracy* is ordinal with scores ranging from 2 for a highly independent bureaucracy to 0 for no permanent regional secretariat.

Dispute Settlement Mechanism. The prevalence of DSMs in regional and other organizations reflects the growing legalization of world politics (Keohane, Moravcsik, and Slaughter 2000). The imperfect design and the unforeseen consequences of international institutions require an impartial body to adjudicate when disagreements arise. Delegating this power to a centralized mechanism reduces uncertainty and fosters cooperation (Hawkins at al. 2006; Yarbrough and Yarbrough 1997, 134–35). Not all DSMs are endowed with the same degree of autonomy and legal authority. Some REOs, like ASEAN and the GCC, adopted a nonbinding third-party review process. Others, like COMESA and the CACM, established a standing tribunal whose rulings are binding. In addition, some organizations, such as ECCAS and AMU, have agreed to form a DSM in principle but have not followed up on their plans (Mortimer 1999, 181; Union of International Associations 2000, 565).

James McCall Smith (2000) evaluates the legalization of different DSMs along five dimensions: the existence of a third-party review, the binding-ness of the ruling, the existence of a standing tribunal, private standing, and the effect of the ruling. Following Smith, these dimensions are collapsed into three ordered categories: no, low, and high levels of independence. A low level of independence refers to an instance in which third-party review is automatic and binding but judges are picked from an ad hoc roster. This design prevents members from bypassing or ignoring the ruling of the DSM, but it gives them power over the selection of the arbiter. A high level of independence entails a standing tribunal as well as automaticity and bindingness. With this design, states have little influence over the composi-tion of the tribunal, ensuring its neutrality. I also consider whether the DSM actually exists.[13] In line with Smith's (2000) own coding rules, to the extent that REOs have an operational DSM, the variable *dispute settlement* scores one point for each level of legalization, for a maximum of two points.

Regional Institutionalization

Chapter 2 pointed to potential synergy between the three institutional as-pects thus far discussed. The combination of a broader scope, regular top-level meetings, and high independence is potentially conducive to regional peace. All the indicators previously described are therefore aggregated into two overarching variables, which capture the degree of functional activity and political authority that states hand over to the organization. The first variable, labeled *designed institutionalization,* merges designed scope with regular meetings of high-level officials (whether they meet in practice or not), corporate bureaucracy, and dispute settlement. It captures the struc-ture and the intended functions of the REO. The second variable, labeled *implemented institutionalization,* takes into account the actual functioning of the organization. It merges implemented scope with regular meetings of high-level officials and the two variables related to institutional indepen-dence. Scores for both variables range from 0 to 29.

Coding and Data

With definitions and measurements in hand, I code the 25 REOs listed in table 3.1 on the institutional variables thus far described. As already dis-cussed, economic cooperation through REOs is a complex, gradual, and

uneven process. Signing agreements, ratifying them, and especially implementing them is time consuming. As a consequence, institutional change
usually takes, at the very least, several years to accomplish. This is especially
the case with respect to implementation, which can be a bumpy process. To
capture this important temporal dimension, I coded each REO at four different time points: 1982, 1987, 1992, and 1997. This undertaking goes beyond a snapshot of the organization's goals at its inception and provides a
sense of its evolution over two decades. The coding of close to 120 indicators for most REOs and over 2,600 indicators overall on both institutional
design and implementation sheds new light on the institutional landscape
of these organizations throughout the 1980s and 1990s.

Ideally, one would measure regional institutionalization and its com-
positional variables in shorter intervals, perhaps annually or biannually.[14]
Annual observations, in particular, would correspond to the convention in
the field and would facilitate research in this area. Producing the original
and fine-grained measures presented here for a large number of REOs on
an annual basis is, unfortunately, impractical for a study with this scope.
As mentioned in previous sections, most extant studies use large (mostly
annual) data sets with crude measures of institutional variation (if any at
all) or employ either one or a small number of detailed case studies. This
study takes a middle path and endeavors to strike a balance between the
depth and the breadth of the information collected on this phenomenon.
In this respect, it complements these two different methods and provides a
fresh angle from which to examine REOs and their role in world politics.
Future expansion of this data set may allow researchers to avoid this
difficult trade-off.

The selection of 1997 as the cutting point emanates from data availabil-
ity on violent conflict, which is purportedly affected by institutional variation across REOs. As I explain in chapter 4, I measure this phenomenon
with a data set on militarized interstate disputes (MIDs), which is widely
used in the study of international conflict. The latest version of this data set
includes disputes up to 2001. Concerns of reversed causality and the five-
year setup require that we go five years back to ensure that regional institutionalization preceded regional conflict. In addition, because it is difficult
to properly evaluate REOs that exist for a short period of time, only organizations that were formed before 1993 are included in this data set. This selection criterion ensures that each REO has at least two observations,
thereby having a temporal dimension. Of the 25 REOs included in the sam-

ple, 18 (75 percent) were formed before 1982 and thus have four observations, 4 have three observations, and 3 have two observations.

When coding the degree of institutionalization of the REOs, I relied on various primary and secondary sources. The main primary source was treaties and agreements, which provide the legal foundation for these organizations. These documents shed light on the organizations' objectives and institutions and on the manners by which they intend to promote economic cooperation. Many of these agreements are publicly available on the organizations' and other websites. This is only a first step, however, since not all agreements are accessible and because they provide an incomplete portrayal of institutional design. International agreements can be ambiguous with respect to the fine details of actual policies and leave ample room for interpretation. In addition, institutional changes are not always reflected in the main treaties and can be relegated to letters of understanding, internal documents, and the like.

To have a fuller picture of institutional design, I first scrutinized the websites of the various REOs for additional information. Most of them provide useful details on the organization's activities in different economic sectors and issue areas. They also describe the REO's institutional structure, including the secretariat, DSM, decision-making procedures, and development bank. Some websites, such as those for EFTA[15] and ASEAN,[16] also shed light on extraregional relations, by listing trade agreements with other countries or REOs. I complemented this survey with several studies that survey the goals, policies, and institutions of REOs included in the data set. These consist of studies by the International Monetary Fund (IMF 1994), the United Nations Conference on Trade and Development (1996), the African Development Bank (2000), and Page (2000b). In addition, I used the Union of International Associations' *Yearbook of International Organizations* (various years) and the IMF's *Directory of Economic, Commodity, and Development Organizations* online. The coding of DSMs follows Smith's (2000).[17]

Determining the degree of implementation is much trickier than determining institutional design. What is considered implementation is often subject to personal opinions and biases. Here, too, I started with the REOs' websites and examined annual reports and similar documents to provide a first cut into the organizations' activities. For example, the CARICOM website claims, "A single market for goods already exists among the CARICOM member states, as more than 95 per cent of the goods produced in the Region move freely across the Region."[18] Similarly, a recent COMESA annual report (2005, 15) indicates that the free trade agreement is largely implemented. REOs' self-reporting of their achievements provides only a very rough indication of implementation. Statements regarding implementation tend to be imprecise and to lack details regarding the timing of implementation. In addition, REOs may overstate the degree of implementation in order to present a rosy picture of their accomplishments (Gutner and Thompson 2010).

REO websites are equally, if not more, useful in establishing the lack of implementation. They often report on agreements that are under discussion or negotiation, suggesting that a given area of cooperation is yet to be executed. For example, reflecting on the status of sectoral cooperation, one ECO annual report (ECO 2000) states that "the implementation of the Almaty Outline Plan and the Programme of Action for the ECO Decade of Transport and Communications . . . is under way, albeit at a pace which is not entirely satisfactory," suggesting little implementation on this indicator. In another telling example, the ANCOM website reports that "the Advisory Council of Labor Ministers is preparing the groundwork to draft the regulations for [free movement of labor],"[19] indicating that this provision remains unrealized. Finally, most REOs publicize the dates of important meetings and often back them up with press releases related to these meetings. I used this information to code the indicator that pertains to regular meetings of high-level officials.

I complement this initial assessment with a large number of secondary resources.[20] First, I used the same surveys employed in the coding of institutional design. The African Development Bank (2000) and the Economic Commission for Africa (2004), for example, evaluate the progress of most African REOs in a number of important issue areas. Similarly, the Institute for the Integration of Latin America and the Caribbean (INTAL) publishes periodical reports on Latin American REOs, and publications by the IMF (1994) and the Organization for Economic Cooperation and Development (OECD 1993) provide an assessment of the achievements of most REOs. Second, I examined numerous independent studies and reports on each REO. These studies are often conducted by experts on the specific region or the specific issue area (or both). To increase the reliability of the coding and to reduce the risk of measurement error, I consulted several sources before determining the value of each indicator. Each coding is a result of cross-examination of these different sources, providing a degree of intercoder reliability. Finally, I utilized the Internet and search engines such as LexisNexis to scrutinize news reports on each of the organizations. These items were especially instrumental in verifying particular dates and events. Taken as a whole, these sources offer a meaningful and largely accurate, even if rough, assessment of implementation. Here, I provide illustrations of this coding procedure.

I pointed out earlier that a 2005 COMESA report claims that the free trade agreement (among some of its members) is largely implemented. To trace this process, I first examined the agreements related to trade liberalization. They indicate that the first agreement was signed in 1983 and involved a limited number of goods. A second agreement, which was signed in 1993, called for a comprehensive free trade agreement by 2000. Turning to implementation, a number of studies indicate that the first agreement faced numerous obstacles and remained largely on paper (Chanthunya 2001; Takirambudde 1999). The second agreement was implemented, albeit sluggishly and unevenly. For example, the African Development Bank (2000, 155) argues, "By 1997, only two of the member states had met the target of an 80 per cent tariff reduction on intra-COMESA trade."[21] Nevertheless, more recent studies indicate that most participants in the FTA reduced most of the agreed-on tariff lines by the early 2000s, corroborating the organization's claim. For example, one IMF paper states that "the FTA was formed in October 2000 as the result of a long period of tariff reductions" (Khandelwal 2004, 8). Based on these resources, COMESA scores 0 on the implemented level of the indicators that pertain to trade liberalization in 1982, 1987, and 1992. It scores 0.5 for 1997 and would score 1 for 2002 on the first two indicators in table 3.2.

Turning to other trade-related issues, the original 1960 CACM treaty called for a customs union among the REO's members. Extant studies indicate that the CET was not functioning in the 1980s (Bulmer-Thomas 1997, 260–64; Sánchez Sánchez 2009, 103–4). The organization renewed its commitment to the customs union in the 1993 Protocol of Guatemala (Articles 15–17). According to several reports, this plan was mired with difficulties and was not implemented by the late 1990s (Bulmer-Thomas 1997; INTAL 2000). The Protocol of Guatemala also calls for the liberalization of trade in services and investment. Similar to the common external tariff, however, these commitments remained on paper. As an INTAL report (2000, 52) points out, "Apart from some purely symbolic initiatives, there is little short-term hope that the Central American countries will secure real deepening by assuming greater commitments to open up [to trade in services and investment] among themselves."[22] Thus, the CACM scores 0 on all the indicators related to the implementation of a common external tariff and trade in services.

Moving beyond trade-related indicators, both the GCC and WAEMU were envisioned as common markets with free movement of labor and capital. The GCC facilitated the movement of labor and capital with a number of policies, such as eliminating visa requirements and relaxing ownership rules for the organization's citizens as early as the middle 1980s (Peterson 1988). Accordingly, Legrenzi (2003, 34) argues, "The aim of creating a regional 'economic citizenship' in accordance with Article 4 of the GCC Charter is one of the few goals that have come close to being fully realized." Nonetheless, these policies fall short of a comprehensive common market (Barnett and Gause 1998, 177; Legrenzi 2003; Peterson 1988). Consequently, the GCC scored 1 for the facilitation of labor movement and 0.5 for free movement of labor from 1987 onward. Several observers indicate that WAEMU achieved a high degree of capital mobility early on, as one aspect of its monetary union (African Development Bank 2000; Bourenane 2002, 25; Langhammer and Hiemenz 1990, 38). Provisions related to the free movement of labor were only partly implemented (African Development Bank 2000, 141; Bach 1997, 86). WAEMU therefore scored 1 for the capital mobility indicator and 0.5 for the two indicators related to labor mobility for all four time periods.

As pointed out earlier, less traditional areas of cooperation are more difficult to quantify. CARICOM offers a good illustration of how indicators related to these areas are coded. This REO aspires to facilitate regional coordination of monetary and fiscal policies and ultimately to form a monetary union. Despite several agreements and repeated commitments, CARICOM has failed to make meaningful progress on these issues. In particular, efforts to coordinate exchange rate and tax policies were unsuccessful throughout the 1980s and the 1990s (El-Agraa and Nicholls 1997, 287–90; Nicholls et al. 2000, 1187; Payne 1994, 97). As Taccone and Nogueira (2002, 44) explain, "Although member states had accepted the proposals and reiterated their commitment to monetary integration in 1994, the preparatory process for monetary union has not yet moved beyond biannual assessments of the convergence indicators and eligibility criteria." Similarly, in the 1980s, CARICOM members agreed on programs of regional industrialization, such as the CARICOM Industrial Programming Scheme and the

CARICOM Enterprise Regime. These programs remained largely on paper and were eventually scrapped in 1995 (Payne 1994, 95; Taccone and Nogueira 2002, 44). Accordingly, CARICOM scores 0 on the implemented indicators pertaining to monetary and macroeconomic coordination as well as industrial cooperation.

CARICOM was more successful in the areas of sectoral cooperation and harmonization, in setting up a development bank, and in negotiation with extraregional actors (Girvan 2008; Nicholls et al. 2001; Taccone and Nogueira 2002, 69–70). With respect to harmonization for example, the Caribbean Market Standards Council, established in 1976, is designed to promote regional standards in various sectors. Efforts in this area resulted in harmonization of some customs, competition, sanitary, and labor standards in the early 1990s (El-Agraa and Nicholls 1997, 290; Girvan 2008). Taccone and Nogueira (2002, 48) note, however, "Much work remains to be done to upgrade and harmonize technical, labor, environmental and sanitary standards for products and production processes." I therefore assigned the scores 0 in the 1980s and 0.5 in the 1990s for this indicator. Regarding a common bargaining position, CARICOM negotiated several important nonreciprocal agreements with the EU, United States, and Canada in the 1980s. The organization continued to negotiate as a bloc in the 1990s in multilateral and bilateral forums. It also formed the Caribbean Regional Negotiating Machinery to further strengthen this important function. Observers agree that through these negotiations, CARICOM improved the bargaining position of its members (Nicholls et al. 2000, 1175–80; Taccone and Nogueira 2002). It thus scored one point on the two indicators related to bargaining power in all four time periods.

The Landscape of Regional Economic Organizations

This section builds on the data collection effort thus far described, to assess the variation in the institutionalization and design of REOs included in the sample. It first examines general trends across regions and over time. It then considers specific design features and the relationships between them. The analysis highlights the substantial institutional variation across existing organizations and reinforces the call for a nuanced treatment of their structure and functions. It also indicates that the measures constructed for this study are compatible with extant research, providing them with face validity. Table 3.3 presents descriptive statistics for all the variables discussed in this chapter.

Regional Institutionalization

To gauge the scale of regional institutionalization worldwide, each of the two overarching variables are divided into three groups along a continuum of institutionalization: low, medium, and high. Figure 3.1 reports the number of organizations that fall in each of these categories.[23] It substantiates the widespread intuition, shared by this study, that all REOs are not alike (Choi and Caporaso 2002; Mansfield and Milner 1999; Page 2000b): many organizations are weakly institutionalized, but others exhibit intermediate or high levels of institutionalization. Figure 3.1 also underscores the gap between institutional design and implementation. Considering only institutional design, it appears that a large number of REOs champion ambitious agreements with lofty goals. About 70 percent of all organizations fall in either the intermediate or high category. This trend is turned on its head when taking into account implementation, however: about 70 percent of the REOs fall in the low category, and only one (the EU) falls in the high category. This observation underscores the reality that many organizations, especially those among developing countries, fall short of their stated objectives (de la Torre and Kelly 1992; Langhammer and Hiemenz 1990; OECD 1993, 65).[24]

An overview of the evolution of REOs throughout the 1980s and the 1990s indicates that economic regionalism is a dynamic phenomenon. This is apparent from the sheer number of organizations included in the sample at each time point, which increases from 18 in 1982 to 25 in 1992. The for-

TABLE 3.3. Descriptive Statistics of Variables Related to Regional Institutionalization

Variable	Range	Min	Max	Mean	Std. Dev.
designed institutionalization	0–29	1	29	13.13	6.86
implemented institutionalization	0–29	0	28	7.43	5.59
designed scope	0–24	1	24	10.56	6.01
implemented scope	0–24	0	23	5.08	4.85
high-level officials	0–1	0	1	0.71	0.43
bureaucracy	0–2	0	2	1.02	0.56
dispute settlement	0–2	0	2	0.62	0.86

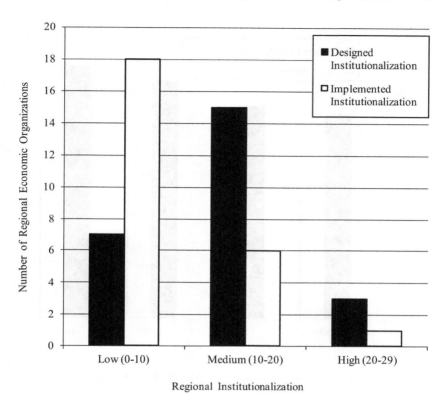

Fig. 3.1. Average distribution of 25 REOs across three categories of regional institutionalization, 1982–97

mation of organizations like Mercosur, SAARC, and AMU illustrates this proliferation and reflects the growing number of economic IGOs, even as the number of other types of IGOs is falling (Pevehouse, Nordstrom, and Warnke 2004). The increasing level of institutionalization over this time period further substantiates this observation. Figure 3.2 depicts the annual average of institutionalization for the 18 REOs that have all four observations.[25] It demonstrates that its average level has substantially increased over this 15-year interval. This is evident for both designed and implemented institutionalization, which exhibit a growth rate of 23 and 33 percent, respectively. REOs like ECOWAS, ANCOM, and ASEAN are but a few examples of this development.[26] This description corresponds to other recent assessments of this trend. Many observers point out that the wave of

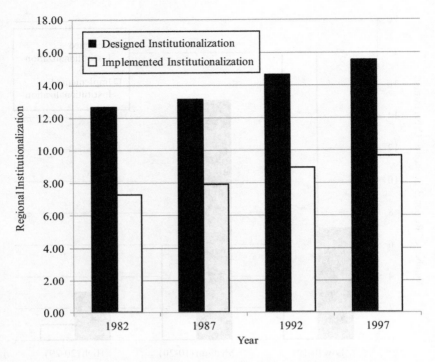

Fig. 3.2. Average institutionalization of 18 REOs by year

regionalism that ensued in the early 1990s deals with more issues and strives for deeper cooperation, compared to previous efforts (Fawn 2009; Hettne 1999, 7–8; Kahler 1995, 81–82; Mansfield and Milner 1999).[27]

Turning to the institutionalization of specific REOs, figure 3.3 presents the designed and implemented levels for each organization (averaged over the coded time points). It further validates the observation that existing REOs exhibit considerable institutional variation. It also illustrates the uneven gap between design and implementation. For some REOs, such as ASEAN, SACU, and the EU, the former diverges from the latter only slightly. Their implementation ratios, which is the percentage of implemented indicators out of those that score 1 on institutional design, are 0.87, 0.93, and 1.00, respectively.[28] In other organizations, most notably AMU and ECCAS, implementation falls far short of institutional design. The implementation ratios of these two organizations hover around 10 percent, indicating a very wide gap between objectives and practice.

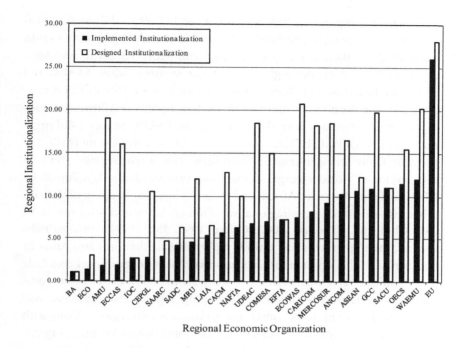

Fig. 3.3. Average institutionalization of 25 REOs, 1982–97

The variation reported in figure 3.3 bestows the measure with a degree of face validity. Consistent with conventional wisdom, the EU emerges as the most institutionalized REO, far ahead of all the other organizations. This gap is particularly pronounced when implementation is taken into account. This result echoes the commonly held view that the EU "has consolidated its status as the champion of regional integration" (Choi and Caporaso 2002, 483) and that it is much more institutionalized than REOs in the Western Hemisphere (Choi and Caporaso 2002; Grieco 1997), Asia (Acharya and Johnston 2007, 245; Katzenstein 1997), and Africa (Page 2000a). Nonetheless, the EU has much in common with other REOs and serves as a useful yardstick. As Kahler (1995, 82) observes, "The EU's evolving institutions provide an important benchmark for other regional institutional arrangements. Despite its virtually unique institutions, the EU continues to confront many of the same dilemmas that other, less institutionalized arrangements face."

Detailed comparisons that go beyond the EU offer additional indications that the measure previously described is sound. Page (2000a) ranks many REOs on their intensity. Consistent with figure 3.3, SACU and Mercosur are located on the higher end of her measure, while SAARC and SADC are found on the other extreme. An analysis of African REOs conducted by the Economic Commission for Africa (2004) reaffirms this coding as well. It identifies WAEMU, ECOWAS, and SADC as successful organizations and CEPGL, ECCAS, IOC, and the Mano River Union (MRU) as laggards. Considering average institutionalization across regions, REOs in the developed world emerge as the most institutionalized, followed by REOs in Latin America, Africa, and Asia.[29] This, too, is compatible with other assessments of cross-regional variation (Acharya and Johnston 2007, 245; Choi and Caporaso 2002; Grieco 1997; IMF 1994). Interestingly, though, the implementation ratio is higher in Asia than in Latin America and Africa.[30] This observation suggests that Asian governments conclude less ambitious agreements but are more likely to realize their visions compared to governments in other developing regions. Nevertheless, one should not lose sight of the substantial variation within regions. Along with moribund REOs, Africa contains two of the most institutionalized organizations, SACU and WAEMU. Similarly, Asia hosts lackluster as well as ambitious REOs: ECO and SAARC exemplify the former, and ASEAN and the GCC represent the latter.

In short, the measure constructed for this study corroborates a good deal of casual observations made by extant research with respect to institutional variation across REOs. At the same time, it provides one of the first nuanced and systematic treatments of this variation and offers a clearer picture of institutional differences across organizations, regions, and time.

Design Features and Relationships among Them

In light of the theoretical framework presented in chapter 2, it is important to move beyond the overarching measures of regional institutionalization and examine the specific design features presumed to affect conflict. This section first considers the variation on each of these variables, further underlining the great deal of variation on their values. It then explores the association between the different features, summarized in table 3.4, and points to a positive but imperfect correlation between them. If these different institutional aspects are highly correlated, we may be able to employ one feature as a surrogate for regional institutionalization, dispensing with the rest. The data indicate that this is not the case: the correlations among the features are positive but far from perfect.

Patterns pertaining to the scope of economic activity largely resemble those of the broader institutionalization measures, as indicated by the very high correlation between these two sets of variables ($R^2 = 0.97$). This is not surprising, as scope comprises about 80 percent of regional institutionalization. Again, substantial variation exists on the designed and implemented scopes, and the gap between them is often considerable. The average score on the variable *designed scope* is more than twice the average score on the variable *implemented scope*. A broader, cross-regional comparison of economic scope offers a slightly different picture than the one pertaining to regional institutionalization. Here, the average level of the variable *implemented scope* in Asia surpasses Africa's, albeit by a very slim margin. This observation further attests to the meager achievements of several African organizations.

In chapter 2, I argued that despite the emphasis of extant research on commercial integration, other areas of cooperation are as (and perhaps even more) instrumental in mitigating violent conflict. Insofar as the values of trade-related indicators go hand in hand with values of other indicators, this theoretical claim may not matter much in practice. To explore the significance of this issue, I examined the association between the indicators related directly to trade and the rest of the indicators.[31] The analysis reveals that the distinction between trade and other economic issue areas is not only theoretically important but also empirically significant. The correla-

TABLE 3.4. Correlation Matrix of Variables Related to Regional Institutionalization

	designed institu- tionalization	imple- mented institu- tionali- zation	designed scope	imple- mented scope	high-level officials	bureau- cracy	dispute settlement
designed institutionalization	1.00						
implemented institutionalization	0.71	1.00					
designed scope	0.98	0.70	1.00				
implemented scope	0.63	0.97	0.66	1.00			
high-level officials	0.43	0.34	0.36	0.20	1.00		
bureaucracy	0.46	0.45	0.34	0.30	0.43	1.00	
dispute settlement	0.52	0.53	0.42	0.37	0.30	0.34	1.00

tion between trade and nontrade indicators is positive but moderate, suggesting that cooperation on trade matches cooperation on nontrade issues only imperfectly.[32] A glance at the various REOs points to several instances where cooperation on trade diverges from cooperation on other issue areas. Some organizations, such as EFTA and Mercosur, made greater advancements on commercial integration compared to cooperation on other issues. Other organizations, such as COMESA, SADC, and the GCC, made headway on nontrade issues but achieved precious little on trade-related measures.

Turning to regular meetings of high-level officials, close to 70 percent (61 out of 90) of all observations score 1, indicating that this feature is rather common among existing REOs. Twenty-three observations score 0 on this variable, 16 times because the organization did not institute top-level meetings and 7 times because high-level officials have failed to meet according to schedule. In the remaining six cases, high-level meetings have taken place occasionally, and the score was therefore 0.5. Cross-regional comparison indicates that top-level meetings are more common in Africa and Latin America than in Asia.

The existence and power of corporate bureaucracy fluctuates across different organizations and over time. While almost all REOs have established a secretariat or a commission, only a handful of these bodies have the authority to make recommendations or initiate policies. Some (e.g., the ASEAN Secretariat and the WAEMU Commission) have obtained such power only in the 1990s. REOs institute a binding DSM only infrequently.[33] About a third of the observations (33 out of 90) score at least 1 on this variable. Nevertheless, about three-quarters of these mechanisms are standing tribunals. This feature, too, exhibits some temporal variation. REOs like EFTA and the CACM have established their DSM only in recent decades. Considering some general trends, it appears that institutional independence has increased over time. The average level of independence for the 18 REOs that have all four observations climbed from 1.61 in 1982 to 2.06 in 1997 (out of four possible points). Cross-regional comparison indicates that Latin American REOs are much more independent than their African and especially their Asian peers. The average independence level for Latin American REOs is about 2.12, almost three times higher than Asia's 0.82. This is consistent with the widely held view that Asian governments prefer less formal and legalized organizations (Kahler 2000; Katzenstein 1997).

The correlation between the different institutional features is always positive, suggesting that wider economic scope is frequently accompanied by regular top-level meetings and greater institutional independence. At the same time, most bivariate correlations range from low to intermediate, underscoring the diverse nature of existing regional organizations. The correlation between economic scope—either designed or implemented—and regular meetings of high-level officials does not exceed 0.40, suggesting that functional cooperation does not necessitate frequent top-level meetings and vice versa. For example, despite having a rather broad economic scope, NAFTA and SACU did not institute regular meetings of high-level officials. The leaders of IOC and UDEAC met regularly, however, even though these REOs have a very limited economic scope. This potential bifurcation merits attention, because subsequent chapters suggest that coupling a wide economic scope with regular meetings among high-level officials is especially conducive to regional peace.

The correlation between economic scope and the two features pertaining to independence is also quite modest, ranging from 0.30 to 0.45. Presenting the average score on implemented scope and institutional independence, figure 3.4 illustrates this multiplicity of arrangements. Some organizations, such as WAEMU and IOC, score high and low on both aspects, respectively. Other REOs, in contrast, score high on one aspect but low on the other. ECOWAS is rather independent but has a limited economic scope. SACU and the GCC have a wider scope but are less independent.

The association between regular meetings of high-level officials and institutional independence is moderate, suggesting that these features go together frequently but not always. Some REOs, such as NAFTA, include a binding DSM but no top-level meetings. Many other organizations provide for regular meetings of high-level officials but have little independence. Interestingly, the correlation between the two variables related to independence is only 0.34. Thus, while some REOs have both an independent secretariat and a standing tribunal, others have one but not the other. LAIA, for example, includes an independent secretariat but not a binding DSM. In contrast, COMESA has a standing tribunal but a weak secretariat. Thus, institutional independence may develop in a number of different ways.

With all factors taken together, this analysis highlights the varied landscape of existing REOs with respect to their functions and structure and indicates that each design feature captures a distinct aspect of regional institutionalization, which merits separate empirical analysis.

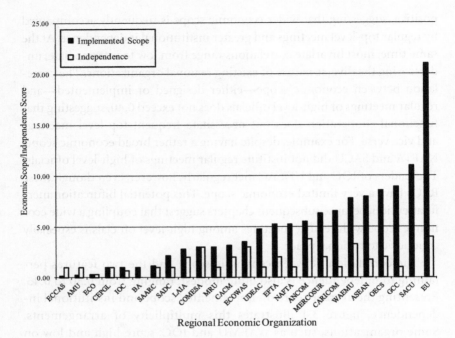

Fig. 3.4. Average implemented scope and independence of 25 REOs, 1982–97

Conclusion

This chapter offers a framework to systematically assess regional economic organizations, their institutional design, and their operation. It thus facilitates the construction of several institutional variables hypothesized to mitigate armed conflict. It advances the study of this nexus by considering the range of activities these organizations address and the institutions that sustain them. It also moves beyond institutional design and takes into account the implementation of signed agreements. The coding of most existing REOs on these variables over two decades results in an original data set that casts new light on the landscape of this important type of international institutions. It reveals substantial variation in the institutional makeup of these organizations and in the gap between design and implementation. The next two chapters employ this data set to evaluate the implications of this variation for regional conflict.

CHAPTER 4

The Effect of Regional Institutionalization on Violent Conflict

The theoretical framework presented in chapter 2 indicates that regional economic organizations can be instrumental in reducing interstate violent conflict, and proposes several causal mechanisms by which they may do so. As discussed in that chapter, the effects of these institutional features on conflict depend, in important ways, on their level of institutionalization. More institutionalized REOs, I argued, increase the opportunity cost of conflict, build trust among their members, and serve as effective conflict managers. In addition, bringing a number of specific features together creates synergies by facilitating issue linkage, side payments, and socialization. Using the data set described in chapter 3, this chapter offers an empirical analysis of the hypotheses made in chapter 2, with respect to the effect of the aggregate level of regional institutionalization on the number of intraregional militarized disputes. This analysis pays particular attention to the considerable gap between institutional design and implementation reported in chapter 3.

The first section of this chapter elaborates on issues of research design and on the dependent, independent, and control variables. The second section reports the results of the empirical analysis, which indicate that regional institutionalization mitigates intraregional violent conflict, but only to the extent that it is implemented. Thus, highly institutionalized agreements that remain on paper do not promote peace. Employing the quantitative results as a springboard, the third section presents a large-N qualitative analysis. In it, I calculate the expected number of disputes based on all the explanatory variables except regional institutionalization. I then contrast REOs that face similar propensity for conflict but have different levels of institutionalization. This comparison offers additional support to the argument that implemented regional institutionalization reduces violent conflict and identifies the conditions under which it does so. Specifically, it shows that high levels of institutionalization are instrumental in mitigating violent conflict when the level of regional hostility is intermediate but that they are less effective when frictions are either minimal or highly intense.

Research Design

To test the hypothesized effect of regional institutionalization on violent conflict, I use the original data set described in chapter 3. Because regional institutionalization is an attribute of an REO, the empirical analysis is conducted at the regional level of analysis, as defined by organizational membership. For the sake of consistency, the dependent variable and the control variables are also defined and measured at the regional level. This setup expands on other quantitative analyses on the link between international organizations and conflict, which commonly employ a dyadic setup (Bearce and Omori 2005; Boehmer, Gartzke, and Nordstrom 2004; Mansfield and Pevehouse 2000; Mansfield, Pevehouse, and Bearce 1999/2000; Russett and Oneal 2001; Russett, Oneal, and Davis 1998).

Although the dyadic level of analysis has provided numerous insights into the sources of violent conflict, it suffers from some limitations. In particular, it reduces all international dynamics to bilateral relations. There are good reasons to believe that some types of interactions are not adequately captured by a dyadic setup and are more amenable to a regional one (Poast 2010). Regional institutionalization is, of course, an organizational trait of the REO and not of any particular dyad. For example, all the members of Mercosur take part in the REO's common external tariff, and all WAEMU heads of state meet in the annual summit to discuss regional matters. Thus, to gauge the consequences of these institutional elements, one has to examine the organization in one piece. The dependent variable, violent conflict, is also not necessarily a bilateral phenomenon (Gleditsch 2002, 41). Many disputes involve multiple participants, often neighboring states. Even when conflicts are bilateral, they tend to have ripple effects and to impact the political and economic stability of adjacent third parties.

Some conventional explanations for the likelihood of militarized interstate disputes point to a similar conclusion. The regional balance of power and the existence of a regional hegemon, for example, require one to identify the region itself. The politics of the EU go beyond German-French diplomacy, and those of ASEAN do not boil down to Malaysian-Indonesian relations. Similarly, economic resources and networks commonly span several countries, not just two. That is why economic and other functional matters are often regulated by regional, rather than bilateral, bodies (reflected by the numerous organizations examined in this book). Recent studies point to additional factors that tend to cluster geographically, such as security relations and regime type, thereby suggesting that regional dynamics are at work (Buzan and Wæver 2003; Gleditsch 2002).

Taken together, these observations point to the significance of interaction in the regional arena and reinforce several calls for greater scholarly attention to this level of analysis (Buzan 1991; Buzan and Wæver 2003; Fawn 2009; Gleditsch 2002; Kacowicz 1998; Lake and Morgan 1997; Lemke 2002; Solingen 1998). Such analysis can serve as a useful complement (rather than a substitute) to the dyadic level of analysis. The definition of particular regions according to membership in regional international organizations emanates from my attempt to evaluate the effect of variation in these organizations on conflict in the region. While there is a lack of consensus on exactly how to define a region and on the specific states that belong to each region, identifying regions by organizational ties is one conventional way to proceed (Mansfield and Milner 1999; Väyrynen 2003). The institutional aspect of regions is especially pertinent to questions of peace and stability. As Acharya (2007, 639) explains, "While regions should not be conflated with regional institutions, the existence, design, and performance of regional institutions can tell us much about the conditions and prospects of regional order, including . . . prospects for conflict management and rule-governed behavior among states."

Some might argue that defining regions by organizational membership may be susceptible to selection bias—that perhaps only states that already have amicable relationships are inclined to form an REO, whereas zones of conflict may be unwilling to form REOs of any kind. If this were the case, the more war-prone regions would be left out of the analysis, which would, in turn, artificially inflate the pacifying effect of regional institutions. But this concern is misplaced for at least two reasons. First, this book is interested less in the consequences of REOs per se than in the implications of differences across REOs for conflict mitigation. Its center of attention is therefore on comparing the institutional design and implementation of these organizations. Second, the landscape of REOs, discussed in chapter 3, defies the claim that only peaceful regions form REOs. Indeed, the sample of REOs examined in this study covers most regions in the world, which reflect varying degrees of conflict and cooperation. These organizations operate in peaceful regions, such as Western Europe and the Southern Cone, as well as conflict-prone regions, such as South Asia and Central Africa. Similarly, out of the handful of regions that are excluded from the analysis, some, such as parts of the Middle East, experience high levels of conflicts, but others, such as Oceania, are very peaceful.

Even if most regions are included in the analysis, it is still possible that zones of peace will form more REOs than zones of conflict, resulting in overrepresentation of the former in the sample. A glance over the organizations examined in this study provides little support for the notion that REOs are formed at a higher rate in more peaceful regions. If anything, the opposite is true. Ten out of 25 REOs were formed in highly unstable parts of sub-Saharan Africa, while only three organizations were formed in the rather peaceful regions of Western Europe and North America.

Finally, it could be that REOs that are formed in conflict-prone regions exclude "troublemakers," which may be shunned by or not interested in cooperating with their neighbors: for example, Cuba is not a member of CARICOM, and North Korea is not a member of any organization. Or it could be that one or both sides to an enduring rivalry are excluded from a certain REO: for example, the GCC excludes Iraq but includes Kuwait, and the EU excludes Turkey but includes Greece. Insofar as conflict-prone states are systematically excluded from REOs, some regions may appear more peaceful than they actually are. Again, these examples appear to be the exception rather than the rule. The membership of Myanmar in ASEAN, Afghanistan in ECO, and the Democratic Republic of Congo in four different REOs attests to the inclusiveness of most regional clubs. More strikingly, almost all regional rivals—such as India and Pakistan, Peru and Ecuador, Morocco and Algeria, and Ethiopia and Eritrea—have joint REO memberships. In sum, conceptualizing regions with organizational membership does not introduce a systematic bias into the empirical analysis. The large number of regions and states included in the analysis further reduces the risk that the sample, in and of itself, artificially lowers the evidentiary bar to the theoretical framework presented in chapter 2.

Estimation Technique

The dependent variable is a count of intraregional violent disputes and is characterized by a Poisson distribution. Therefore, an *event count model* is used for estimation. In addition, the significance of the goodness-of-fit parameters in the statistical models discussed later in this section indicates that a *negative binomial regression model* is most appropriate. This model assumes a Poisson distribution but allows a conditional variance that is greater than the conditional mean (J. S. Long 1997). Finally, the data is arranged in a panel setup and thus "pools" numerous REOs together.[1] While the statistical models include a battery of explanatory factors (discussed shortly), they are unlikely to account for all the determinants of violent conflicts, some of which may be unique to specific organizations. This may lead to the so-called omitted variable bias. This pitfall is addressed statistically with random effects or fixed effects models, which account for cross-sectional unobservable contextual heterogeneity. I am using the more efficient (in a statistical sense) random effects specification.[2]

As discussed in previous chapters, claims about the causal effect of international institutions are susceptible to risks of reversed causality and endogeneity. Because REOs are created by and serve their member states, they may reflect prior relationships rather than affect them. Even if the theoretical expectations with respect to the manners by which political conditions affect regional institutionalization are contested, the empirical analysis ought to offer some ways to untangle the causal relationships between these variables. This chapter begins to tackle this issue in two ways. To reduce the risk that peace leads to institutionalized cooperation rather than vice versa, the variables that capture the institutional features—as well as the rest of the independent variables—precede the dependent variable. This ensures that armed disputes are observed after REO activities and institutions are already in place. For example, the level of regional institutionalization observed in 1987 for SADC is linked to the number of militarized disputes observed from 1987 to 1991 between the members of this organization. To minimize the risk of spurious relationships between regional institutions and conflict, the statistical models include several control variables that are thought to account for both phenomena. These factors include, among other things, power relationships, the type of political regime, and the degree of political affinity in the region. If, indeed, any or all of these factors determine both the level of institutionalized cooperation and the amount of militarized conflict, the effect of regional institutionalization (to the extent that there is one) should disappear.

Given the complex interaction between international politics, institutions, and conflict, these two procedures provide only preliminary assurance that the effect of regional institutionalization is genuine. Ideally, one would use more sophisticated techniques to address this issue, such as structural equation, instrumental variable, and selection models. These models relax the assumption that the dependent variable (in our case, militarized conflict) has no effect on the explanatory variables, and they thus obtain a more accurate estimate of the effect of these variables.[3] Unfortunately, if used appropriately, these techniques require a large number of observations, many more than the data set used in this study have. In addition, these methods are commonly applied in the context of linear models and cannot easily accommodate nonlinear models, such as the count model required for the analysis here.

To shed additional light on the link between regional institutionalization and conflict, I therefore conduct a separate analysis of the sources of the former. This approach, which the next chapter presents, is common in studies that cannot implement the more sophisticated techniques previously discussed (Boehmer, Gartzke, and Nordstom 2004; Boehmer and Nordstom 2008; Mansfield and Pevehouse 2000; Russett and Oneal 2001; Russett, Oneal, and Davis 1998). Reversing the causal arrow, this analysis pays particular attention to the potential impact of militarized disputes on economic cooperation through institutions but also sheds light on the sources of variation across current REOs.

Dependent Variable

The dependent variable is the number of intraregional militarized disputes. To accommodate the setup of the variables pertaining to regional institutionalization, the number of disputes are aggregated over a five-year period.[4] Because violent disputes are rather rare events, such aggregation also provides meaningful variation on this variable. For each REO, all intraregional dyadic disputes are counted in all years in which they took place. The theoretical framework generates expectations regarding relationships between REO members, rather than between member and nonmember states. Disputes between members and nonmembers are therefore not included in the count. In infrequent cases where a dispute involves several participants that are both members and nonmembers, only dyads in which both participants are members are counted.

A dispute between Sierra Leone, on the one hand, and Nigeria, Guinea, and Ghana, on the other, that lasted from 1997 to 1998 illustrates this counting method. As all four states are members of ECOWAS, this dispute produces a count of six for this REO (one dyadic dispute between Sierra Leone and each of the other three members for each year). Only Sierra Leone and Guinea are also members of MRU, so the same dispute produces two counts for this REO (one dyadic dispute between the two members for each year). Again, the logic is that one might expect MRU to influence the relationship between Sierra Leone and Guinea but not that between Sierra Leone and Nigeria. To operationalize this variable, labeled *MID*, I employ version 3.10 of the Correlates of War (COW) data set on MIDs (Ghosn, Palmer, and Bremer 2004; Jones, Bremer, and Singer 1996). This data set, which is widely used in the study of international conflict, contains incidents that involve the threat, display, and actual use of force up to 2001. While many of these incidents fall short of a full-blown war, they reflect an open and serious rift between the participating parties.[5]

It may still be argued that threats to use or the display of force are not significant manifestations of armed conflict (Gleditsch 2002). As in previous studies, a count of the disputes that involve only the use of force, labeled *violent MID*, addresses this concern (Mansfield and Pevehouse 2000). In addition, disaggregating regional conflicts into dyadic ones may inflate the number of disputes in some regions but not in others. To ensure that the results are not affected by the method of aggregation, I created a third variable, labeled *regional MID*. This variable counts the annual number of disputes regardless of the number of participants. In the example previously mentioned, the dispute between Sierra Leone and the other ECOWAS members will generate only two, rather than six, counts for this variable (one for each year). The tables in the appendix to this chapter report summary statistics for the three dispute variables.[6]

Figures 4.1 and 4.2 depict the variation on interstate armed conflict within existing REOs across organizations and over time, respectively. The former presents the average number of MIDs for each organization for all five-year intervals, normalized by the number of members. It also breaks down this number to violent and nonviolent disputes. This figure highlights the reality that almost all REOs have experienced at least some mili-

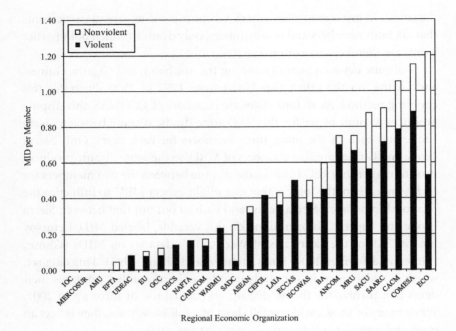

Fig. 4.1. Average number of militarized interstate disputes per member in 25 REOs, 1982–2001

tarized disputes over the course of two decades and that most of these disputes involved the use of force. These observations substantiate the premise, made in this study, that armed disputes do not prevent states from forming international organizations. It also reveals a great deal of cross-regional variation. Some REOs, such as Mercosur and EFTA, have witnessed little conflict among their members. Other organizations, ECO, the CACM, and COMESA for example, have experienced a great deal of tension and numerous disputes. It is noteworthy that the occurrence of armed disputes is not confined to one region but spans a number of different regions, mainly in the developing world.

Figure 4.2 offers a glimpse into the temporal changes in the number of regional conflicts. It reports the number of militarized disputes in each five-year interval, normalized by the number of organizations. The figure shows a falling number of disputes in the late 1980s but a steady increase through the early and late 1990s. The peak by the decade's end is indicative of grow-

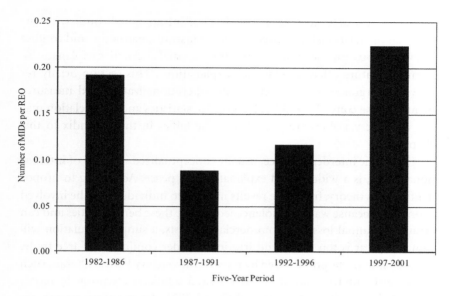

Fig. 4.2. Number of intraregional MIDs per REO in four five-year intervals

ing regional tensions during this time, especially in sub-Saharan Africa, South Asia, and Central Asia. This observation provides additional confirmation to the assessment that the post–Cold War era is rife with regional conflicts and that this problem is intensifying over time. This general trend masks some cross-regional differences. In many regions, the number of disputes has increased in the last decades of the twentieth century. In others, such as the GCC, the number of conflicts is rather constant, and in still others, such as SACU, the EU, and WAEMU, the number of disputes actually declined over time. It appears, then, that intraregional armed conflict is an important phenomenon that varies a great deal across organizations and over time.

Independent Variables

The main independent variables examined in this chapter are the two overarching measures of regional institutionalization, *designed institutionalization* and *implemented institutionalization*. The setup of these variables was discussed in detail in the previous chapter. The theoretical framework expects these variables to decrease the level of intraregional conflict. To ensure that the relationship between regional institutionalization and conflict is not spurious, one needs to account for potential alternative explanations. Extant literature offers several such explanations. This section briefly reviews the arguments and discusses the operationalization and measurement of these control variables. Descriptive statistics and a correlation matrix of these variables are provided in the tables in the appendix to this chapter.

Economic interdependence, usually conceptualized in terms of international trade, is a widely cited explanation for peace. According to proponents of this theory, free trade results in gains to individuals in the involved countries. Because war and violence jeopardize these beneficial ties and can create substantial losses to commercial interests, a simple calculation will show that war is too costly and irrational under conditions of free trade. This argument was popularized by nineteenth-century British liberals, such as Richard Cobden, and attracted renewed scholarly attention in recent years (Polachek 1980; Russett and Oneal 2001; for a recent review, see Mansfield and Pollins 2003). Indeed, as discussed in previous chapters, several scholars argue that REOs mitigate conflict partly because they reduce barriers to regional trade and increase economic interdependence (Mansfield and Pevehouse 2000). From this perspective, accounting for regional economic interdependence allows one to evaluate the effect of regional institutionalization on conflict independent of its indirect effect through trade.

The level of regional economic interdependence is usually captured by regional trade share, which is the intraregional trade as a percentage of the total regional trade (Grieco 1997; Page 2000b). A greater proportion of intraregional trade indicates that REO members trade more among themselves relative to their trade with the rest of the world, which, in turn, suggests greater regional interdependence. The World Bank's *World Development Indicators* (various years) provides information on trade share for most REOs, based on their exports.[7] I use the World Bank data to operationalize this variable, labeled *trade share*.

Proponents of the "democratic peace" research program contend that democracies rarely go to war against other democracies and are less likely to fight each other relative to other groups of states.[8] Most of the empirical research on this issue, however, is conducted at the dyadic level. While the empirical findings using dyadic setup are generally robust for alternative specifications, the explanatory power of the theory at other levels of analysis remains disputed (Gleditsch and Hegre 1997; Gortzak, Haftel, and Sweeney 2005). Particularly, although both regime type and conflict tend to cluster geographically, the effect of regime type at the regional level has attracted only scant attention (Gleditsch 2002). Nonetheless, several studies that examine the sources of regional conflict posit that higher levels of democracy in the region should result in less conflict (Gleditsch 2002; Kacowicz 1998; Lemke 2002).

To measure the level of regional democracy, I employ the widely used Polity IV definitions and data (Jaggers and Gurr 1995; Marshall, Gurr, and Jaggers 2010).[9] This variable is operationalized in a number of ways. The composite measure of regime type is the difference between the level of democracy and the level of autocracy and can range from −10 to 10 for strong autocracy and strong democracy, respectively. The first variable, labeled *democracy*, is simply a five-year regional average of this composite variable. Numerous analyses employ the so-called weakest link assumption, meaning that the most war-prone state is likely to determine the risk of armed conflict. From this point of view, it is possible that the least democratic country in the region will play the most significant role in setting off regional conflict. This logic is captured with the variable *democracy min*, which is the Polity score of the least democratic member of a given organization. Finally, the authors of the Polity data set point out that only those states that score at least 6 on this scale should be considered coherent democracies (Jaggers and Gurr 1995). To account for this threshold, regions inhabited by mature democracies are distinguished from other regions. Thus, *democracy dummy* is a dichotomous variable that scores 1 if the average level of democracy is greater than a score of 6, while scoring 0 otherwise.[10]

Mansfield and Snyder (1995, 2002) argue that states that undergo democratic transition are more likely to engage in interstate disputes than are either fully autocratic or fully democratic states. According to them, states that go through a process of democratization usually lack the necessary institutions that are required to function as a mature and stable democracy. Facing such institutional challenges, leaders have incentives to resort to nationalist ideologies. These ideologies, in turn, lead to aggressive foreign policies and militarized disputes. This is especially the case for states that experience an incomplete democratization and have a partially democratic regime (labeled *anocracy*) for several years. The logic of this argument suggests an inverse U-shaped relationship between regime type and conflict;[11] that is, if we conceptualize regime type as a continuum in which mature democracies and complete autocracies are in the extremes and in which anocracies are in the middle, we can expect low levels of conflict in the extremes and high levels of conflict in the center. The variable *democracy²*, the square of the variable *democracy*, is designed to capture these potential curvilinear relationships.

Theories of power transition hold that preponderance of power is associated with more stability and less violence (Gilpin 1981; Pollins 1996). According to proponents of this perspective, global hegemons have both the ability and the willingness to impose order that mitigates the concerns of other states with respect to their survival and security. Therefore, greater power disparity should result in lower levels of war and other militarized disputes (Pollins 1996). Several recent studies examined the implications of this logic at the regional level (Kacowicz 1998; Lemke 2002; Mansfield and Pevehouse 2000). Lemke (2002), for example, develops a "multiple hierarchy model," in which he argues that regional hegemony should result in lower levels of interstate war. In the context of economic regionalism, Mansfield and Pevehouse (2000, 800–801) find empirical support for the notion that greater power disparity reduces the likelihood of militarized disputes among regional members. The regional balance of power is measured with the so-called concentration ratio, which takes into account both the relative economic size of all members and the number of members in the organization (Mansfield and Pevehouse 2000; Smith 2000). The value of this variable, labeled *concentration*, is bounded between 0 and 1 and increases as power asymmetry grows. Data on gross domestic product from the Penn World Tables is used to calculate this variable (Heston, Summers, and Aten 2002).

The internationalization of civil wars in Central Africa and West Africa as well as in Central Asia and South America attests to the potential effect of domestic violence on neighboring states (M. E. Brown 1996, 590). From a theoretical standpoint, the logic of diversionary war points to the possibility that governments will turn to international conflict in order to ameliorate domestic unrest or to take advantage of states that experience high levels of domestic strife (Dassel and Reinhardt 1999; Davies 2002). To measure the level of regional conflict, I count the number of domestic armed conflicts as reported in the Uppsala Conflict Data Program's data set on armed conflict (Gleditsch et al. 2002). This data set distinguishes among four types of wars: interstate armed conflict, extra-state armed conflict, internationalized internal armed conflict, and internal armed conflict. It also divides armed conflicts into three levels of intensity: minor armed conflict, intermediate armed conflict, and war.[12] I count all the incidents among members of an REO that are defined as internal armed conflict.[13]

As noted in previous chapters, neighboring states that have shared political interests or friendly relations may be more inclined to institutionalize their economic cooperation than states that have less in common. It is thus important to take into account the degree of affinity among REO members. I employ an S-score to capture the intraregional similarity of interests (Signorino and Ritter 1999). The S-score ranges from −1 to 1. A value of 1 indicates that the interests of two states are perfectly aligned, and a value of −1 indicates that the interests of the two states are diametrically opposed. As is the case with other variables, the dyadic scores are averaged for the region. The S-score is measured with the two most conventional methods: similarity of alliance portfolios (Bueno de Mesquita 1981; Signorino and Ritter 1999)[14] and similarity of voting in the United Nations General Assembly (Gartzke 2006). The former is labeled *affinity alliances* and the latter *affinity UN*. Since these two variables measure the same concept, they are included in separate models.

It is widely agreed that regional political dynamics do not operate in isolation and are affected by external forces, such as great-power intervention. The exact effect of these forces on regional conflict is not clear, however. Some studies argue that great-power competition tends to exacerbate local conflict and to inflame otherwise peaceful regions. Others, by contrast, contend that great powers restrain their local clients in order to prevent local conflict from expanding to the global arena.[15] Although these opposing effects may cancel out, it is important to account for the possibility of great-power intervention. The ease of intervention is captured with Douglas Lemke's (2002) calculations of the ability of great powers to project their power in different regions.[16] Using his estimates, the number of great powers that can intervene in any particular region is calculated.[17] Thus, the variable *intervention* is a count of great powers that are capable of interfering in any REO, and it can vary from 0 to 5.[18]

Joseph Schumpeter (1951) has argued that capitalism and the rise of a powerful middle class will result in the overthrow of warlike interest groups that support imperialism. According to him, war jeopardizes economic prosperity, and the middle class will therefore find war too costly. Schumpeter's contention is echoed in a number of recent studies that identify strong theoretical foundations and find empirical support to the link between capitalism, economic prosperity, and peace (Gartzke 2007; McDonald 2007, 2009; Mousseau 2000). The link between economic development and peace at the regional level is yet to be considered in a systematic manner. This study takes a first step in that direction. The pacifying effect of wealth is captured with the natural log of the average regional gross domestic product per capita, labeled *development*. Data from the Penn World Tables is used to calculate this measure (Heston, Summers, and Aten 2002).

It is reasonable to expect that the number of states in a region will be associated with the number of disputes. A greater number of states may result in additional opportunities of interaction and friction and, thus, in more conflict. The variable *members* is a lagged five-year average count of the states that are members of an REO. In addition, it is widely accepted that geographical proximity provides more opportunities for interaction and, in turn, for conflict (see, e.g., Gleditsch 2002). Thus, the variable *borders* is a count of the number of borders in the region.[19] I operationalize this variable with version 3 of the COW data set on direct contiguity (Stinnett et al. 2002).

Results

Tables 4.1 and 4.2 report the results of the empirical analysis for designed and implemented regional institutionalization, respectively. These tables begin with a basic model that controls for the most conventional explanations for regional conflict. The next model substitutes regional affinity based on shared alliances with similarity of voting in the UN. The third model includes the variable *intervention*. The final model examines the effect of the independent variables included in the basic model on disputes that involve the use of force. Table 4.3 provides substantive interpretation of the significant variables in the basic model. Because a negative binomial regression is nonlinear, the substantive interpretation of these results requires the exponentiation of the coefficients. The numbers in table 4.3 reflect the expected value of the incidence of the dependent variable as conditioned by the values of certain independent variables. Table 4.4 reports additional model specifications that check the robustness of the results. Taken as a whole, the results indicate that implemented institutionalization reduces conflict while designed institutionalization does not.

Main Findings

Table 4.1 indicates that the estimate of the variable *designed institutionalization* is negative in most models. This is consistent with the expectations of the theoretical framework, which predicts that higher levels of regional institutionalization will reduce conflict. This negative effect is not statistically significant, however. Different model specifications do not change this basic conclusion. The possibility that regional institutionalization has no effect on intraregional conflict cannot be ruled out. This finding seems to

TABLE 4.1. Random-Effects Negative-Binomial Estimates of the Effect of Designed Regional Institutionalization on Intraregional MIDs, 1982–2001

	Model 1 All MIDs	Model 2 All MIDs	Model 3 All MIDs	Model 4 Violent MIDs
designed institutionalization	−0.012 (−0.66)	−0.007 (−0.40)	−0.015 (−0.80)	0.004 (0.20)
trade share	−0.009 (−0.71)	−0.009 (−0.66)	−0.010 (−0.76)	−0.003 (−0.26)
concentration	−2.011*** (−3.13)	−1.681*** (−2.71)	−2.020*** (−3.14)	−1.396* (−1.88)
democracy	0.061** (2.33)		0.055* (1.94)	
democracy dummy		0.511† (1.40)		0.585† (1.55)
civil war	0.043*** (4.59)	0.052*** (5.19)	0.045*** (4.50)	0.060*** (5.21)
members	0.013 (0.29)	−0.012 (−0.26)	0.020 (0.43)	−0.040 (−.72)
borders	0.047** (2.25)	0.060*** (2.73)	0.045** (2.09)	0.066** (2.56)
affinity alliances	0.509 (0.47)		0.494 (0.46)	2.076† (1.33)
development	−0.564** (−2.54)	−0.446** (−2.15)	−0.550** (−2.45)	−0.416* (−1.87)
affinity UN		−0.769 (−0.60)		
intervention			0.055 (0.63)	
constant	5.285** (2.28)	5.034** (2.19)	5.035** (2.12)	1.591 (0.61)
log likelihood	−154.28	−155.93	−154.08	−143.81
Wald χ^2	230.87***	217.17***	225.48***	160.43***
NT	82	82	82	82

Note: Figures in parentheses are *z* statistics.

***$p < .01$; **$p < .05$; *$p < .1$ (two–tailed test); †$p < .1$ (one-tailed test).

lend empirical support to the possibility that the pacifying impact of international agreements and institutions is weak. At the same time, this result may also emanate from the disparity, discussed in chapter 3, between the design and implementation of many REOs. In other words, it is possible that signed agreements cannot alleviate conflict in and of themselves but that the implementation of these agreements may indeed be conducive to peace. In line with the arguments made in chapter 2, REOs are more likely to promote peace to the extent that they foster economic interdependence (which, in turn, increases the opportunity cost of conflict) and insofar as they actually bring top officials together or actively involve them in the management of bilateral disputes. Thus, the conclusion of far-reaching agreements offers no assurances that these mechanisms will be activated when discord rears its head.

The results reported in table 4.2 offer ample support for this interpretation. As institutional theory expects, the estimate of the variable *implemented institutionalization* is negative, indicating that this variable reduces the number of militarized interstate disputes. This time, the coefficient is much larger and is statistically significant in most models. In two models, it is significant at a 95 percent level of confidence. The results are weaker and fall somewhat short of conventional levels of statistical significance in the model that includes the variable *affinity UN* and in the model that considers only violent MIDs.[20] The substantive effect of the variable *implemented institutionalization* on the number of militarized disputes is meaningful as well. As reported in table 4.3, one standard deviation increase on this variable reduces the number of predicted armed disputes by about a third.

Thus, to the extent that REO members follow up on their signed agreements and implement them, they actually produce the pacifying effect expected by the theoretical framework developed in this study. Controlling for a myriad of factors that arguably account for both regional institutionalization and conflict does not change this basic conclusion. The supplementary models presented in table 4.4 further corroborate it. The effect of implemented institutionalization remains intact after substituting the average regional democracy with the score of the least democratic member or with the curvilinear term and upon replacing the basic dependent variable with the one that does not account for the number of members involved in the dispute (*regional MID*).

One may correctly point out that the EU is qualitatively different from all other REOs. Arguably, its supranational nature resembles a federal state more than an instance of international cooperation (Parsons 2003; cf. Acharya and Johnston 2007; Kahler 1995). The extremely high value on the regional institutionalization measures, particularly the implemented one, suggests that the EU is, in fact, an outlier. Perhaps the results previously reported are driven by the EU's high level of institutionalization, on the one hand, and the largely peaceful coexistence in Western Europe over the 1980s and 1990s, on the other. To rule out this possibility, I ran the basic model with the exclusion of the EU. As the results in model 12 show, dropping the

TABLE 4.2. Random-Effects Negative-Binomial Estimates of the Effect of Implemented Regional Institutionalization on Intraregional MIDs, 1982–2001

	Model 5 All MIDs	Model 6 All MIDs	Model 7 All MIDs	Model 8 Violent MIDs
implemented institutionalization	−0.065** (−2.00)	−0.053† (−1.47)	−0.067** (−2.07)	−0.053† (−1.45)
trade share	0.009 (0.59)	0.009 (0.50)	0.008 (0.50)	0.011 (0.65)
concentration	−2.193*** (−3.53)	−1.775*** (−2.90)	−2.209*** (−3.57)	−1.740** (−2.38)
democracy	0.074*** (2.70)		0.069** (2.39)	0.063** (2.04)
democracy dummy		0.608† (1.65)		
civil war	0.041*** (4.90)	0.051*** (5.98)	0.044*** (4.71)	0.045*** (4.36)
members	0.031 (0.71)	−0.002 (−0.05)	0.037 (0.83)	0.016 (0.31)
borders	0.042** (2.09)	0.058*** (2.76)	0.039* (1.92)	0.047* (1.96)
affinity alliances	0.737 (0.74)		0.676 (0.68)	2.496* (1.85)
development	−0.640*** (−2.85)	−0.493** (−2.29)	−0.626*** (−2.77)	−0.553** (−2.25)
affinity UN		−0.053 (−0.04)		
intervention			0.055 (0.68)	
constant	5.932** (2.57)	4.84** (2.04)	5.720** (2.45)	2.957 (1.08)
log likelihood	−152.52	−154.92	−152.29	−142.20
Wald χ^2	235.49***	214.91***	231.17***	165.86***
NT	82	82	82	82

Note: Figures in parentheses are *z* statistics.

***$p < .01$; **$p < .05$; *$p < .1$ (two–tailed test); †$p < .1$ (one-tailed test).

EU somewhat weakens the effect of the variable *implemented institutionalization*, but this variable remains in the expected direction and falls just short of conventional levels of statistical significance. It is also important to keep in mind that with a data set that contains a small number of observations, any drop of observations is likely to decrease the significance of the results. It seems, then, that the pacifying effect of implemented regional institutionalization is at work beyond the confines of Western Europe.

Additional Determinants of Regional Conflict

The performance of the control variables is generally consistent across the various model specifications. The results on these variables shed new light on the sources of regional conflict. They corroborate a number of existing arguments regarding the factors that affect the number of militarized disputes, but they cast doubt on others.

The estimate of the variable *trade share* is negative in the models that pertain to designed institutionalization and positive in the models that include implementation, but it never reaches statistical significance. The evidence on the link between international commerce and peace appears to be weak, then. This result is compatible with several recent studies that challenge the theoretical foundations and the empirical findings that link commercial interdependence and peace (Barbieri 2002; Keshk, Pollins, and Reuveny 2004). At first blush, it also casts doubt on the opportunity cost mechanism advanced in this study. If economic scope is purported to promote peace through higher levels of economic interdependence, why is the

TABLE 4.3. Substantive Interpretation of the Effects of Significant Independent Variables on the Expected Count of Militarized Interstate Disputes, 1982–2001

Variable	Change in Count of Regional Conflict Resulting from a One Std. Dev. Increase	Change = _____ % of Expected Count in the Baseline Model
implemented institutionalization	−0.77	−32%
concentration	−0.87	−36%
civil war	1.17	48%
democracy	1.37	56%
borders	0.80	33%
development	−1.06	−44%

Note: Predictions are based on model 5 in table 4.2. The expected count in the baseline model is 2.41 armed disputes.

latter ineffective? Here, it is worthwhile recalling that the theoretical framework actually insists on the need to expand the conceptualization of economic interdependence beyond trade. Commerce is undoubtedly significant but is only one of several aspects of cross-border economic ties. Furthermore, as I argued in chapter 2, commerce can potentially elevate the sensitivity of governments to conditions in and policies of neighboring states, but it is less likely to affect the vulnerability of states to the suspension of these economic ties. The theoretical discussion suggests that other

TABLE 4.4. Estimates of the Effect of Implemented Institutionalization on Intraregional MIDs, 1982–2001, Additional Models

	Model 9 All MIDs	Model 10 All MIDs	Model 11 Regional MIDs	Model 12 EU Dropped
implemented institutionalization	−.069**	−0.049†	−0.051†	−0.054†
	(−2.04)	(−1.47)	(−1.61)	(−1.61)
trade share	0.008	0.005	0.013	0.027†
	(0.42)	(0.34)	(0.86)	(1.33)
concentration	−1.885***	−2.055***	−1.637**	−1.934***
	(−3.18)	(−3.32)	(−2.55)	(−3.34)
civil war	0.053***	0.036***	0.043***	0.039***
	(5.95)	(3.97)	(4.92)	(5.00)
members		0.049	0.025	0.049
		(1.12)	(0.56)	(1.18)
borders	0.060***	0.030†	0.028†	0.035*
	(5.95)	(1.48)	(1.35)	(1.81)
affinity alliances	0.692	0.670	1.600†	
	(0.66)	(0.68)	(1.42)	
affinity UN				0.369
				(0.28)
development	−0.497**	−0.528**	−0.532**	−0.664***
	(−2.40)	(−2.30)	(−2.43)	(−3.04)
democracy MIN	0.062**			
	(2.22)			
democracy		0.071**	0.051*	0.071***
		(2.56)	(1.90)	(2.60)
democracy^2		−0.007†		
		(−1.45)		
constant	4.806**	5.274**	4.069*	6.209**
	(2.07)	(2.31)	(1.71)	(2.52)
log likelihood	−153.86	−151.51	−148.05	−146.21
Wald χ^2	225.98***	246.07***	149.06	236.18***
NT	82	82	82	78

Note: Figures in parentheses are z statistics.

***$p < .01$; **$p < .05$; *$p < .1$ (two-tailed test); †$p < .1$ (one-tailed test).

issue areas—such as monetary cooperation, foreign investment, and development projects—are more important in this respect. Thus, the weak performance of intraregional trade does not invalidate the opportunity cost mechanism. Rather, it reinforces the call, made in chapter 2, for a broader and more inclusive conceptualization of economic interdependence.

The analysis indicates that democratic regions are not more peaceful than their nondemocratic counterparts. Surprisingly, the opposite appears to be true. The variable *democracy* is always positive and statistically significant, revealing that more democratic regions face a higher risk of violent conflict. The substantive impact of this variable is also sizable: one standard deviation increase on this variable raises the number of disputes by over 50 percent. This finding is robust to different specifications of the conflict variable as well as alternative measures of the democracy variable. Given the large number of South–South REOs in the sample, this result suggests that outside the industrialized regions of the North, democracy actually increases the risk of militarized disputes. Most democracies in these regions are not well established, and many of them have transitioned from autocratic and other nondemocratic regimes during the last two decades of the twentieth century. Perhaps such political conditions tend to provoke cross-border militarized disputes. Indeed, a series of studies by Mansfield and Snyder (1995, 2002) show that states that have mixed or transitioning regimes are especially prone to conflict.

Model 10 in table 4.4 further corroborates this interpretation. Consistent with the curvilinear hypothesis, the coefficient of the variable *democracy* is positive and statistically significant, and the coefficient of the variable *democracy*^{2} is negative and approaches statistical significance. Thus, regions that are either highly democratic or highly autocratic tend to be rather peaceful. In contrast, regions that inhabit weakly democratic countries are likely to experience a higher number of violent interstate disputes. These results suggest that the domestic political structure of REO members does affect the prospects of regional peace, but in manners that are more complex than commonly thought.[21]

Regional concentration of power has a negative and highly significant effect on the level of regional conflict across all models. Substantively, an increase of one standard deviation on this variable reduces the number of expected disputes by 36 percent. This suggests that regions with a local hegemon enjoy low levels of MIDs, while regions in which power is more evenly distributed are more vulnerable to the outbreak of hostilities. These findings are consistent with recent theoretical and empirical studies on this question (Buzan and Wæver 2003; Lemke 2002; Mansfield and Pevehouse 2000). The estimate of the variable *civil war* is positive and highly significant across all models. This variable has a sizable substantive effect as well. This result points to the potential international repercussions of domestic conflicts, which may spill over to produce interstate violence (M. E. Brown 1996; Dassel and Reinhardt 1999; Davies 2002).

The number of members in the organization does not increase the number of regional disputes: this variable is positive but statistically insignificant. The number of borders, however, is positive and statistically significant. This result corroborates the conventional wisdom, which points to territorial proximity as an important source of friction and conflict. Thus, contiguity appears to be more detrimental to peace than is the number of members per se. Importantly, the inclusion of the number of members and borders in the regression models does not nullify the pacifying effect of regional institutionalization, suggesting that this effect is not an artifact of the REO's size or its members' adjacency. The vulnerability of a region to great-power intervention does not seem to affect the level of violent conflict. This result provides initial support for the notion that the main sources of regional conflict are domestic and regional, rather than global, in nature (Miller 2001).

The effect of similarity of interests—measured either with alliance portfolios or with voting in the UN—is mixed. The estimates of affinity alliances are almost always positive and reach statistical significance in the models that pertain to violent conflict (models 4 and 8). Interestingly, then, similar alliance portfolios appear to be associated with higher levels of violent conflict. The variable *affinity UN* is negative but statistically insignificant. These results indicate that the similarity of interest is not a good predictor of violent conflict. Moreover, they mitigate concerns that both peace and regional institutionalization thrive among friends but not among rivals. Finally, as expected, higher levels of economic development are associated with lower levels of violent conflict. Substantively, an increase of one standard deviation on this variable reduces the count of militarized disputes by about 44 percent. This finding offers additional empirical support for the growing number of studies that highlight the pacifying role of a vigorous middle class and a thriving market economy.

Table 4.5 summarizes the findings of the statistical analysis. It highlights the central result: higher levels of regional institutionalization, when implemented, lead to a lower number of intraregional militarized disputes. Accounting for a host of alternative explanations and different model specifications does not change this main conclusion. At the same time, simply signing ambitious agreements but stopping short of implementing them is unlikely to mitigate violent conflict. Thus, implementation is essential to the functionality of the causal mechanisms discussed in the theoretical framework.

Large-*N* Qualitative Analysis

This section employs the previously reported statistical analysis as a springboard to examine the pacifying effect of regional institutionalization more closely. One useful way to do this is to compare REOs with a similar baseline risk of conflict but different levels of regional institutionalization (Fortna 2004). The baseline risk of conflict refers to the number of intraregional conflicts expected based on the values of all the independent variables *except* regional institutionalization. This baseline tells us how conflict-prone different regions are regardless of the level of cooperation through international institutions. Adding the level of institutionalization to this baseline offers a clearer perspective on its effect on conflict.

Table 4.6 presents a summary of this analysis. It first groups REOs according to their average baseline risk of conflict. It then sorts the REOs in

TABLE 4.5. Summary of Findings of the Statistical Analysis

Explanation	Effect on the Number of MIDs	Statistical Significance
designed institutionalization	Decrease	No
implemented institutionalization	Decrease	Yes
intraregional trade	Mixed	No
regional democracy	Increase	Yes
concentration ratio	Decrease	Yes
domestic armed conflict	Increase	Yes
regional affinity	Increase	No
great power intervention	Increase	No
number of members	Increase	No
number of borders	Increase	Yes
economic development	Decrease	Yes
regime type	Inverse U-shape	Yes

each group according to their level of implemented regional institutionalization. Finally, it reports the actual number of intraregional militarized disputes for each organization. As one might expect, the predictions of the baseline model are generally on track: the actual number of conflicts increases as the expected level of conflict moves from lower to higher categories. This close match indicates that the control variables capture much of the dynamics that drive intraregional militarized disputes. It is also ap-

TABLE 4.6. Regional Institutionalization and Militarized Interstate Disputes, by Baseline Risk of Conflict

Regional Economic Organization	Baseline Risk of Conflict	Average Implemented Regional Institutionalization	Average Actual Number of Militarized Disputes
IOC	**Very low**	Low	0.00
NAFTA	(0–1 disputes	Medium	0.50
GCC	predicted in a	High	0.75
EFTA	five-year period)	High	0.25
MERCOSUR		High	0.00
AMU	**Low**	Low	0.00
CEPGL	(1–1.5 disputes	Low	1.25
MRU	predicted)	Medium	2.25
UDEAC		Medium	0.50
EU		Very high	1.00
CACM	**Medium**	Medium	4.75
ANCOM	(1.5–2.5 disputes	High	3.75
ASEAN	predicted)	High	2.25
CARICOM		High	2.00
BA		Low	3.00
ECCAS	**High**	Low	5.00
LAIA	(2.5–4 disputes	Medium	4.75
SADC	predicted)	Medium	2.50
WAEMU		High	1.75
ECO	**Very high**	Low	7.66
SAARC	(more than 4 disputes	Low	6.33
ECOWAS	predicted)	Medium	8.00
COMESA		Medium	21.75

Note: The baseline risk of conflict is determined by model 5 in table 4.2 excluding *implemented institutionalization* and substituting *democracy* with *democracy dummy* (the model with the former variable does not converge). The categories for implemented regional institutionalization are as follows: Low 1–4; Medium 4–8; High 8–13; Very High 13 or higher.

parent that there is a great deal of variation in the level of regional institutionalization within each category of baseline risk of conflict. In particular, some regions that experience intermediate or high risk of conflict also have medium or high levels of institutionalization. This observation challenges the view that international institutions thrive only when and where peace is already well established. The cases of ASEAN, ANCOM, and WAEMU stand out as examples of relatively institutionalized organizations in conflict-prone regions.

This within-group variation is also instrumental for a more fine-grained analysis of the effect of regional institutionalization on conflict. According to the theoretical framework, when all else is equal, higher levels of institutionalization should reduce conflict. Comparing REOs with a similar baseline risk of conflict means that all else is largely equal. Thus, within each category, we should observe a lower number of conflicts as regional institutionalization increases. Table 4.6 offers considerable support for this expectation but also reveals some differences across the baseline categories. The patterns in the medium and high categories correspond rather nicely to the theoretical expectations. In both categories, the number of actual conflicts tends to drop as the level of institutionalization increases.[22] In the high category, for example, the weakly institutionalized ECCAS experiences a higher number of conflicts compared to REOs with a medium level of institutionalization, which, in turn, experience more conflicts than the highly institutionalized WAEMU.

Some concrete examples cast light on this general observation. On the lower end, weakly institutionalized REOs can do little to alleviate conflict among their members. ECCAS, for instance, did not play a pacifying role in the numerous conflicts that revolved around the Democratic Republic of Congo from the middle 1990s to the early 2000s. During these years, ECCAS was largely dormant because of nonpayment of membership dues. As a result, meetings among officials at all levels took place very infrequently, and activity grinded to a halt (Panafrican News Agency, February 24, 2001). While its members envisioned ECCAS as an instrument that would promote peace and stability in the region, the low level of institutionalization rendered it ineffective in this respect. The CACM provides a second illustration of this reality. Its members experienced recurrent violent disputes in the 1980s and 1990s. These disputes were a result of interstate rivalries, such as the one between Honduras and El Salvador, and the spillover of civil wars, particularly the one in Nicaragua. This organization, while initially one of the more promising REOs in the developing world, entered into a period of protracted hibernation in the early 1980s. Mainly as a result of the economic crisis, regional integration had lost much of its dynamism: signed agreements were not implemented, and meetings among officials were very infrequent. Even though the CACM was revived in the early 1990s, its level of institutionalization remains low (Bulmer-Thomas 1998; Sánchez Sánchez 2009, 186). This low level of institutionalization did not allow the CACM to play a pacifying role in the region.

In contrast, REOs with a high level of regional institutionalization have proved valuable in mitigating violent conflict among their members. AN-COM and WAEMU offer two useful illustrations of this point.[23] In many ways, ANCOM is comparable to the CACM. Both REOs are in the same region, have five members, have a number of ongoing rivalries, and suffer from continuous domestic strife.[24] Yet the members of ANCOM have experienced fewer militarized disputes than CACM members. Arguably, this difference can be attributed to the more dynamic nature of ANCOM compared to the CACM. One notable disparity is between the institutional frameworks of the two organizations. Since 1979, ANCOM instituted regular meetings among its foreign ministers, a commission, and a court of justice. In contrast, until the early 1990s, the CACM's highest decision-making body was composed of economic ministers, and it had no DSM. Its corporate secretariat still lacks the power to make recommendations or take initiatives (Nicholls et al. 2001). Similarly, the economic scope of ANCOM is wider and better implemented than the CACM's. For example, even though both REOs agreed to form a customs union, only ANCOM has actually moved forward in this direction, while the CACM remains a free trade area.

The high level of implemented regional institutionalization allows AN-COM to ease some of the tensions in the region. The dispute between Peru and Ecuador illustrates this point. In 1995, a border dispute between the two states erupted into an open armed conflict. While this conflict has resulted in some casualties, it was contained and was followed by peace talks between the two sides. ANCOM has played an important role in keeping this conflict in check. First, meetings between the Peruvian and the Ecuadorian leaders within the framework of ANCOM have allowed them to communicate their desire for compromise. These meetings have also fostered reconciliation talks between officials from the two states, which were mediated by officials from other ANCOM members (Agence France Presse, March 11, 1996). Second, the two belligerents have restrained themselves in order to prevent the collapse of ANCOM and the loss of the many accompanied benefits. As one news report points out, "Tempers were calmed largely due to the pressure of economic agents that benefited from Andean integration" (Gutíerrez 1997). In sum, it is apparent that ANCOM's high level of regional institutionalization was instrumental in mitigating violent conflict in the Andean region.

WAEMU encompasses francophone West Africa. As table 4.6 makes clear, the baseline risk of conflict in this region is very high. States in this region are among the least economically developed in the world, and several of them suffer from continuous domestic unrest. Despite the high vulnerability of this region to interstate violent conflict, it has experienced only a limited number of such incidents. Actually, it experienced the smallest number of MIDs among all REOs in the medium and high baseline categories. What distinguishes WAEMU from other organizations with a similar baseline risk of conflict is its high level of institutionalization. WAEMU covers a variety of issues, including trade liberalization, a monetary union, and economic development. Unlike most of their counterparts in sub-Saharan Africa, the members of WAEMU have implemented many of the agreements they signed (Bourenane 2002).

In addition, WAEMU has a solid institutional framework that supports the integration process. These institutions have proved useful in mitigating conflict in the region. In one instance, the ministerial council of the organization was instrumental in defusing a border dispute between Burkina Faso and Mali in 1985. A meeting of this council allowed high-level officials from the two states to meet in a relaxed atmosphere. It also facilitated mediation between the two rivals by officials from other member states (BBC, January 1, 1986; Ero, Sidhu, and Toure 2001, 5). The increasing level of institutionalization in the 1990s further reduced the frequency of militarized interstate disputes.[25] It is thus apparent that the highly institutionalized WAEMU promotes peace among its members.

So far, I have examined medium and high levels of baseline risk of conflict. What about other categories? Table 4.6 suggests that the effect of regional institutionalization in the extreme categories is muted. This is not very surprising. In the two lower categories, conflict is very unlikely to begin with. In them, states may have little to fight about, as in the cases of the small island states of which IOC is composed and the members of EFTA that are spread across Europe. Even if they have disagreements, other conditions make violent disputes unlikely. The preponderance of the United

States in NAFTA, the high levels of democracy and economic development in the EU, and the absence of civil wars in Mercosur illustrate this point. In such instances, REOs may provide other valuable benefits to their members, but their pacifying effect is probably redundant regardless of the level of their institutionalization. From this perspective, the lack of a clear pattern in these categories seems reasonable.

Regional institutionalization does not seem to alleviate violence in regions in which the baseline for conflict is very high. Instead, REOs that are more institutionalized are actually associated with more conflict. I am not suggesting that higher levels of regional institutionalization result in higher violence. A closer inspection of this baseline category indicates that it differs from other categories in at least two respects. First, in contrast to other categories, the baseline risk of conflict varies a great deal within this category. The baseline risk is below 6 armed disputes for ECO and SAARC, almost 7 for ECOWAS, and over 19 for COMESA. It is therefore not surprising that the latter two organizations experience more conflicts even if they are more institutionalized. In particular, while conflicts within SAARC are driven mainly by the rivalry between India and Pakistan, conflict within ECOWAS and COMESA is driven by multiple rivalries and several ongoing civil wars.

Second, the variation on regional institutionalization is rather limited, and there is no representation of REOs with a high level of institutionalization. This absence indicates that in regions in which conflict is very intense and widespread, international institutions are unlikely to thrive. This observation corresponds to the notion that adversaries, while willing to join regional organizations, are loath to make substantial and long-term commitment to economic cooperation. Moreover, the lack of an obvious relationship between regional institutionalization and the actual number of militarized disputes in this category suggests that REOs may not be effective in reducing conflict in regions that experience extreme levels of violence.

Recalling the endogenous nature of international institutions discussed in chapter 2, it seems that both the supply-side and demand-side logics can be at work, but under different conditions. In regions where militarized disputes are especially common, considerations of power and relative gains trump the prospects of mutually advantageous economic cooperation. In regions where militarized conflict is less common, governments are prepared to forgo short-term advantages in exchange for the prospects of prosperity and peace in the long haul. This bifurcation may account for the growing disparity between zones of war and zones of peace around the world. The former experiences a vicious cycle in which conflict and enmity rule out sustainable economic cooperation, which, in turn, perpetuate the hostile political environment in these regions. In contrast, regions where aggression is more restrained benefit from a virtuous cycle. There, the initial commitment to meaningful economic cooperation through REOs paves the way to a more peaceful regional environment, which fosters further regional institutionalization.

Conclusion

This chapter examined the effect of regional institutionalization on violent conflict. Its first part utilized a multivariate regression technique to evaluate this effect. The analysis indicated that regional institutionalization, when implemented, mitigates violent conflict. This result, which is largely robust to a host of control variables and various model specifications, provides empirical support for the theoretical framework presented in chapter 2; that is, it corroborates the notion that the level of institutionalization determines the value of international institutions as instruments of peace and stability. The statistical analysis also showed that high levels of regional institutionalization have a pacifying effect only to the extent that signed agreements are implemented. An elaborated institutional design, in and of itself, does not mitigate violent conflict.

The statistical analysis facilitated a large-N qualitative analysis, which offered a closer look at some of the cases and compared several REOs that—apart from their level of regional institutionalization—are expected to experience similar levels of conflict. This analysis indicated that in instances in which the baseline risk of conflict is intermediate or high, the level of institutionalization makes an important difference. Regions that have more institutionalized organizations experience less conflict than their counterparts. The cases of ANCOM and WAEMU, on the one hand, and ECCAS and the CACM, on the other, illustrate this point. It appears that REOs, to the extent that they are highly institutionalized, matter when and where they are needed. In contrast, the level of regional institutionalization is inconsequential in regions that have either low or very high baseline risk of conflict. This finding, while preliminary, underscores the need to identify the conditions under which the theoretical framework applies and points to the need to consider the effect of conflict on the institution-alization of regional economic organizations. The next chapter takes up these issues.

Appendix

TABLE 4.A1. Descriptive Statistics for Dependent and Control Variables

Variable	N	Mean	Std. Dev.	Min	Max
MID	90	3.54	6.01	0	48
violent MID	90	2.68	4.96	0	41
regional MID	90	2.95	3.93	0	23
trade share	86	10.31	12.88	0.04	61.70
concentration	90	0.44	0.19	0.04	0.96
democracy	86	−0.00	5.99	−9.60	10
democracy dummy	86	0.25	0.43	0	1
civil war	90	8.56	10.03	0	40
members	90	7.38	4.05	2.20	21.80
borders	90	8.80	7.29	0	35
borders per member	90	1.08	0.43	0	1.91
affinity alliances	90	0.93	0.10	0.52	1
affinity UN	88	0.956	0.139	−0.01	1
intervention	90	2.61	1.40	1	4
development	90	8.50	0.91	6.70	10.73
democracy^2	86	35.54	31.94	0.03	100
democracy MIN	86	−4.87	6.18	−10	10

TABLE 4.A2. Correlation Matrix

	MID	violent MID	regional MID	designed institutionalization	implemented institutionalization	trade share	concentration	democracy	civil war	members	borders	affinity alliances	affinity UN	intervention	development	democracy dummy	democracy²
violent MID	0.97																
regional MID	0.92	0.87															
designed institutionalization	0.01	0.05	-0.02														
implemented institutionalization	-0.07	-0.05	-0.09	0.73													
trade share	-0.10	-0.09	-0.11	0.38	0.73												
concentration	-0.22	-0.17	-0.18	-0.13	-0.20	-0.11											
democracy	-0.05	-0.04	-0.07	-0.01	0.34	0.53	-0.13										
civil war	0.54	0.48	0.62	-0.34	-0.23	-0.13	0.00	-0.02									
members	0.58	0.55	0.58	0.34	0.26	0.11	0.00	-0.09	0.28								
borders	0.55	0.52	0.52	0.38	0.23	0.09	-0.27	-0.00	0.17	0.89							
affinity alliances	0.07	0.12	0.12	0.33	0.01	-0.24	-0.24	-0.40	-0.05	0.15	0.20						
affinity UN	0.07	0.07	0.10	0.10	0.00	-0.47	0.20	-0.24	0.09	0.19	0.17	0.35					
intervention	-0.13	-0.11	-0.11	0.29	0.33	0.37	-0.25	0.48	-0.28	0.02	0.10	-0.10	-0.17				
development	-0.26	-0.25	-0.32	0.18	0.45	0.52	-0.29	0.48	-0.33	-0.11	-0.16	-0.37	-0.28	0.23			
democracy dummy	-0.16	-0.13	-0.20	0.18	0.43	0.51	-0.07	0.81	-0.31	0.02	-0.06	-0.30	-0.29	0.50	0.57		
democracy²	-0.33	-0.31	-0.38	0.41	0.52	0.33	-0.10	0.24	-0.51	-0.09	-0.12	-0.18	-0.06	0.21	0.61	0.61	
democracy MIN	-0.19	-0.16	-0.21	0.17	0.48	0.56	-0.18	0.84	-0.28	-0.12	-0.18	-0.36	-0.19	0.49	0.56	0.85	0.60

CHAPTER 5

Institutional Design, Violent Conflict, and Reversed Causality

Chapter 4 examined the effect of regional institutionalization on conflict. Quantitative and qualitative evidence corroborated the claim made in this book that higher levels of institutionalization reduce the number of militarized disputes. It also identified some conditions under which REOs promote peace. Most notably, it pointed to the need to implement signed agreements. In addition, it suggested that the pacifying effect of regional institutions is likely to be muted in the most war-prone regions. Extending the quantitative analysis presented in chapter 4, this chapter probes further into the specific manners by which regional institutions are linked to armed conflict. It does so, first, by disaggregating regional institutionalization into a number of specific design features and by inquiring into their effect on conflict. Tackling concerns of endogeneity, it then reverses the causal arrow and explores the effect of conflict on the institutionalization and design of REOs.

The first part of this chapter presents a fine-grained analysis of the effect of regional institutions on armed disputes. Specifically, it shifts the focus to the separate components of regional institutionalization, namely, the scope of economic activity (designed and implemented), regular meetings of high-level officials, and institutional independence. It thus tests hypotheses 1–4 in table 2.1 and corroborates two of them. Echoing the results of the preceding chapter, greater economic scope mitigates interstate conflict, but only to the extent that agreements on economic cooperation are implemented. In addition, repeated meetings at the highest level promote regional peace, suggesting that such forums are well equipped to smooth regional differences and manage bilateral conflicts. In contrast, regional bureaucracies and DSMs do not contribute to conflict mitigation. Surprisingly, more independent secretariats and more legalized DSMs are (weakly) associated with more, rather than less, militarized disputes. Taken as a whole, the first part of this chapter highlights the analytical advantage afforded by the appreciation of institutional design.

The second part of this chapter addresses concerns of reversed causality. As discussed in previous chapters, a positive association between institutions and peace may emanate from the effect of amity on cooperation through international institutions, rather than the other way around. I deal with this issue by examining the effect of violent disputes on the variables related to regional institutionalization.[1] The relationships between conflict and institutions are assessed in the context of a multivariate statistical analysis, which takes into account several factors that are alleged to affect the level of institutionalization, institutional design, and implementation. In one of the first rigorous analyses of these phenomena, the results highlight some dynamics that encourage member states to institutionalize their economic cooperation, as well as other factors that deter them from doing so.

The findings show that not all institutional features are driven by the same forces. Some variables, such as regional trade, appear to facilitate a wider scope of economic activity, while others, democracy for example, foster institutional independence. Most pertinent to this study is the finding that the number of militarized disputes has no significant effect on most of the institutional variables. Violent conflict is thus not a hurdle to regional institutionalization. The only exception is DSM legalization, which is strongly and consistently endogenous to armed disputes. The effect of the latter on the former is *positive*, however, indicating that more conflict results in greater legalization. This effect is therefore compatible with the demand-side logic, which expects greater investment in international institutions when and where conflict is more prevalent. It also helps making sense of the positive association between DSMs and conflict identified in the first part of this chapter, suggesting it is driven by reversed causality. On the whole, the analysis in the second part of this chapter demonstrates that REOs, while endogenous to their members' interests, have an independent causal impact on conflict behavior.

In tandem, the two parts of this chapter provide a nuanced and refined picture of the relationship between REOs and violent conflict. The statistical results, summarized in table 5.12, indicate that not all design features are equally instrumental in mitigating conflict: some promote regional peace, while others do not. Nonetheless, the effect of the former is genuine and not a mere reflection of preexisting friendly or peaceful relations.

The Effect of Specific Design Features on Conflict

This part of the chapter examines the effect of militarized disputes on the separate institutional features described in chapter 3. Thus, the key explanatory variables are designed scope, implemented scope, high-level officials, bureaucracy, and dispute settlement. The dependent and control variables are largely identical to those used in the preceding chapter and are therefore not revisited here. Table 5.A1 in this chapter's appendix reports bivariate correlations between the variables pertaining to institutional design, on the one hand, and the dependent and control variables, on the other.[2] Given that the dependent variables remain MID counts, I continue to use the negative binomial technique employed in chapter 4.

TABLE 5.1. Estimates of the Effect of Economic Scope on Intraregional MIDs, 1982–2001

	Model 1 All MIDs	Model 2 Violent MIDs	Model 3 All MIDs	Model 4 Violent MIDs	Model 5 EU Excluded	Model 6 Regional MIDs
designed scope	−0.017	−0.001				
	(−0.84)	(−0.05)				
implemented scope			−0.095**	−0.081*	−0.079*	−0.090**
			(−2.35)	(−1.79)	(1.92)	(−2.27)
trade share	−0.008	−0.005	0.014	0.016	0.025†	0.022
	(−0.66)	(−0.40)	(0.88)	(0.90)	(1.40)	(1.36)
concentration	−1.983***	−1.587**	−2.049***	−1.621**	−1.928***	−1.527**
	(−3.09)	(−2.15)	(−3.40)	(−2.26)	(−3.24)	(−2.47)
democracy	0.061**	0.052*	0.072***	0.060**	0.070***	0.050*
	(2.31)	(1.84)	(2.68)	(2.00)	(2.64)	(1.90)
civil war	0.042***	0.049***	0.042***	0.045***	0.041***	0.043***
	(4.53)	(4.39)	(5.07)	(4.47)	(5.06)	(5.00)
members	0.014	−0.006	0.024	0.011	0.036	0.021
	(0.32)	(−0.12)	(0.57)	(0.22)	(0.87)	(0.51)
borders	0.048**	0.053**	0.044**	0.049**	0.039**	0.030
	(2.27)	(2.10)	(2.28)	(2.08)	(2.03)	(1.50)
affinity alliances	0.487	2.257†	0.528	2.311*	0.252	1.429
	(0.46)	(1.58)	(0.55)	(1.74)	(0.26)	(1.33)
development	−0.568**	−0.473**	−0.595***	−0.514**	−0.613***	−0.507**
	(−2.57)	(−2.05)	(−2.73)	(−2.14)	(−2.86)	(−2.35)
constant	5.336**	2.270	5.644**	2.698	5.950***	4.001*
	(2.30)	(0.85)	(2.49)	(1.00)	(2.64)	(1.71)
log likelihood	−154.15	−143.25	−151.71	−141.61	−145.65	−146.73
Wald χ^2	229***	167***	233***	162***	237***	149***
NT	82	82	82	82	78	82

Note: Figures in parentheses are *z* statistics.

***$p < .01$; **$p < .05$; *$p < .1$ (two-tailed test); †$p < .1$ (one-tailed test).

Tables 5.1, 5.2, and 5.3 report the estimated effects of the design features related to regional institutionalization on all militarized interstate disputes as well as on those that involve only the use of force. Models 1–14 in these tables examine the effect of each feature separately, and models 15 and 16 in table 5.3 consider all of them jointly.[3] Table 5.4 provides substantive interpretation of the variables that are statistically significant. The results on the control variables echo the ones obtained in chapter 4, and their performance is not discussed further. The following discussion thus focuses on the effect of specific institutional features on armed disputes.

The results offer ample support for the theoretical arguments made in chapter 2. Consistent with the first hypothesis, the coefficients on the variables that capture the scope of economic activity have a negative sign, indicating that greater economic scope is associated with fewer armed disputes. As table 5.1 shows, this result holds for all militarized disputes as well as for violent ones, even though the effect on the latter is less pronounced. Paralleling the findings on the broader level of regional institutionalization, the estimates on the variable *implemented scope* are statistically significant, but the ones on the variable *designed scope* are not. Agreements on economic integration and cooperation that remain on paper fail to decrease violent conflict between REO members. Thus, organizations that involve very ambitious plans but accomplish little, such as UDEAC and AMU, are unlikely to restrain aggression between their members.

To the extent that REOs address a large number of economic issues and follow up on their agreements, however, the pacifying effect of this design feature is not only statistically significant but also substantially meaningful. As table 5.4 shows, an increase of one standard deviation on the implemented scope of economic activity decreases the expected number of disputes by close to 40 percent (and decreases by 34 percent the number of disputes that involve the use of force). This means that, all else being equal, an organization that scores about 5 on implemented scope (e.g., the CACM in the 1990s) will experience about two and a half militarized disputes in a five-year time period. In contrast, an organization that scores about 10 on this variable, such as the GCC in the 1990s, will experience only one and a half disputes during the same time period. As models 5 and 6 in table 5.1 indicate, the statistical and substantive effect of economic scope remains intact even when the EU is omitted from the sample and when multiparty disputes are counted only once. Moreover, this variable continues to be significant when it is combined with other institutional features, shown in models 15 and 16 in table 5.3.

This finding further substantiates the claims made in the theoretical framework regarding the scope of economic activity. They suggest that as member states commit to long-term deeper and wider functional cooperation, the opportunity cost of violent conflict is rising and making the use of force less likely. Notably, the scope of economic activity encompasses cooperation on a myriad of issue areas, such as foreign investment, economic development, and monetary affairs, which go beyond international trade. Arguably, these schemes provide their members with benefits they are reluctant to sacrifice. Disaggregating implemented scope to trade-related and nontrade areas is revealing in this respect.[4] While both coefficients are negative, the former falls just short of conventional levels of statistical significance, while the latter remains highly significant. This result underscores the need to take into account a wide array of functional issue areas when empirically assessing the opportunity cost argument.

It may also be the case that the ties built through extensive economic cooperation foster better communication and exchange of credible information during times of conflict. The weaker result on the variable that includes only MIDs that involve the use of force gives one pause with respect to this mechanism, however. While the estimate of implemented scope is only somewhat weaker in these models, one could speculate that economic interdependence is more instrumental in preventing lower-level militarized disputes than in preventing more severe ones. Insofar as disputes are susceptible to escalation, it is possible that wide economic scope is more useful in preventing disputes from erupting in the first place than as a bargaining chip during international crises. If this interpretation is correct, the manner by which the scope of economic activity promotes peace is less visible than the information mechanism suggests. Obviously, this is one possible and very tentative reading of these results. Further research is needed to sort out the manners by which economic ties inhibit militarized disputes.

Corresponding to this study's expectations, the variable *high-level officials* has a strong effect on the number of intraregional violent conflicts. This variable is negative and statistically significant, indicating that regular meetings among high-level officials contribute to regional peace in a meaningful manner. This effect is not only statistically significant but also substantively sizable. Organizations that provide for top-level meetings reduce the expected number of conflicts by 34 percent. As model 9 in table 5.2 shows, this pacifying effect is even stronger if only violent conflicts are considered, in which case high-level meetings reduce the number of violent disputes by 57 percent. Adding the other design features somewhat weakens the effect of this variable on all MIDs, but the effect on violent MIDs continues to be very strong.

The findings indicate that face-to-face diplomacy at the highest level is conducive to the peaceful management of regional conflict. Conceivably, top-level officials are well equipped to intervene in local conflicts and are prepared to utilize their periodic conferences to promote compromise and

TABLE 5.2. The Effect of Regular Meetings of High-Level Officials and Regional Bureaucracy on Intraregional MIDs, 1982–2001

	Model 7 All MIDs	Model 8 EU Excluded	Model 9 Violent MIDs	Model 10 All MIDs	Model 11 Violent MIDs	Model 12 Violent MIDs
high-level officials	−0.491*	−0.479*	−0.860***			
	(−1.87)	(−1.82)	(−3.08)			
bureaucracy				0.220	0.235	0.510*
				(0.98)	(0.80)	(1.95)
trade share	−0.009	0.013	−0.002	−0.019†	−0.009	−0.017
	(−0.81)	(0.77)	(−0.21)	(−1.42)	(−0.65)	(−1.16)
concentration	−2.189***	−1.980***	−1.862***	−1.873***	−1.445*	−1.200*
	(−3.41)	(−3.18)	(−2.62)	(−3.10)	(−1.88)	(−1.68)
democracy	0.057**	0.056**	0.053*	0.052**	0.045†	0.037
	(2.16)	(2.15)	(1.79)	(1.97)	(1.51)	(1.22)
civil war	0.042***	0.040***	0.039***	0.047***	0.050***	0.048***
	(5.04)	(4.97)	(4.24)	(5.50)	(4.87)	(4.80)
members	0.021	0.042	0.039	0.010	−0.001	0.017
	(0.47)	(0.97)	(0.77)	(0.24)	(−0.04)	(0.35)
borders	0.045**	0.037*	0.042*	0.046**	0.050**	0.045*
	(2.16)	(1.82)	(1.82)	(2.19)	(2.04)	(1.89)
affinity alliances	0.583	0.251	2.440*		1.493	
	(0.56)	(0.24)	(1.92)		(0.87)	
affinity UN				−1.626		−1.97
				(−1.14)		(−1.26)
development	−0.597***	−0.632***	−0.595***	−0.535***	−0.477**	0.522**
	(−2.82)	(−3.01)	(−2.68)	(−2.60)	(−2.13)	(−2.34)
constant	5.858**	6.262***	4.079†	6.719***	2.687	5.912**
	(2.52)	(−3.01)	(1.55)	(2.81)	(1.01)	(2.24)
log likelihood	−152.92	−146.04	−139.47	−153.85	−142.93	−142.71
Wald χ^2	247***	251***	201***	235***	163***	160***
NT	82	78	82	82	82	82

Note: Figures in parentheses are z statistics.
***$p < .01$; **$p < .05$; *$p < .1$ (two–tailed test); †$p < .1$ (one-tailed test).

peace. These findings correspond to other studies that examine this design feature (Bearce and Omori 2005; Bercovitch and Houston 1996, 26–27). Furthermore, in contrast to the results on economic scope, the pacifying effect of this variable is more pronounced with respect to violent MIDs compared to all militarized conflicts. This gap suggests that regional summits are especially instrumental in preventing open disputes from escalating into more severe clashes and perhaps even war. This reading of the results is consistent with the causal mechanisms of information and, especially,

TABLE 5.3. The Effect of Dispute Settlement and All Design Features Combined on Intraregional MIDs, 1982–2001

	Model 13 All MIDs	Model 14 Violent MIDs	Model 15 All MIDs	Model 16 Violent MIDs
implemented scope			−0.101**	−0.070†
			(−2.24)	(−1.69)
high-level officials			−0.404†	−0.990***
			(−1.41)	(−2.97)
bureaucracy			0.321	0.494*
			(1.24)	(1.76)
dispute settlement	0.053	0.152	0.190†	0.329**
	(0.40)	(0.99)	(1.39)	(2.12)
trade share	−0.016	−0.010	0.010	0.004
	(−1.23)	(−0.76)	(0.63)	(0.23)
concentration	−1.814***	−1.319*	−1.807***	−1.268*
	(−2.93)	(−1.70)	(−2.83)	(−1.74)
democracy	0.056**	0.042†	0.046†	0.024
	(2.06)	(1.43)	(0.58)	(0.72)
civil war	0.045***	0.051***	0.044***	0.046***
	(5.43)	(4.86)	(4.97)	(4.38)
members	0.003	−0.032	0.003	−0.002
	(0.06)	(−0.53)	(0.06)	(−0.04)
borders	0.049**	0.060**	0.052**	0.055**
	(2.20)	(2.24)	(2.46)	(2.22)
affinity alliances		2.077†	−0.427	0.953
		(1.46)	(−0.34)	(0.63)
affinity UN	−0.933			
	(−.71)			
development	−0.508**	−0.344†	−0.530**	−0.438*
	(−2.16)	(−1.38)	(−2.26)	(−1.79)
constant	6.002**	1.252	5.962**	3.717
	(2.32)	(0.45)	(2.34)	(1.27)
log likelihood	−154.25	−142.76	−149.66	−135.78
Wald χ^2	235***	169***	241***	197***
NT	82	82	82	82

Note: Figures in parentheses are z statistics.

***$p < .01$; **$p < .05$; *$p < .1$ (two–tailed test); † $p <.1$ (one-tailed test).

conflict management, which often operate in the shadow of conflict. Here, policymakers utilize the regional forum to discuss bilateral disagreements in an informal and open manner and to facilitate mediation by other top officials. It is more difficult to square the findings with the logic of socialization, which expects mutually respectful and like-minded leaders to avoid conflict in the first place.[5]

The empirical analysis indicates that institutional independence does not mitigate intraregional violent disputes. The estimates of the variable *bureaucracy* and the variable *dispute settlement* are actually positive, suggesting that greater independence and more conflict go hand in hand. These effects are not statistically significant in most models but reach conventional levels of significance in models related to violent MIDs and when the four design features are integrated into one model. As table 5.3 shows, a more legalized DSM, in particular, is strongly associated with more armed conflict. These findings cast doubt on the efficacy of corporate secretariats and DSMs as conflict managers. They offer support to the view that is skeptical of the pacifying role of these institutional features, discussed in chapter 2.

What should we make of the rather puzzling positive association between REO independence and militarized dispute? Chapter 2 pointed to a number of factors that may render these institutions ineffective instruments of peace, but one is hard pressed to offer a compelling story in which more independent secretariats and DSMs actually trigger more violent dis-

TABLE 5.4. Substantive Interpretation of the Effects of Significant Independent Variables on the Expected Count of Militarized Interstate Disputes, 1982–2001

Variable	Change in Count of Regional Conflict Resulting from a One Std. Dev. Increase / Moving from Zero to One	Change = ____ % of Expected Count in Baseline Model
implemented scope	−0.93	−38%
high-level officials	−1.36	−38%
concentration	−0.79	−33%
civil war	+1.26	+52%
democracy	+1.37	+56%
borders	+1.26	+52%
development	−0.98	−41%

Note: Expected counts are based on model 3 in table 5.1 for all variables except *high-level officials*, which is based on model 7 in table 5.2. In the baseline models, all continuous variables are held at their mean, and dichotomous variables are held at zero. The baseline count in model 3 is 2.45, and the baseline count in model 7 is 3.51 armed disputes. Standard deviations are reported for continuous variables and one for *high-level officials*.

putes. It is more plausible, I would argue, that governments establish these bodies when differences are frequent and when mistrust runs deep. Under these circumstances, future expectations of open rifts and discord may motivate states to delegate legal authority to such institutions. Indeed, as demonstrated shortly, it appears that this result is an artifact of reversed causality: war-prone regions are more likely to institute highly legalized DSMs. This reasoning corresponds to the demand-side logic, which views the institutionalization of REOs as a response to conflict.

Taken as a whole, the empirical analysis demonstrates that some institutional features reduce conflict and that others do not. These findings cast new light on the ability of regional economic organizations to mitigate conflict between their members. As discussed in chapter 3, the institutional design of existing REOs varies a great deal. Some organizations score high, while others score low on all design features. Still others score high on some features but low on others. The results suggest that REOs that score high on the scope of economic activity, such as the GCC and CARICOM, are conducive to regional peace even if they are not very independent (Barnett and Gause 1998; Bearce 2003). Organizations that include independent institutions but a limited economic scope, such as COMESA and ECOWAS, are unlikely to be as effective in promoting peaceful coexistence. Similarly, REOs that provide for regular meetings of high-level officials, such as SADC, are likely to facilitate a peaceful management of intraregional disputes even though their corporate bureaucracy or DSM may be weak.

The divergent effect of different institutional features on conflict has important implications for the consequences of the broader level of regional institutionalization. In chapter 2, I argued that connecting several institutional features under one organizational umbrella may produce beneficial synergy. In particular, I pointed out that regional intermediaries may find a wide economic scope instrumental in the process of dispute management—for example, by using it as leverage during negotiations. The results suggest that economic scope and top-level diplomacy are likely to reinforce each other. Organizations that combine cooperation on a large number of issue areas and regular meetings of high-level officials—such as the EU, Mercosur, and ASEAN—may be especially successful in preventing the escalation of intraregional disputes. The weak effect of institutional independence points to the limits of this logic, however. To the extent that regional bureaucrats or legal bodies are ineffective mediators, the scope of economic cooperation may not matter in this context.

The findings shed some light on the causal mechanisms by which REOs reduce conflict. The strong pacifying effect of economic scope offers support to the claim that extensive cooperation increases the opportunity cost of violence. That regular meetings of high-level officials mitigate conflict whereas regional bureaucracy and DSMs do not points to the conditions under which information and conflict management are most effective. It appears that regional diplomacy at the highest level, while frequently dismissed as a futile and extravagant ritual, actually fosters negotiations, mediation, and the exchange of valuable information. It is also possible that these forums help top officials to socialize and build mutual trust over time, but the weaker effect on all MIDs compared to only violent ones casts some doubt on this mechanism.

The weak performance of regional bureaucracy and dispute settlement suggests that they are neither effective intermediaries and arbitrators nor transmitters of information that pertains to national security issues. Thus, despite the normative appreciation of institutionalist research to the neutrality and autonomy of these institutions (either implicitly or explicitly), my findings suggest that these characteristics can sometimes be detrimental to the goals of the organization. This lends initial support to recent mediation studies, which argue that greater neutrality and strong preference for peace renders potential mediators ineffective (Kydd 2003; Savun 2008). The enthusiasm of governments in war-prone regions for these institutions (reflected in the positive estimates on these variables) is not easy to reconcile with this conclusion. Is it wishful thinking on their part, or do these institutions provide benefits that are not directly related but are nevertheless associated with conflict? While a complete inquiry into the role of these bodies is beyond the scope of the study, I offer some tentative thoughts on this matter in the next part of this chapter.

The conclusion that REO independence is not conducive to peace is strengthened by strong results on top-level meetings. This feature reflects more control of member states over the organization and, therefore, less institutional independence. Thus, the participation of high-level officials in the functioning of the organization is beneficial from the aspect of regional security. This does not mean that the organization is superfluous in this respect. Rather, it provides an institutional framework for regular interaction at the regional level, which would be unavailable otherwise.[6] This observation bolsters the claim that even though they have control over international organizations, states benefit from acting through them (Keohane 1984; Thompson 2006, 2009).

Reversing the Causal Arrow

Like other international institutions, regional organizations are created and designed by governments. As discussed in chapter 2, prior relationships between member states are likely to affect their willingness to endow their organizations with greater authority and responsibilities. There is no consensus on the direction of this relationship, however. Some research highlights enmity and conflict as significant constraints on and suggests that affinity and peace are important prerequisites for institutionalized international cooperation (Gowa and Mansfield 1993; Grieco 1988; Schweller 2001). Other studies emphasize the incentives to create institutions and indicate that governments are likely to invest in them where tensions are high and where conflict is more likely (Fortna 2004; Lake 1999; Wallander and Keohane 1999, 30–32). To fully grasp the relationships between regional institutionalization and conflict, it is therefore necessary to examine the factors that facilitate or hamper institutional building. It is especially important to guard against the possibility that the results reported thus far are driven by the effect of conflict on institutionalized cooperation, rather than the other way around. This section examines the determinants of regional institutionalization as well as its separate features.

Research Design

Evaluating the implications of violent conflict for institutional variation requires a more general framework that identifies the sources of this variation. In contrast to the extensive research on the causes of conflict, studies that explore the determinants of international institutions in a systematic manner are few and far between. Building on and extending existing arguments, I here consider a number of factors that are believed to account for the nature of international institutions. As we shall see, there is a great deal of overlap between the factors alleged to shape institutions and the ones presumed to affect conflict. The presentation of these factors is preceded by a brief discussion of the dependent variables and estimation techniques.

The results of the analysis, summarized in table 5.12, are then reported. The analysis indicates that, as one might expect, the structure and functions of REOs are shaped by a variety of domestic and international factors. It also shows that violent conflict does not inhibit the institutionalization of regional economic organizations. In one notable exception, it appears that militarized disputes actually foster greater REO legalization. These results increase the confidence that the previously reported pacifying effect of regional institutions is real and not an artifact of reversed causality.

Dependent Variables

The dependent variables are the seven variables related to regional institutionalization. These variables have different distributions and are thereby handled with different statistical tools. The four variables that pertain to the overarching REO structure and functions—*designed institutionalization, implemented institutionalization, designed scope,* and *implemented scope*—are continuous. They are thus estimated with an ordinary least squares regression technique. The variable *high-level officials* is dichotomous and estimated with a probit regression model. The estimations of all these variables include a random effects specification, which accounts for unobservable cross-regional variation. The values of the two remaining variables—*bureaucracy* and *dispute settlement*—are ordered on a 0–2 scale. They are therefore estimated with an ordered probit model. The random effects specification is not available with this technique. Instead, the standard errors of the estimates are robust and clustered by REO.

Independent Variables

The main independent variables are concerned with the amount of armed conflict within a given region. They are captured with the number of annual militarized interstate disputes between members of the organization over a five-year period. The year in which the level of institutionalization is assessed follows the five-year period.[7] To ensure that the results are not driven by the size of the organization, the number of militarized conflicts is normalized by the number of members.[8] The first independent variable is therefore *MID members,* which is the total number of armed disputes divided by the number of members. The second independent variable is *violent MID members,* which is the number of disputes that involve the use of force, again divided by the number of REO members. Table 5.A2 in this chapter's appendix reports descriptive statistics for these two variables.

Control Variables

One conventional explanation for regional institutionalization is the level of economic interdependence.[9] First developed by neofunctionalists, this approach maintains that increasing cross-border economic interactions result in a growing societal demand for regulation of such interaction. As a result, national governments form international organizations to manage their economic relationships (Caporaso 1998, 344–45; Haas 1966, 109–10). This approach still serves as a starting point for recent explanations for variation across international institutions (Boehmer and Nordstrom 2008; Mattli 1999; Moravcsik 1998; Stone Sweet and Sandholtz 1998). The logic of this argument suggests that greater commercial connectedness will lead to greater economic scope, more frequent meetings of high-level officials, and greater institutional independence.[10] This hypothesis is tested with the variable *trade share*, which accounts for the intraregional trade as a percentage of the total regional trade. Keeping in mind that trade and REOs are closely associated and that commerce is widely believed to mitigate armed conflict (Crescenzi 2005; Mansfield and Pollins 2003; Polachek 1980; Russett and Oneal 2001), accounting for this factor is imperative.

Turning to some specific design features, extant research suggests that it is not necessarily the intensity of economic relationships but, rather, the proposed level of institutionalized cooperation that determines the authority and independence of regional institutions. Specifically, it is argued that greater economic scope requires greater legalization and institutional strength (Kahler 2000; Smith 2000; Stinnett 2007). As economic exchange increases and becomes more complex, societal actors demand such international governance in order to reduce transaction costs and lower risks of opportunism, uncertainty, and noncompliance (Abbott and Snidal 2000; Haftel 2011; Stone Sweet and Sandholtz 1998; Yarbrough and Yarbrough 1992, 86–88). To account for this possibility, the variable *implemented scope* is included in the models that examine the sources of top-level meetings and institutional independence. Because intraregional trade and economic scope are highly correlated, they are included in separate statistical models.

Two competing explanations emphasize the distribution of power among the group members and offer opposing views. First, according to assumptions of both realism and bargaining theory, powerful states should prefer weak international institutions designed to reflect the distribution of power among their members. Because they have viable unilateral and bilateral options, powerful states face greater opportunity costs than other states when it comes to creating or working through REOs. Weaker states might be expected to favor powerful organizations in order to constrain their more dominant counterparts (Genna 2008). Insofar as the preferences of the powerful members prevail, greater power asymmetry between the members of an REO should be associated with lower levels of institutionalization. This argument is most applicable to the design features related to institutional independence, because powerful states are especially worried about excessive institutional autonomy and legalization (Haftel and Thompson 2006; Smith 2000; Urpelainen 2011).

An alternative argument focuses on the importance of the hegemonic power as a supplier of regional institutions. This view can be traced back to Karl Deutsch, who argued that successful political integration tends to develop around one core area that pushes it forward (Deutsch et al. 1957, 38). More recently, several scholars grounded this argument in theories of collective action and hegemonic leadership, arguing that hegemons bear the cost associated with higher levels of integration (Mattli 1999; Yarbrough and Yarbrough 1992, 61–66). This argument indicates that greater power asymmetry within a region is likely to be associated with greater institutionalization. The effect of power asymmetry on regional institutions is assessed with the regional concentration of power discussed in chapter 4.

A number of recent studies highlight the link between democracies, international organizations, and regional institutions (Baccini, forthcoming; Ikenberry 2001; Mansfield, Milner, and Pevehouse 2008; Mansfield, Milner, and Rosendorff 2002; Mansfield and Pevehouse 2006; Russett and Oneal 2001). Mansfield, Milner, and Rosendorff (2002), who argue that democratic governments are more likely to tie their hands to REOs, find that democratic dyads are more likely to sign preferential trade agreements. Accordingly, one might expect REOs among democratic states to be more institutionalized than those among nondemocracies (Boehmer and Nordstrom 2008; Mansfield, Milner, and Pevehouse 2008). Regime type is claimed to have particular implications for institutional independence. Democracies, it is argued, are more likely to delegate authority to international organizations and to create and use international adjudicating bodies (Kahler 2000; Pevehouse and Russett 2006). The variable *democracy* is employed to evaluate the role regime type plays in the institutional makeup of regional economic organizations.[11]

The potential effect of domestic conflict on international cooperation remains largely unexplored. Nevertheless, civil wars are likely to inhibit regional institutionalization, for at least three reasons. First, states that experience domestic instability may have to devote their material and political resources to addressing these problems rather than to empowering regional organizations (Nye 1971, 82). Second, insofar as REOs require the delegation of national autonomy, governments whose authority is challenged at home may be more jealous of their sovereignty and thus less willing to entrust international institutions with political independence. Third, neighboring states may be reluctant to institutionalize their economic relationships with countries that experience domestic strife, fearing that the conflict will spill over national borders and destabilize the broader region. As one observer of regional integration in Africa notes, "Instability and insecurity have emerged as the greatest impediments to regional integration in Central Africa . . . The fear of a few states' contagious warmongering . . . hindered the desire to construct a common political and economic space" (Ropivia 1999, 126). Domestic violence is measured with the count of all the incidents of domestic armed conflicts involving any of the organization's members. This variable, labeled *civil war members*, aggregates the number of conflicts over a five-year period, which is then divided by the number of member states.

The conventional wisdom holds that there is a trade-off between the expansion and deepening of REOs. More inclusive organizations may face greater difficulties in institutionalizing their cooperation (Acharya and Johnston 2007; Langhammer and Hiemenz 1990, 69; Mansfield and Milner 1999, 615–16). In addition, as the number of members increases, so does the possibility of greater diversity within the group (Haggard 1997, 24; Kahler 1995, 126; Koremenos, Lipson, and Snidal 2001). Thus, larger organizations may result in a more limited scope of economic activity. However, organizations that include numerous members can benefit from greater centralization and independence, which reduce the transaction costs associated with separate bilateral negotiations (Koremenos, Lipson, and Snidal 2001, 788–89). Accordingly, REOs that consist of more states may institute regular meetings of high-level officials and be more independent. The implications of membership for institutional design are considered with the variable *members*, previously discussed.

Like interdependence, economic development is expected to increase regional institutionalization. More diversified and technologically advanced countries are more likely to benefit from integration and economies of scale (Mattli 1999). More affluent countries may also have the wherewithal needed to form and especially implement regional integration schemes. Considering the growing evidence on the pacifying effect of economic development and markets (Gartzke 2007; McDonald 2007, 2009), it is important to account for this factor. I test for this possibility with the variable *development*. Similarity of the organization's members is an oft-cited condition for cooperation through international institutions. Arguably, states that share values and interests will find it easier to institutionalize their economic relationships (Genna 2008; Haggard 1997, 46). In line with the previously presented analyses, the similarity of interests within the REO is captured with the average regional S-score (Signorino and Ritter 1999), measured with either of the variables *affinity alliances* or *affinity UN*.

Path dependence and other temporal dynamics may also help explain the degree of institutionalization and institutional design. As Douglass North (1990) has argued, institutions may have built-in, self-reinforcing mechanisms that promote persistence and growth over time. Institutions become "sticky" and tend to accrete new constituents, providing an impetus for expansion (Haftel and Thompson 2006). These dynamics are captured with the variable *duration*, which is the number of years passed from the year in which the REO was formed to the year in which the institutional variable is observed. In addition, chapter 3 points to a noticeable increase of institutionalization in the post–Cold War era. A categorical variable, labeled *Cold War*, accounts for this systemic change. It is coded 1 for the 1980s and 0 for the 1990s.

Results

Tables 5.5–5.11 present the results for the various dependent variables. Tables 5.5 and 5.6 consist of several regression models that pertain to the sources of regional institutionalization and the scope of economic activity, respectively. Table 5.7, 5.8, and 5.9 include models related to the determinants of regular meetings of high-level officials, regional bureaucracy, and DSM legalization, respectively. Finally, table 5.10 provides substantive interpretation for the variables found to affect REO independence and table 5.11 shows the substantive effect of variables that were statistically significant in the models pertaining to regional institutionalization and economic scope.

The discussion that follows first considers the effect of militarized disputes on the various institutional variables. It indicates that a higher number of disputes does not hamper regional institutionalization, thereby alleviating concerns of reversed causality. In line with demand-side arguments, there are some instances in which more disputes actually result in greater institutionalization. The rest of this section then turns to the performance of other factors believed to affect the structure and functions of REOs. It identifies economic and political dynamics that have a bearing on regional institutionalization, and it mulls over the implications of these findings for this book's argument. The discussion points to some of the conditions under which REOs are likely to thrive and, in turn, promote peace.

The (Non)Effect of Militarized Disputes on Regional Institutions

As tables 5.5 and 5.6 show, the estimates of the variables related to militarized disputes are negative in the models pertaining to the aggregate level of regional institutionalization and economic scope, suggesting that militarized disputes impede regional cooperation through institutions. For the most part, however, the estimates do not reach conventional levels of statistical significance (economic scope comes close to such levels in two models), indicating that they cannot be distinguished from zero. This null result holds whether or not implementation is taken into account. Thus, interstate violent conflict does not hamper plans for and the realization of regional economic cooperation. This result echoes other recent studies, which find that armed disputes do not affect governments' inclination to conclude trade agreements (Mansfield, Milner, and Pevehouse 2008; Mansfield and Pevehouse 2000).

This nonfinding does not necessarily mean that violent conflict is inconsequential for the institutionalization of REOs. As mentioned earlier, some studies argue that enmity operates as a constraint on institutionalized cooperation, while others emphasize the need to form institutions when conflict is rampant. Perhaps both dynamics are at work in some times and some regions but not in others.[12] Whether armed conflict does not weigh heavily in the design and implementation of REOs or whether it pushes governments in opposite directions, the view that regional institutionalization can thrive only where peace is already well established is not supported by the empirical analysis. This result increases the confidence that the pacifying effect of regional institutionalization is genuine.

Turning to regular meetings of high-level officials, table 5.7 indicates that armed disputes do not impinge on the propensity of member states to establish these institutions and to actually attend them repeatedly. The estimates of the conflict variables are negative in some models and positive in others and never come close to conventional levels of statistical significance. Thus, conflict does not systematically prevent top officials from gathering and tackling regional issues. Keeping in mind the political character of such meetings, this result is not obvious. One can single out instances—for example, involving SAARC and AMU in the 1990s—in which violent disputes or diplomatic tensions led to cancellations or delays of regional summits. Nonetheless, one can also point to occasions when top government officials insisted on meeting according to the schedule during times of conflict, possibly to iron out their differences. For example, an AN-

TABLE 5.5. Random-Effects Estimates of the Sources of Regional Institutionalization, 1982–97

	Model 1 designed institutionalization	Model 2 implemented institutionalization	Model 3 implemented institutionalization	Model 4 implemented institutionalization
MID members	−0.744	−0.600	−0.682	
	(−1.08)	(−0.79)	(−0.84)	
violent MID members				−1.038
				(−1.28)
trade share	0.054	0.231***	0.261***	0.236***
	(0.79)	(4.23)	(4.67)	(4.28)
concentration	−1.757	−5.541*	−7.271**	−5.876*
	(−0.51)	(−1.77)	(−2.26)	(−1.87)
democracy	−0.071	−0.098	0.004	−0.096
	(−0.72)	(−1.02)	(0.005)	(−1.01)
civil war members	−0.587***	−0.722***	−0.670***	−0.742***
	(−2.86)	(−3.24)	(−2.82)	(−3.41)
members	0.135	0.114	0.155	0.096
	(0.82)	(0.83)	(1.09)	(0.69)
affinity alliances	9.287*	9.047*	12.112**	8.828*
	(1.71)	(1.79)	(2.34)	(1.76)
development	1.131	0.834	0.693	0.745
	(1.18)	(1.07)	(0.86)	(0.95)
duration	0.222***	0.161***		0.159***
	(4.77)	(3.58)		(3.58)
Cold War			−1.112**	
			(2.20)	
constant	−8.196	−10.750†	−9.381	−9.436
	(−0.91)	(−1.33)	(−1.11)	(−1.16)
Wald χ^2	81.07***	88.01***	74.68***	89.11***
R^2 (overall)	0.51	0.70	0.64	0.70
NT	82	82	82	82

Note: Figures in parentheses are z statistics.
*$p < .1$; **$p < .05$; ***$p < .01$ (two-tailed); †$p < .1$ (one-tailed test).

COM summit was convened shortly after the 1995 armed conflict between Peru and Ecuador and facilitated negotiations between the two rivals. Presumably, conflict impedes regular top-level meetings in some circumstances but not in others. These opposite motivations may cancel each other out in a broad comparative analysis. All the same, it appears that the strong negative association between regular meetings of high-level officials and armed conflict reported in the first part of this chapter is not caused by the effect of the latter on the former.

TABLE 5.6. Random-Effects Estimates of the Sources of Economic Scope, 1982–97

	Model 5 designed scope	Model 6 implemented scope	Model 7 implemented scope	Model 8 implemented scope	Model 9 implemented scope
MID members	−1.041†	−0.852	−0.434		
	(−1.52)	(−1.28)	(−0.61)		
violent MID members				−1.026†	−0.563
				(−1.45)	(−0.74)
trade share	0.117*	0.236***	0.310***	0.239***	0.310***
	(1.81)	(5.23)	(7.02)	(5.24)	(6.94)
concentration	−2.907	−4.899*	−1.410	−5.129*	−1.633
	(−0.88)	(−1.86)	(−0.59)	(−1.94)	(−0.67)
democracy	−0.109	−0.121†	−0.046	−0.118†	−0.044
	(−1.13)	(−1.49)	(−0.64)	(−1.45)	(−0.60)
civil war members	−0.378*	−0.424**	−0.432**	−0.456**	−0.446**
	(−1.87)	(−2.20)	(−2.16)	(−2.42)	(−2.29)
members	0.103	0.050	0.030	0.033	0.024
	(0.67)	(0.44)	(0.29)	(0.29)	(0.23)
affinity UN			11.458***		11.265***
			(3.70)		(3.59)
affinity alliances	9.973*	6.628†		6.323†	
	(1.90)	(1.56)		(1.49)	
development	0.920	0.774	0.705	0.706	0.667
	(1.02)	(1.20)	(1.22)	(1.08)	(1.13)
duration	0.182***	0.126***		0.126***	
	(4.04)	(3.29)		(3.32)	
Cold War			−0.705*		−0.788*
			(−1.83)		(−1.86)
constant	−9.194	−10.028†	−14.217**	−8.961†	−13.553**
	(−1.07)	(−1.48)	(−2.28)	(−1.30)	(−2.12)
Wald χ^2	63***	89***	103***	89***	101***
R^2 (overall)	0.50	0.70	0.74	0.70	0.74
NT	82	82	82	82	82

Note: Figures in parentheses are z statistics.
*$p < .1$; **$p < .05$; ***$p < .01$ (two–tailed); †$p < .1$ (one-tailed test).

Interestingly, the estimates of the variables related to institutional independence are almost always positive and reach conventional levels of statistical significance in some of these models. Table 5.8 suggests that the relationships between conflict and the independence of regional bureaucracy are rather weak. The coefficient in one model is negative and statistically insignificant. The other estimates are positive, but only one reaches statistical significance. Even there, the substantive effect of this variable appears modest (see table 5.10). We can therefore have little confidence that violent conflict affects the independence of REO bureaucracies either positively or

TABLE 5.7. Random-Effects Probit Estimates of the Sources of Regular Meetings of High-Level Officials, 1982–97

	Model 10	Model 11	Model 12	Model 13	Model 14
MID members	0.198	1.061	−0.055		
	(0.22)	(0.90)	(−0.06)		
violent MID members				−0.267	−0.360
				(−0.30)	(−0.44)
trade share	0.006	0.063†		0.008	
	(0.18)	(1.32)		(0.25)	
implemented scope			0.381**		0.381**
			(2.00)		(2.02)
concentration	−0.975	−1.329	−5.516**	−1.065	−5.480**
	(−0.50)	(−0.71)	(−2.12)	(−0.54)	(−2.12)
democracy	−0.031	−0.087†	0.005	−0.026	0.007
	(−0.45)	(−1.34)	(0.07)	(−0.37)	(0.10)
civil war members	−0.253	−0.451*	−0.148	−0.220	−0.112
	(−1.04)	(−1.68)	(−0.49)	(−0.95)	(−0.39)
members	0.226*	0.177†	0.226†	0.227*	0.224†
	(1.80)	(1.49)	(1.47)	(1.78)	(1.45)
affinity UN		7.600†			
		(1.36)			
affinity alliances	5.480*		7.339*	5.667*	7.327*
	(1.73)		(1.86)	(1.76)	(1.87)
development	−0.029	−0.136	−0.794†	−0.061	−0.798†
	(−0.06)	(−0.29)	(−1.29)	(−0.12)	(−1.30)
duration	−0.014		−0.099*	−0.017	−0.099*
	(−0.39)		(−1.82)	(−0.49)	(−1.84)
Cold War		−0.438			
		(−0.85)			
constant	−4.301	−6.833	2.370	−4.049	2.440
	(−0.80)	(−0.99)	(0.37)	(−0.74)	(0.39)
Wald χ^2	8.80	8.81	8.87	8.72	9.07
log likelihood	−27.90	−26.56	−25.44	−27.88	−25.36
NT	82	82	86	82	86

Note: Figures in parentheses are z statistics.
*$p < .1$; **$p < .05$; ***$p < .01$ (two-tailed); †$p < .1$ (one-tailed test).

negatively. The weak association between armed disputes and regional bureaucracy goes both ways, then. More independent regional bureaucracies are not effective in mitigating violent conflict, and armed disputes do not figure heavily in the existence and authority of REO secretariats. Possibly, these bureaucratic bodies remain focused on economic and functional matters and, for the most part, are insulated from the region's security affairs.

The models related to the legalization of regional DSMs present a somewhat different and quite intriguing picture. As table 5.9 indicates, the effect of militarized conflict on the variable *dispute settlement* is always positive

TABLE 5.8. Ordered Probit Estimates of the Sources of Regional Bureaucracy, 1982–97

	Model 15	Model 16	Model 17	Model 18	Model 19
MID members	0.328	1.084*	−0.031		
	(0.53)	(1.82)	(−0.06)		
violent MID members				0.295	0.365
				(0.48)	(0.77)
trade share	0.018	0.128***		0.018	
	(0.91)	(2.82)		(0.91)	
implemented scope			0.092*		0.112*
			(1.78)		(1.69)
concentration	−3.213**	−1.762	−5.963***	−3.318**	−4.792***
	(−1.97)	(−1.19)	(−3.46)	(−2.01)	(−2.90)
democracy	0.064†	0.080†	0.090*	0.064†	0.075**
	(1.36)	(1.63)	(1.92)	(1.36)	(2.08)
civil war members	−0.121	−0.317**	0.003	−0.106	−0.106
	(−0.91)	(2.47)	(0.03)	(−0.82)	(−0.83)
members	0.058	0.014	0.029	0.060	0.041
	(0.94)	(0.22)	(0.50)	(1.01)	(0.70)
affinity UN		31.817***			18.703**
		(3.85)			(2.41)
affinity alliances	10.533***		10.520***	10.584***	
	(3.51)		(3.43)	(3.47)	
development	0.300†	−0.115	0.197	0.306†	−0.035
	(1.40)	(−0.51)	(0.73)	(1.43)	(−0.14)
duration	0.041†		−0.003	0.039†	
	(1.36)		(−0.12)	(1.29)	
Cold War		−0.105			0.134
		(−0.26)			(0.47)
Wald χ^2	42.83***	21.25**	35.00***	43.94***	33.74***
pseudo R^2	0.44	0.52	0.44	0.44	0.37
log likelihood	−36.19	−31.27	−40.67	−36.25	−46.04
NT	82	82	86	82	86

Note: Standard errors are clustered and robust. Figures in parentheses are *z* statistics.

*$p < .1$; **$p < .05$; ***$p < .01$ (two-tailed); †$p < .1$ (one-tailed test).

and reaches statistical significance in most models. This result holds whether one considers all MIDs or only violent ones, and it is robust to alternative model specifications. Thus, states that inhabit regions that experience a larger number of armed disputes are actually more likely to form and legalize DSMs. As table 5.10 indicates, the substantive effect of this variable is quite large. Moving from one standard deviation below the mean to one standard deviation above the mean on the variable *MID members* increases the probability of a highly legalized DSM fourfold, from about 6 to about 20 percent, whereas making the same move for the variable *violent MID*

TABLE 5.9. Ordered Probit Estimates of the Sources of Dispute Settlement Mechanisms, 1982–97

	Model 20	Model 21	Model 22	Model 23	Model 24
MID members	0.965*	0.858†	0.989**		
	(1.62)	(1.44)	(2.46)		
violent MID members				0.906**	0.773*
				(2.00)	(1.87)
trade share	0.101***	0.109**		0.099***	
	(3.12)	(2.44)		(2.97)	
implemented scope			0.162**		0.201***
			(2.41)		(2.67)
concentration	−2.947†	−4.373***	−2.022†	−3.045†	−3.806***
	(−1.50)	(−3.03)	(−1.34)	(−1.56)	(−3.12)
democracy	0.192**	0.204**	0.138**	0.184**	0.167*
	(2.52)	(2.31)	(2.03)	(2.30)	(1.91)
civil war members	−0.722***	−0.727**	−0.420**	−0.674***	−0.373**
	(−2.63)	(−2.43)	(−2.44)	(−2.63)	(−2.06)
members	0.074	0.048	0.064	0.081	0.074
	(0.96)	(0.62)	(0.84)	(1.06)	(0.96)
affinity UN		0.630			−3.068**
		(0.42)			(−2.41)
affinity alliances	−0.325		−1.268	−0.239	
	(−0.15)		(−0.62)	(−0.11)	
development	−1.961***	−1.934***	−1.060**	−1.866***	−1.476**
	(−3.15)	(−2.96)	(−2.16)	(−2.94)	(−2.36)
duration	0.044†		0.006	0.040†	
	(1.44)		(0.23)	(1.36)	
Cold War		−0.429			−0.296
		(−0.86)			(−0.65)
Wald χ^2	36.58**	42.50***	22.76***	32.01**	64.18***
pseudo R^2	0.40	0.38	0.33	0.40	0.39
log likelihood	−40.48	−41.63	−46.36	−40.81	−41.99
NT	82	82	86	82	86

Note: Standard errors are clustered and robust. Figures in parentheses are z statistics.
*$p < .1$; **$p < .05$; ***$p < .01$ (two-tailed); †$p < .1$ (one-tailed test).

TABLE 5.10. Predicted Probability of REO Independence Due to Changes in Independent Variables

Variable	Value	Independence of Regional Bureaucracy		
		No (RB = 0)	Low (RB = 1)	High (RB = 2)
MID members	low	0.0458	0.9484	0.0058
	high	0.0062	0.9504	0.0434
trade share	low	0.2328	0.7669	0.0002
	high	0.0001	0.6903	0.3096
implemented scope	low	0.0618	0.9239	0.0143
	high	0.0075	0.8947	0.0978
concentration	low	0.0008	0.7131	0.2861
	high	0.1849	0.8182	0.0023
democracy	low	0.0558	0.9399	0.0044
	high	0.0054	0.9463	0.0483
civil war members	low	0.0063	0.9506	0.0432
	high	0.0566	0.9391	0.0043
affinity UN	low	0.9890	0.0110	0.0000
	high	0.0002	0.7482	0.2561
affinity alliances	low	0.1683	0.8289	0.0028
	high	0.0030	0.8331	0.1640

Variable	Value	Legalization of Dispute Settlement Mechanism		
		No (DSM = 0)	Low (DSM = 1)	High (DSM = 2)
MID members	low	0.8805	0.0625	0.0570
	high	0.6749	0.1293	0.1958
violent MID members	low	0.8372	0.0770	0.0858
	high	0.6871	0.1212	0.1917
trade share	low	0.9711	0.0182	0.0107
	high	0.3207	0.1544	0.5249
implemented scope	low	0.9559	0.0258	0.0184
	high	0.4022	0.1520	0.4458
concentration	low	0.6250	0.1398	0.2325
	high	0.9249	0.0424	0.0328
democracy	low	0.9766	0.0150	0.0084
	high	0.3737	0.1586	0.4677
civil war members	low	0.4457	0.1594	0.3948
	high	0.9740	0.0165	0.0095
development	low	0.1722	0.1216	0.7062
	high	0.9957	0.0031	0.0012
duration	low	0.8989	0.0545	0.0466
	high	0.6582	0.1331	0.2088
affinity UN	low	0.6307	0.1328	0.2364
	high	0.8147	0.0849	0.1004

Note: Effects are generated using Spost (Long and Freese 2006). Effects for *bureaucracy* are based on models 16 and 17 in table 5.8; effects for *dispute settlement* are based on models 20 and 24 in table 5.9. All continuous variables except the variable of interest are held at mean values. High and low values are one standard deviation above and below the mean, respectively. If one standard deviation is above (below) the maximum (minimum) potential value, the maximum (minimum) value is used.

members increases that probability twofold, from about 9 to 19 percent. Violent conflict therefore appears to push for greater REO legalization.

Indeed, some of the organizations that have experienced the highest number of disputes, such as ANCOM, COMESA, and ECOWAS, have instituted the most legalized DSMs. This finding offers some support to demand-side arguments, which emphasize the greater need for dispute resolution mechanisms where conflict is rampant. As I speculated earlier, states empower regional legal bodies in regions where they experience or anticipate trouble. Conceivably, they are less needed in regions where relations are more harmonious. It is difficult to square this interpretation with the ineffectiveness of these mechanisms in reducing the number of armed disputes, however. It is possible that member states put too much faith in the ability of these bodies to settle their differences. Alternatively, a third, underlying factor may lead to more violent conflict as well as greater DSM legalization. More intense economic friction, for example, may be susceptible for escalation into armed conflict and, at the same time, may encourage member states to create a highly legalized economic DSM. Further research on this link is required to move beyond conjectures.

Other Sources of Regional Institutionalization

The performance of the control variables is generally consistent with theoretical expectations and offers interesting insights into the sources of regional institutionalization and institutional design and their relationships with armed conflict. The effect of economic interdependence on regional economic organizations is largely compatible with the institutionalist conventional wisdom as well as recent empirical studies (Boehmer and Nordstrom 2008; Genna 2008; Haftel 2011). The variable *trade share* has a positive and statistically significant effect on the implemented levels of regional institutionalization and economic scope in all models. As table 5.11 shows, among all the independent variables, intraregional trade also has the largest substantive effect on the scope and institutionalization of REOs. Interestingly, the effect of trade share on the variables that do not account for implementation is much weaker and is statistically insignificant in some models. This disparity suggests that governments sometimes conclude agreements that are detached from the economic realities of their region but that they take the costly steps associated with implementation only when the anticipated benefits are meaningful.

The effect of economic interdependence on top-level meetings, regional bureaucracy, and REO legalization is also positive, though somewhat less consistent. The variable *trade share* is statistically significant in all models related to DSMs but falls short of conventional levels of significance in most models pertaining to regular meetings of high-level officials and regional bureaucracy. Nevertheless, economic scope has a positive and significant effect on all three variables. This finding suggests that these regional bodies are driven more by the economic activities tackled by the REO and less by commercial ties. Table 5.10 shows that the substantive effect of these variables can be fairly large. For example, moving up one standard deviation from the mean on the variable *implemented scope* increases the probability of a highly independent secretariat from about 1.5 to about 9.8 percent and increases the probability of a highly legalized DSM from about 1.8 to about 44 percent. On the whole, then, the analysis points to a strong positive association between economic ties and regional institutionalization.

The propensity of regional commerce to enhance regional institutionalization and especially a wider economic scope has implications for the relationships between these two phenomena and armed disputes. It suggests that the effect of trade on peace may be indirect. Even if regional trade does not inhibit conflict, as indicated by the preceding analyses, it appears to re-

TABLE 5.11. Substantive Interpretation of the Effects of Significant Independent Variables on the Expected Levels of Regional Institutionalization and the Scope of Economic Activity

Variable	Change in the Level of Implemented Regional Institutionalization Resulting from a One Std. Dev. Increase/Moving from Zero to One	Change = ____ % of Expected Count in Baseline Model	Change in Level of Implemented Scope of Economic Activity Resulting from a One Std. Dev. Increase/ Moving from Zero to One	Change = ____ % of Expected Count in Baseline Model
trade share	2.96	42	3.03	67
civil war members	−1.12	−16	−0.65	−14
concentration	−1.14	−16	−1.00	−22
affinity alliances	0.69	10	0.51	11
duration	1.55	22	1.22	27
Cold War	−1.11	−18	−0.78	−16
affinity UN			0.53	11

Note: Expected values are based on models 2 and 3 in table 5.5 for regional institutionalization and models 6 and 7 in table 5.6 for the scope of economic activity. In the baseline models, all continuous variables are held at their mean, and dichotomous variables are held at zero. For the variables *affinity UN* and *affinity alliances* one standard deviation above the mean is greater than the maximum possible value for these variables. The maximum value of one is therefore used.

sult in greater cooperation on a variety of economic issues through regional institutions, which, in turn, increases the opportunity cost of conflict. Solid commercial links are therefore instrumental in facilitating REO institutionalization, and in so doing, they contribute to regional amity (Mansfield and Pevehouse 2000). Greater economic scope promotes peace not only directly but also through encouraging top government officials to meet regularly. Chapter 2 points to potential synergy between these two variables, mainly through issue linkage and side payments during regional summits. The positive and significant effect of economic scope on regular meetings among high-level officials indicates that these two design features tend to go together in practice as well. On the whole, these findings highlight the complex interaction between economic activity, economic institutions, and security relationships and begin to disentangle the multiple ways by which they are linked.

Turning to the regional balance of power, the estimates of the variable *power concentration* are negative across all dependent variables and, with some exceptions, are statistically significant. It appears, then, that power preponderance tends to hamper institutionalized cooperation on a wide number of functional issues. It is especially unfavorable to the establishment of regular meetings among high-level officials as well as independent bureaucracies and DSMs. Perhaps dominant regional powers are not inclined to establish or participate in regional forums, which their weaker neighbors might utilize to coalesce and increase their relative influence. Similarly, powerful states may be loath to give up their control of regional politics and endow international organizations with greater independence (Ikenberry 2001; Smith 2000). Most pertinent to this study, the distribution of regional power pushes conflict and REOs in opposite directions. Regional hegemony promotes peace but not regional institutionalization. It is thus unlikely that regional hegemony drives the positive association between regional institutions and peace. Rather, the latter may serve as a substitute for the former, allowing regions that lack a local "policeman" to manage security relations through institutions.

The relationships between democracy and REOs vary across design features as well. Surprisingly, the effect of the variable *democracy* is negative in the models that pertain to regional institutionalization and economic scope, although this effect is not statistically significant. This variable flips signs in the models related to top-level meetings and, again, falls short of statistical significance. These results cast doubt on the argument that democracies engage in more extensive institutional building and greater economic cooperation. In contrast, democracy is always positive and statistically significant in the models related to institutional independence, suggesting that more democratic regions tend to form more independent regional bureaucracies and especially more legalized DSMs. Substantively, for example, moving up one standard deviation from the mean on the variable *democracy* increases the probability of a highly legalized DSM from close to zero to about 46 percent.

These findings are consistent with the notion that democratic countries are more likely to rely on commitment mechanisms to promote economic cooperation (Kahler 2000; Mansfield, Milner, and Rosendorff 2002; Mansfield and Pevehouse 2006; Pevehouse and Russett 2006). Keeping in mind the analysis thus far, it is apparent that democracy has no bearing on the design features that reduce armed conflict and that it fosters institutional independence, which does little to promote peace. Like concentration of power, then, it is doubtful that democracy accounts for the association between REOs and peace. Highly institutionalized organizations can promote peace in regions where democracy has yet to take roots (Boehmer and Nordstrom 2008).

In line with my expectations, civil wars exert a negative effect on regional cooperation through institutions. Domestic violence is detrimental to regional institutionalization in general, the scope of economic activity, and legalization.[13] The substantive impact of the variable *civil war* is rather pronounced as well. For instance, an increase of one standard deviation on this variable reduces the expected level of implemented scope by about 14 percent and the probability of a highly legalized DSM by 40 percent. These findings suggest that governments that face internal resistance cannot afford to invest time and resources in regional projects and are reluctant to delegate power to regional organizations.

These findings have significant implications for regional cooperation and conflict. Domestic violence is the one variable in the analysis that triggers interstate armed disputes and, at the same time, hampers institutionalized economic cooperation in a sizable and consistent manner. Even though civil wars did not wipe out the pacifying effect of regional institutions in the statistical models previously presented, they potentially condition the relationships between REOs and interstate disputes. In particular, domestic strife may prevent institutionalized functional cooperation from taking hold and, in turn, from restraining cross-border aggression. Thus,

civil wars perpetuate a vicious cycle of regional violence and little cooperation. In contrast, domestic political stability is conducive to the emergence
of a virtuous cycle between regional institutionalization and peace. Considering the silence of extant studies on the role of domestic violence in regional dynamics, exploring this nexus is a promising and perhaps necessary
avenue of future research.

The estimates of regional affinity, measured with either similarity of alliance portfolios or voting in the UN General Assembly, are positive and
statistically significant in all models except those related to DSMs. The substantive effect of these two variables on regional institutionalization and
economic scope is rather small, however.[14] Moving from their average value
to the maximum value increases regional institutionalization and economic scope by about 10 percent and the probability of top-level meetings
by about 5 percent. These findings offer some support for supply-side views
of international institutions. Neighboring states that share political interests and concerns may find international cooperation through institutions
less threatening than states that do not.

In contrast to the other variables, the estimates of regional affinity are
negative in models pertaining to DSM legalization and reach statistical
significance in one model. This result may suggest that like-minded governments do not feel the need to form highly legalized regional courts or
that states that have divergent interests are likely to experience more frequent disagreements, which, in turn, require a more legalized DSM to resolve them. This finding echoes and further corroborates my interpretation
of the positive association between militarized disputes and dispute settlement bodies. Recall that regional affinity was not found to mitigate conflict.
It is therefore possible that states that have common as well as divergent interests institutionalize functional cooperation to manage their disagreements more peacefully. These ambiguous theoretical implications, the
mixed statistical results, and the modest substantive impact of regional
affinity alleviate concerns that the pacifying effect of REOs is an artifact of
shared political interests.

The variable *duration* exerts a positive and significant effect on economic scope and aggregate levels of regional institutionalization. Substantively, an increase of one standard deviation in the duration of an REO,
which is about 10 years, increases economic scope and regional institutionalization by 22 and 27 percent, respectively. The effect of the variable *duration* on institutional independence is also positive but falls short of statisti-

cal significance, and the effect of this variable on top-level meetings is actually negative and significant in two models. On the whole, this finding points to the tendency of international organizations to gradually expand their reach. This result is important insofar as REOs with greater economic scope are more instrumental in promoting peace. As time passes and economic cooperation becomes more institutionalized, the opportunity cost of conflict increases and makes armed disputes less likely. This is also consistent with the idea of vicious and virtuous cycles. To the extent that REOs become established, they are in a better position to reinforce existing peace. Newer organizations tend to be less institutionalized and not as valuable in this respect.

The effect of the number of members on regional institutionalization is positive but statistically insignificant in all models except those pertaining to top-level meetings. This finding suggests that membership, in and of itself, has no noticeable effect on the functions and structure of regional economic organizations. The estimate of the variable *Cold War* is negative and significant in the models related to regional institutionalization and economic scope and insignificant in the others. This result indicates that regional economic organizations were more institutionalized and included more numerous issue areas in the 1990s compared to the 1980s. This finding corresponds to the conventional wisdom regarding the "new regionalism" and further substantiates the descriptive analysis reported in chapter 3. Perhaps one reason for this development was member states' need for a firmer institutional framework to manage their economic and political relationships in the face of diminished involvement of great powers in local matters and greater exposure to global economic forces.

Discussion

On the whole, the analysis of the sources of regional institutionalization and institutional design offers several valuable insights. It provides additional appreciation for the importance of implementation. When implementation is accounted for, the estimates of most variables are sharper, and the fit of the entire model is better. The findings also call attention to the distinct sources of specific design features. Much of the extant research identifies some explanatory variables, such as hegemony and democracy, and applies them to REOs as a whole. The nuanced institutional analysis reported here and summarized in table 5.12 demonstrates that the effect of

TABLE 5.12. Summary of Findings of the Statistical Analyses

Explanatory Variable	Effect on the Number of MIDs	Statistical Significance
designed scope	Decrease	No
implemented scope	Decrease	Strong
regular meetings of high-level officials	Decrease	Strong
corporate bureaucracy	Increase	Weak
dispute settlement mechanism	Increase	Weak

Explanatory Variable	Effect on Implemented Regional Institutionalization and Economic Scope	Statistical Significance
militarized dispute	Decrease	No
economic interdependence	Increase	Strong
regional democracy	Decrease	Weak
concentration ratio	Decrease	Weak
domestic armed conflict	Decrease	Strong
regional affinity	Increase	Strong
number of members	Increase	No
development	Increase	No
duration	Increase	Strong
Cold War	Decrease	Strong

Explanatory Variable	Effect on Regular Meetings of High-Level Officials	Statistical Significance
militarized dispute	Mixed	No
economic interdependence	Increase	No
economic scope	Increase	Strong
regional democracy	Mixed	No
concentration ratio	Decrease	Weak
domestic armed conflict	Decrease	No
regional affinity	Increase	Strong
number of members	Increase	Strong
development	Decrease	No
duration	Decrease	Weak
Cold War	Decrease	No

Explanatory Variable	Effect on the Independence of Regional Bureaucracy	Statistical Significance
militarized dispute	Increase	No
economic interdependence	Increase	Weak
economic scope	Increase	Strong
regional democracy	Increase	Strong
concentration ratio	Decrease	Strong
domestic armed conflict	Decrease	No
regional affinity	Increase	Strong
number of members	Increase	No
development	Mixed	No

TABLE 5.12.—*Continued*

Explanatory Variable	Effect on the Independence of Regional Bureaucracy	Statistical Significance
duration	Increase	Weak
Cold War	Mixed	No

Explanatory Variable	Effect on the Legalization of Dispute Settlement Mechanism	Statistical Significance
militarized dispute	Increase	Strong
economic interdependence	Increase	Strong
economic scope	Increase	Strong
regional democracy	Increase	Strong
concentration ratio	Decrease	Strong
domestic armed conflict	Decrease	Strong
regional affinity	Mixed	No
number of members	Increase	No
development	Decrease	Strong
duration	Increase	Weak
Cold War	Decrease	No

Note: *strong* indicates that a variable is statistically significant at a 90 percent level of confidence or higher in most models; *weak* indicates that a variable is statistically significant in some models but is not robust to different model specifications; *no* indicates that a variable is statistically insignificant in all or most models.

such variables varies across design features. For example, regional hegemony has a weak effect on economic scope but tends to hamper greater independence. In comparison, regional democracy and interstate violence are associated with higher levels of independence and legalization.

Most important, the analysis offers additional support to the findings reported in chapter 4 and the first part of this chapter. Militarized interstate disputes do not impede regional economic cooperation through international organizations. In fact, armed conflict appears to strongly shape one institutional variable—DSM—but in the opposite direction. In line with the demand-side logic, more frequent disputes beget greater legalization of these bodies. Reassuringly, then, the negative association between regional institutions and armed conflict does not emanate from reversed causality.

REOs are still endogenous inasmuch as their structure and functions correspond to their members' interests, incentives, and constraints. The statistical analysis points to a number of domestic and institutional factors that shape these regional institutions. Some of the findings corroborate views that emphasize constraints on institutionalized international cooperation, such as the negative effects of civil war and regional hegemony. Other results are more consistent with perspectives that emphasize incentives for functional cooperation, such as the positive effect of trade and development. Nevertheless, interpretation of these results in the context of the relationships between regional institutionalization and violent conflict offers little evidence that the positive association between these variables stems from these other phenomena and is thus spurious. Most variables either affect REOs and conflict in different directions or affect one but not the other. The only potential exception is domestic strife, which appears to hamper cooperation as well as set off armed conflict in regions in which it is rampant. Accordingly, domestic political stability may be an important condition for the institutionalization of REOs and their ability to cultivate regional peace and stability. Additional research is needed to shed light on this poorly understood link.

Conclusion

This chapter has accomplished two important goals. Building on the empirical analysis presented in the previous chapter, it first investigated the pacifying effect of specific institutional features. The results reveal that not all design features are equally instrumental in promoting regional peace. In line with the theoretical framework, the scope of economic activity and regular meetings of high-level officials reduce the number of armed conflicts. In comparison, more independent regional bureaucracies and DSMs have no effect on the number of militarized disputes. These findings indicate that the consequences of regional institutions for conflict are determined not only by the broader level of institutionalization but also by the specific features of which these organizations are composed. As such, they reinforce recent calls to pay close attention to sources and implications of institutional design (Acharya and Johnston 2007; Koremenos, Lipson, and Snidal 2001).

The second part of this chapter took up the potential endogeneity of regional institutionalization. Because international institutions are created by their members to promote their shared interests, it is important to isolate the independent effects of REOs from the factors that led to their creation and design in the first place. One potential pitfall involves reversed causality, meaning that militarized disputes affect regional institutionalization rather than the other way around. In addition, it is possible that the association between REOs and conflict is spurious, that is, that other, underlying factors account for both variables. In chapter 2, I argued that even though international institutions are endogenous, determining the effect of conflict and other factors on institutionalized cooperation requires one to the specify the interests on which states act. Theoretical perspectives that emphasize constraints are often skeptical with respect to the ability of REOs to promote peace in conflict-prone regions. An alternative stance, which calls attention to states' incentives rather than constraints, indicates that governments may form REOs in order to promote peace. In this view, institutions both are affected by and independently affect international interaction.

In light of these mixed theoretical expectations, I turned to an empirical examination of the sources of regional institutionalization and specific design features. The analysis indicates that the number of militarized disputes does not affect institutionalized functional cooperation in a negative and systematic manner. It thus alleviates concerns of reversed causality and is at odds with the view that only zones of peace invest in regional economic organizations. In one notable exception, armed disputes bring about greater legalization, as the perspective that emphasizes incentives would lead us to expect. The examination of other potential sources of institutional variation across REOs shows that, indeed, they are endogenous to their members' preferences and interactions. Nonetheless, they show little indication that the association between REOs and conflict is caused by other, more fundamental forces. As such, they further substantiate the finding that international institutions can have a real and substantial impact on matters of regional security, even as they are shaped by these forces.

Finally, the results begin to shed light on the complex interconnections between conflict, REOs, and other regional dynamics. For example, the positive association between economic scope and regular meetings of high-level officials points to a positive feedback loop between the two design features, which reinforces their separate pacifying effect. In other examples, it appears that international trade promotes peace indirectly by stimulating greater functional cooperation and that domestic political stability is an important precondition for regional economic cooperation and, in turn, for peace. These preliminary observations call for greater scholarly attention to these issues.

These observations also underscore the limited ability of the statistical analysis presented in this chapter to address concerns of endogeneity, interactions, and reversed causality. Ideally, one would employ more sophisticated statistical techniques to account for these issues. Unfortunately, these methods cannot be applied fruitfully to the data set employed in this book. As discussed in previous chapters, when faced with choosing between many observations that capture institutional variation rather crudely and fewer observations that offer a nuanced and more precise measure of this variation, I took the latter approach for this study. That being said, even the most sophisticated statistical methods go only so far in sorting out complex and multifaceted relationships, such as the ones considered here. Furthermore, statistical methods are not well suited to disentangle the causal mechanisms by which independent and dependent variables are linked. An in-depth case study is one good way to shed additional light on these issues and to complement the statistical analysis (Lieberman 2005; Tarrow 1995). The next chapter carries out this task.

Appendix

TABLE 5.A1. Correlation Matrix for Tables 5.1–5.3

	designed scope	implemented scope	high-level officials	bureaucracy	dispute settlement
MID	−0.02	−0.14	0.05	0.00	0.28
violent MID	0.01	−0.12	0.00	0.04	0.28
regional MID	−0.08	−0.18	0.01	0.03	0.29
trade share	0.37	0.75	−0.00	0.30	0.39
concentration	−0.07	−0.15	−0.11	−0.28	−0.28
democracy	−0.04	0.35	−0.25	0.24	0.27
civil war	−0.37	−0.26	−0.11	−0.13	0.02
members	0.29	0.18	0.31	0.25	0.39
borders	0.32	0.14	0.33	0.32	0.34
borders per member	0.39	0.14	0.40	0.42	0.14
affinity alliances	0.29	−0.07	0.44	0.35	0.03
affinity UN	0.06	−0.05	0.31	0.34	−0.06
development	0.21	0.52	−0.12	0.17	0.00

TABLE 5.A2. Descriptive Statistics for Variables Not Included in Previous Chapters

Variable	N	Mean	Std. Dev.	Min	Max
MID members	90	0.35	0.40	0	1.67
violent MID members	90	0.28	0.36	0	1.57
civil war members	90	1.29	1.59	0	7.6
duration	90	15.46	9.74	1	40
Cold War	90	0.44	0.49	0	1

CHAPTER 6

Regional Economic Organizations and Conflict in Southeast Asia

The quantitative analysis presented in previous chapters indicates that some institutional features reduce conflict and that others do not. This chapter complements the quantitative analysis with an in-depth case study. The first section discusses the main objectives of this chapter and elaborates on the selection of the ASEAN region for this qualitative analysis.[1] The second section examines the effect of regional institutionalization and institutional design on intraregional conflict. It largely corroborates the statistical findings: economic scope and regular meetings of high-level officials made a significant contribution to intraregional peace. Greater institutional independence, as well as security cooperation, did not have a noticeable pacifying effect. The third section reverses the causal arrow and assesses the effect of conflict on the evolution of regional institutions in Southeast Asia. It suggests that conflict constrains in some instances, encourages in others, and is inconsequential for regional cooperation in still others. The third section also identifies the conditions that determined the manner by which conflict affected Southeast Asian institutions. The fourth section further addresses concerns of endogeneity by considering a number of alternative explanations for conflict and peace in Southeast Asia. It shows that the pacifying effect of regional institutionalization is genuine and that there are instances in which it substitutes for or complements other determinants of regional security dynamics. The fifth section reflects on the narrative and draws lessons for the broader study and for conflict and cooperation in the ASEAN region.

Method and Case Selection

Considering the broader context of this study, this chapter endeavors to uncover evidence of the putative causal mechanisms offered in chapter 2.

Quantitative analysis can provide valuable insights with respect to the causal effect of one variable (or more) on another variable. It is less suitable to shed light on the ways by which these variables are interrelated, however (George and Bennett 2005; Gerring 2004). The case study method is particularly useful in this regard. This method allows one to trace the causal processes that presumably connect the variables of interests and to evaluate the hypothesized motivations of the relevant actors (Gerring 2004, 348–49; Tarrow 1995). To the extent that a case study shows how the explanatory variables cause the explained variable, it comprises additional evidence that bears on the plausibility of the theory (Lieberman 2005). In addition, an in-depth historical account can provide a more nuanced analysis of the relationship between the variables of interest. It may allow one to refine the hypotheses and to further develop existing theories (Coppedge 1999; George and Bennett 2005, 20–21).

The specific method used in this chapter is within-case theory testing.[2] This approach focuses on one case included in the larger data set and investigates the manners by which temporal changes in the key independent variables affect the phenomenon they are purported to explain. It is especially suited to illuminate time-related dynamics, such as endogeneity and reversed causality, which are not captured adequately by the cross-regional analysis employed in the preceding chapters (Coppedge 1999). According to Lieberman (2005, 444), two criteria ought to guide the choice of the particular case to be investigated. First, the case should fit the statistical model well, thereby allowing the researcher to cast light on the causal processes underlying the observed statistical correlation. Second, the case should have wide variation on the explanatory variables that are central to the study. Starting from the independent variables ensures that the process tracing goes from cause to effect.

The ASEAN region meets these criteria very well. As the large-N qualitative analysis conducted in chapter 4 shows, the predicted and the actual number of militarized disputes are closely matched. Moreover, in comparison with other REOs in the group predicted to experience an intermediate level of conflict, ASEAN is ranked high on regional institutionalization and low on the number of disputes (see table 4.6). This negative association is consistent with the expectations of the theoretical framework presented in chapter 2. Turning to the second criterion, ASEAN embodies a lengthy experience in economic regionalism, which dates back to the 1960s, thereby permitting an effective longitudinal examination of the relationships be-

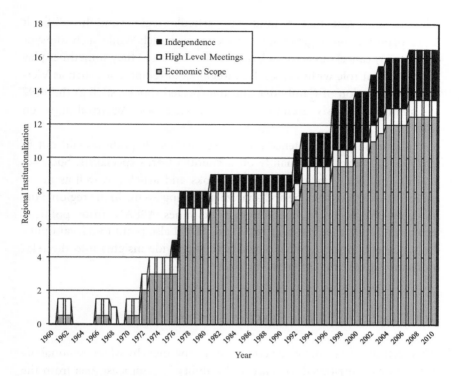

Fig. 6.1. Regional institutionalization in the ASEAN region, 1960–2010

tween institutionalized cooperation and violent conflict in this region. More important, Southeast Asian history in the last five decades reflects substantial variation on the independent variables of interest. Regional institutions thrived during some periods but faced serious challenges in others. In addition, as figure 6.1 demonstrates, the nature and design of REOs in this region have changed over the years.

The ASEAN case study has two further advantages. First, table 6.1 indicates that the region has experienced numerous militarized disputes over the years, on diverse issues and with different levels of intensity. It also shows that some periods were characterized by conflict and animosity, while others were rather peaceful. This wide-ranging variation and the dynamic nature of conflict and cooperation in the ASEAN region are especially conducive to the investigation of the reciprocal relationships between the two. Second, this case study allows for the consideration of the effects of idiosyncratic events that are unique to particular regions and thus difficult to incorporate into a general, cross-sectional model. While such idiosyncrasies may cancel out across a large number of cases,[3] they sometimes play an important role within cases. Extraregional developments, such as Vietnam's occupation of Cambodia, and unexpected shocks, such as the 1997 Asian financial crisis, exemplify such idiosyncrasies (Aggarwal and Koo 2008).

In searching out evidence for (or against) the hypotheses laid out in chapter 2, I have relied mainly on accounts of area specialists. Such accounts commonly include academic books and articles as well as newspaper articles that describe and analyze unfolding events in the region. Fortunately, the body of research that examines ASEAN from political, economic, and other perspectives is extensive. I also point to relevant public statements of policymakers where they provide insights into the relationship between the different variables.[4]

The Effect of ASEAN on Peace in Southeast Asia

This section offers a detailed account of the manners by which regional organizations contributed to peace and stability in Southeast Asia from the early 1960s to the first decade of the twenty-first century. It examines five time periods that correspond to the evolution of institutionalized cooperation in this region (Khong 1997; Narine 2002). For each of these periods, it describes the nature of regional cooperation and violent conflict. It then evaluates if and in what ways regional institutionalization mitigated armed disputes. The narrative pays particular attention to the institutional features considered in earlier chapters and offers ample support for the findings reported in the statistical analysis; that is, the scope of economic activity and regular meetings of high-level officials make a significant contribution to regional peace. A corporate secretariat and formal mechanisms of dispute resolution, economic as well as political, are largely inconsequential in this respect.

1960–67: ASA and Maphilindo

The experience of Southeast Asia with both indigenous regional organizations and interstate armed disputes dates back to the early 1960s. The

TABLE 6.1. Militarized Interstate Disputes in the ASEAN Region, 1960–2011

State A	State B	Date	Description	Source
Indonesia	Malaysia	1963–65	Confrontation. Multiple incidents, several hundred battle deaths.	Gordon 1966; Jones, Bremer, and Singer 1996; Lyon 1969
Malaysia	Philippines	April 1968	The Corregidor Affair. Two Malaysian gunboats and an aircraft invaded Philippine territory.	Brown 1994, 102; Caballero-Anthony 1998, 54; Jones, Bremer, and Singer 1996
Malaysia	Philippines	November 1979	Malaysian task force occupied a reef in the Spratly Islands.	Jones, Bremer, and Singer 1996; Mak 2009
Malaysia	Philippines	June 1980	A Philippine navy vessel shot at a Malaysian fishing boat from Sabah.	Indorf 1984, 18; Jones, Bremer, and Singer 1996
Malaysia	Philippines	September 1985	Malaysian gunboats and helicopters raided the island of Maddanas, killing or abducting 53 people in a piracy suppression operation.	Jones, Bremer, and Singer 1996
Malaysia	Philippines	May–August 1988	Malaysian forces seized 49 Filipino fishermen in the South China Sea. Both sides boosted military presence in the area.	Jones, Bremer, and Singer 1996; Simon 1990, 128
Malaysia	Singapore	April 1992	A Singaporean patrol craft engaged a Malaysian patrol boat near the disputed island of Pedra Branca.	Jones, Bremer, and Singer 1996; Tan 2000, 22–23
Thailand	Vietnam	May 30, 1995	Exchange of fire between naval vessels in the Gulf of Thailand.	Collins 2003b, 105; Ghosn, Palmer, and Bremer 2004
Philippines	Vietnam	August 1998	Philippines increased patrol near the disputed Spratly Islands.	Ghosn, Palmer, and Bremer 2004
Myanmar	Thailand	December 1998	A Burmese vessel attacked a Thai navy vessel, killing two Thai naval officials.	Alford 1999
Myanmar	Thailand	January 1999	Thai patrol boat exchanged fire with Burmese frigates. Three Burmese sailors died.	Collins 2003a, 104–5; Ghosn, Palmer, and Bremer 2004
Philippines	Vietnam	October 1999	Vietnamese troops shot a Philippine air force plane in the Spratly Islands.	Collins 2003b, 197; Ghosn, Palmer, and Bremer 2004; Mak 2009
Myanmar	Thailand	February 2001	Border clashes. Tens of Burmese battle deaths.	Collins 2003a, 100; Ghosn, Palmer, and Bremer 2004; Haacke 2003, 210–11
Indonesia	Malaysia	April 2005	Naval vessels collided near the disputed sea block of Ambalat.	Mak 2009; Gale 2009
Indonesia	Malaysia	June 2009	Naval standoff near the disputed sea block of Ambalat.	Osman 2009
Thailand	Cambodia	October 2008–May 2011	Multiple incidents of fire exchange and skirmishes near the disputed Preah Vihear temple. Tens of battle deaths and dozens of wounded soldiers.	Sukma 2008; Haywood 2011

process of decolonization, which was nearly complete by that time, resulted in bilateral tensions between the newly independent states in the region. The formation of Malaysia in the early 1960s brought about two serious conflicts. The first conflict involved the Philippines' claim for the territory of Sabah, which became a part of the Malaysian federation. The Philippines raised what had been a dormant issue in 1962 and pursued it vigorously in the following years. Malaysia rejected the Philippines claim single-handedly.[5] Although this conflict did not lead to a militarized incident, it triggered the breakdown of the diplomatic relationship between the two governments from 1963 to 1965 (Gordon 1966, 9–10; Solidum 1974, 148). The second and much more severe conflict of this period was the Konfrontasi (Confrontation) between Indonesia and Malaysia, which took place from September 1963 to 1965 (Gordon 1966; Jorgensen-Dahl 1982). This is, by far, the most severe conflict to date between any of the ASEAN founding members.[6]

During the same years, initial experimentations with regional cooperation took place. The formation of the Association of Southeast Asia (ASA)[7] in 1961 and Maphilindo[8] in 1963 epitomize the first indigenous international organizations in the region.[9] Maphilindo intended to enhance the security of its members and did not have economic components. Nevertheless, it represents an early attempt to address political conflict between its member states (Fifield 1979, 4–5). The main purpose of the organization was to provide a forum for political consultation and to prevent the escalation of existing disputes between Malaysia, Indonesia, and the Philippines (Solidum 1974, 29). Beyond this, its intended substance remained ambiguous (Lyon 1969, 157). The organization collapsed in September 1963, only several weeks after its inception (Fifield 1979, 6; Leifer 1989, 19).

ASA was essentially a functional organization, whose main objectives were to promote the economic, social, and cultural development of its members (Gordon 1966; Solidum 1974, 28). It included a plan for a preferential trade agreement (which was not implemented) and sectoral cooperation in various areas, such as agriculture, tourism, transportation, education, culture, and health (Solidum 1974, 43–44). The foreign ministers were the highest authority and were scheduled to meet annually. There were also a standing committee, expert committees for different issue areas, and national secretariats (Gordon 1966, 172–73; Solidum 1974, 132). ASA experienced institutional instability during its six years of existence. Its meetings and activities were suspended from 1963 to 1965, resumed in 1966, and finally subsumed by ASEAN in 1967.

Have these abortive organizations exerted any effect on the disputes between their members? The answer with respect to Maphilindo is decidedly negative. This short-lived organization had little opportunity to have an effect on these conflicts (Fifield 1979, 6; Leifer 1989, 19). As a consequence, Malaysia and Indonesia did not share membership in a regional organization during the Konfrontasi. Despite having strong commercial ties (Kivimäki 2001), the two states did not institutionalize their economic relations in manners that the theoretical framework in chapter 2 suggests are conducive for peace. ASA, however, was instrumental in mitigating conflict between its members. ASA did not promote peace through institutional independence, simply because it had neither a corporate secretariat nor a DSM in place. Its pacifying effect, however minimal, stems from the economic benefits anticipated by its members and from opening channels of communication between high-level officials.

Even though ASA's scope of economic activity was extremely narrow and provided few concrete benefits, leaders valued the organization and believed that they would reap its fruits in coming years (Gordon 1966; Solidum 1974). These expectations rendered the organization a valuable bargaining chip during the Malaysia-Philippines Sabah dispute. Consistent with the argument that severing economic ties can function as a substitute for violence (Morrow 1999, 2003; Stein 2003), the contending parties used the organization to demonstrate their resolve. As Jorgensen-Dahl (1982, 195) explains, "[ASA] added to their bargaining strength in holding out a promise of benefits even though these did lie in the future. Both Malaya and the Philippines used their common membership in ASA as a lever, evidently in the hope that the other party's commitment to the association was strong enough to make it change its position on the Sabah issue."

As the theoretical framework presented in chapter 2 indicates, however, the organization's limited scope and lack of implementation undermined the effectiveness of this strategy. Jorgensen-Dahl (1982, 196) further elaborates, "At the time of the Sabah crisis the level of functional specificity of ASA was low . . . The use of sanctions may have become synonymous with abandoning ASA because few or no sanctions were available which could be isolated and divorced from the activities, real and potential, of the association." This observation demonstrates that governments can substitute the use of force with economic ties during crisis bargaining and avoid risky escalation. Yet the utility of this instrument hinges on the scope of economic activity. A narrow scope, which remains mostly on paper, reflects a low level of interaction as well as fewer benefits to REO members and thus is of limited value as a check on aggression.

ASA also facilitated the establishment of channels of communication and understandings between top-level policymakers. In particular, it allowed Thailand to play the role of an honest broker (Gordon 1966, 186).[10] According to Gordon (1966, 185 n. 63), the Thai foreign minister "believes that political relations between Malaya and the Philippines probably would have deteriorated much further had it not been for the existence of an organizational tie (ASA) between them." His observation corroborates the argument that direct diplomacy fosters better communication among government officials and provides a channel for informal negotiations. It seems, however, that the organization played only a minor role in this respect, as meetings of high-level officials were not held from 1963 to 1966. The diplomatic deadlock ended only after a newly elected Philippine government decided to shelve the Sabah issue (temporarily, as demonstrated shortly). In sum, despite its many limitations, ASA was instrumental in restraining violence between its members in manners consistent with the mechanisms of opportunity cost, information, and conflict management. There is little evidence of socialization at this early stage. The rapprochement between Malaysia and the Philippines and the end of the Konfrontasi opened the door for more meaningful regional cooperation.

1967–76: ASEAN's Early Years

Following a year of intense diplomatic negotiations, ASEAN was formed in 1967. This organization had a broad purpose, which included economic as well as security goals. Specifically, ASEAN endeavored to promote economic, social, and cultural cooperation, as a means to achieve economic growth, political stability, and regional peace. Due to political sensitivities and disagreements, the founding document emphasized the former at the expense of the latter.[11] To get functional cooperation underway, ASEAN borrowed the institutional structure of ASA and many of its projects.[12] In the early 1970s, the organization's activities have expanded to include negotiations of economic agreements with extraregional actors, such as the European Economic Community, and cooperation in multilateral forums, such as the General Agreement on Tariffs and Trade and the United Nations Conference on Trade and Development (Jorgensen-Dahl 1982, 145–49).[13] Nevertheless, the formative years of ASEAN brought very few tangible accomplishments beyond the organization's survival. As Frost (1990, 5) suggests, for example, "For the first eight years of its existence ASEAN made only modest progress towards developing substantive co-operation."[14]

The ability of ASEAN to mitigate violent conflict was tested shortly after its inception. In 1968, the dispute between the Philippines and Malaysia regarding the Sabah territory reared its head again. During the so-called Corregidor Affair, indications that the Philippines were training guerilla forces to infiltrate Sabah caused alarm in Malaysia. The latter's demand that the Philippines formally recognize the Malaysian sovereignty over Sabah, followed by the refusal of the Philippines to do so, resulted once again in the suspension of diplomatic relations from April 1968 to December 1969 and in a low-level militarized dispute in 1968 (Caballero-Anthony 1998; R. Irvine 1982, 19–20; Jorgensen-Dahl 1982, 197–212; Leifer 1989, 34–35).[15]

When this conflict erupted, then, ASEAN was less than one year old. Like ASA, it had a very loose institutional structure that did not include a regional secretariat and a DSM. In addition, even though ASEAN is frequently (and rightfully) portrayed as a political organization whose initial objective was to manage regional conflict (Amer 1998; Caballero-Anthony 1998; Severino 2006), the organization had no formal mechanism to promote collective security or resolve bilateral disputes. In fact, such security cooperation was proposed but rejected by the founders of ASEAN, who perceived it as too controversial (Jorgensen-Dahl 1982, 114–15; Leifer 1989, 69). Nevertheless, ASEAN did promote the peaceful management of the Sabah dispute in manners similar to its predecessor.

First, ASEAN provided a forum for informal communication and mediation between the two parties. In ASEAN's meeting of foreign ministers, the other members convinced Malaysia and the Philippines to tone down their rhetoric and accept a "cooling-off period" (Acharya 2001, 50; M. L. Brown 1994, 109; Severino 2006, 165–66). President Suharto of Indonesia played the role of a mediator (Caballero-Anthony 1998; Tuan 1996, 69). The mediation efforts were only partly successful, however (R. Irvine 1982, 19–20; Leifer 1989, 34–35; cf. Simon 1982, 38). In addition, Jorgensen-Dahl (1982, 208) argues that in the second part of 1969, ASEAN "acted as an important face-saving device, especially to the Philippines, by serving as a channel through which relations between the two disputants could be gradually brought back to normal."

Second, although ASEAN achieved very little by the time of this conflict, policymakers had high hopes. These expectations of future benefits had a moderating effect on the dispute. For example, Malaysia's prime minister announced that "Malaysia and the Philippines had agreed to restore diplomatic relations without any preconditions, out of consideration for the need for regional co-operation." A joint communiqué issued by the ministerial meeting recorded that "the restoration of diplomatic relations had been agreed 'because of the great value which Malaysia and the Philippines placed on ASEAN.'"[16] While these statements do not refer to any specific issue area, most of ASEAN's actual and planned activities revolved around sectoral cooperation. It is thus conceivable that these future benefits were expected from a range of activities pursued by the organization. Reflecting on these events, Roger Irvine (1982, 20) concludes that "some argued plausibly that the Association [of Southeast Asian Nations] had been a moderating influence that had prevented the Sabah dispute from escalating further."

The Sabah dispute was followed by several years free of major bilateral tensions. Both observers and policymakers acknowledge the role that ASEAN played in this respect. They point to two particular manners by which ASEAN promoted peace. First, a UN report that examined ways by which ASEAN can best promote regional cooperation and made several specific recommendations was submitted to the organization in 1972 (Jorgensen-Dahl 1982, 142–43). The adoption of this study and initial steps toward its implementation had incrementally expanded ASEAN's scope of economic activity (Castro 1981; Suriyamongkol 1988). Moreover, Jorgensen-Dahl (1982, 177) points out that "the scope for bargaining or compromise became considerably wider once the perceptions of the political and economic leaders had accommodated or adjusted to the opportunities and potential for economic cooperation suggested by the UN study."[17] Given the still embryonic stage of economic cooperation and the low level of implementation, the pacifying effect of economic scope appears to be limited. Nevertheless, member governments had expected this first step to lead to a durable and expanded economic partnership (Castro 1981, 244; Suriyamongkol 1988, 106–7).

Second and much more important, ASEAN served as a forum that fostered socialization and informal communication between high-level officials. For example, Acharya (2001, 204) contends that "ASEAN did contribute to [regional peace] by fostering a climate of socialization and trust that might have suppressed Sukarno-like militant nationalist sentiments among the member states towards each other and led them to realize the benefits of cooperation over confrontation."[18] Policymakers expressed similar views. Malaysia's deputy prime minister, Tun Ismail, asserted that "the constant contact and communication between our officials has helped to develop a habit of co-operation and solidarity."[19] The organization's annual ministerial meeting (AMM) for foreign ministers played a particularly important role in this respect. As one observer explains,

> The need to ensure a stable and friendly relationship among ASEAN members has been the primary political function of the AMM. That function has been carried out through a number of roles. Firstly, the AMM served as a useful vehicle by which ASEAN high officials become more acquainted with one another, recognize one another's problems better, become more sensitive to one another's interests, and promote greater mutual understanding. Secondly, the AMM constitutes a forum for the institutionalization of a habit of dialogues among member states. Thirdly, the AMM provides a venue for consultation and exchange of views over bilateral and regional problems whenever they arise. Fourthly, and more importantly, the AMM plays a central role as a forum for regional confidence-building measures in Southeast Asia. All these functions have, in turn, contributed greatly to the institution of a regional mechanism for conflict management and reduction among its member states. (Soesastro 2001, 282)

An important element of socialization was the decision-making process—widely known as the "ASEAN Way"—that was developed during ASEAN's early years. Two main principles guided decision making at the highest levels: *musjawarah* (consultation) and *mufakat* (consensus). These principles represent the tendency to discuss disagreements in a relaxed manner, to arrive at an agreed-on solution through an informal dialogue, and to set aside outstanding differences (Acharya 2000, 63–72; Jorgensen-Dahl 1982, 165–69).[20] Golf games and singing sessions, for example, were instrumental in facilitating socialization and informal discussions (Caballero-Anthony 1998, 58–60; Indorf 1975, 26; Yew 2000, 331). This style of negotiation further promoted reconciliation and peace.

Overall, it seems that ASEAN was instrumental in bringing its members closer to each other and in reducing the risk of violent conflict during this decade. As Leifer (1989, 151) explains, "the cohesion and viability of ASEAN have come to constitute a hostage to worst case predatory intent." With respect to specific design features, the examination of this REO throughout this period provides support for the hypothesis that regular meetings of high-level officials are instrumental in defusing regional frictions. It also shows that these meetings promoted peace through the mechanisms of information, conflict management, and, for the first time, socialization. There is little evidence that socialization among the elite trickled down to lower-level officials or the general public, however. Consistent with the statistical results, the limited and largely unimplemented scope of functional cooperation did not make a significant mark on regional security matters.

1976–92: The Bali Summit and Vietnam's Invasion to Cambodia

ASEAN's Bali summit in 1976 ushered in a new phase in the evolution of the organization. In the years that followed that summit, ASEAN has developed a reputation of a viable organization and an important player in regional politics. David Irvine (1982, 68) contends that "the strength of both the internal commitments and the external recognition suggests that ASEAN by 1980 was proving to be one of the most successful experiments in regional cooperation amongst Third World countries."[21] From an institutional vantage point, it broke new ground on several fronts.

ASEAN embarked on several significant new initiatives that broadened its economic scope. For the first time, its members signed a (rather modest) preferential trade agreement (Castro 1981; Frost 1990).[22] They also agreed to initiate regional industrial projects, signed a swap agreement, and expanded their collective economic bargaining efforts (Chatterjee 1990; D. Irvine 1982). In addition, ASEAN went through a structural reorganization that enhanced its institutional independence by forming a small corporate secretariat.[23] Finally, the member states signed the Treaty of Amity and Cooperation (TAC). In this treaty, they called for a peaceful resolution of intraregional political conflicts and agreed to form a mechanism for the resolution of such disputes (Frost 1990, 9; D. Irvine 1982, 45–46; Leifer 1995, 134–35).[24]

This high visibility continued throughout the 1980s, when the ASEAN governments joined forces to address the Vietnamese occupation of Cambodia. Despite some disagreements on how to approach this problem and despite few tangible accomplishments,[25] ASEAN was able to speak with one voice on this issue and to keep it on the agenda of the international community. According to several observers, these were the heydays of the organization (Antolik 1990; Huxley 1996; Leifer 1989). The preoccupation with Indochina had two somewhat contradictory implications for the institutionalization of ASEAN. On the one hand, it diverted the attention of member governments from the economic aspects of the organization (Huxley 1990, 90; Indorf 1984, 5; Jorgensen-Dahl 1982, 219). In turn, ASEAN's economic scope has expanded in an incremental manner until the early 1990s. On the other hand, the ongoing Vietnamese challenge enhanced the informal mechanisms and habits of diplomatic consultation and coordination among top-level officials (Narine 2002, 58–59).

Turning to conflict, only a handful of militarized disputes erupted from 1976 to 1991. These were mostly isolated, low-intensity incidents between Malaysia and the Philippines (Huxley 1990, 93–95). The low level of armed conflict does not reflect the absence of bilateral disagreements or the resolution of competing territorial claims. Rather, the members of ASEAN deliberately deemphasized their differences and agreed to shelve them (Acharya 2001, 130; Antolik 1990; Indorf 1984, 16; Simon 1982, 39). Huxley (1990, 93) points out, "A wide range of potentially dangerous disputes and clashes of interest remain between various ASEAN members, despite the best efforts of their governments and news media to play down their scope and significance." Thus, despite persisting animosities and disagreements, the members of ASEAN were able to minimize interstate violence during this time period.

What accounts for this prolonged period of relative peacefulness? Certainly, the emergence of Vietnam as a common external threat brought the members of ASEAN closer to each other in their thinking (Leifer 1989). The bonding effect of this common enemy should not be exaggerated, however. For one thing, clear divisions were exposed within the organization with respect to the manner by which Vietnam should be contained (Huxley 1990). Thailand and Singapore pushed for a hard-line approach toward Vietnam, which was resisted by more moderate members, such as Indonesia and Malaysia (Indorf 1984). For another, as pointed out already, bilateral tensions remained. Indorf (1984, 16) points out, "Even Thailand, while focusing its attention almost entirely upon the Indochina Problem and recurrent insurgency, has not been able to evade some antagonistic strains with its southern ASEAN neighbor [Malaysia]." Notwithstanding these caveats, there is little doubt that the conflict in Indochina tempered intra-ASEAN frictions.

A second moderating factor on Southeast Asian politics was the increase in ASEAN's institutionalization after the Bali summit. The progress made by ASEAN enhanced the value of the organization to its members and influenced, for example, the Philippines decision not to pursue the Sabah claim (Jorgensen-Dahl 1982, 211–12; Simon 1982, 38). As Ferdinand Marcos, president of the Philippines, announced in 1977, "[The Philippines] is . . . taking definite steps to eliminate one of the burdens of ASEAN, the claim of the Philippine Republic to Sabah. It is our hope that this will be a permanent contribution to the unity, the strength, and the prosperity of all ASEAN."[26]

The value of ASEAN did not emanate from the weak corporate secretariat, which did not play any noticeable role with respect to intraregional politics (Indorf 1984, 68; D. Irvine 1982, 56; Leifer 1989, 26–27). One is also hard pressed to attribute the low level of conflict to the TAC. Despite the symbolic value of this treaty, it contains very few concrete measures to promote peace, and its provisions for dispute settlement are yet to be implemented.[27] As in the previous period, ASEAN's tightening cordiality between high-level officials and, to a lesser extent, its expanded economic scope have continued to play important roles in reducing intraregional conflict.

With respect to scope, the growing number of issues addressed by ASEAN has slowly increased its value in the eyes of member governments. Progress on some areas of cooperation was unimpressive. The preferential trade agreement remained rather narrow, and the regional industrial schemes were mired with difficulties (Chatterjee 1990; Suriyamongkol 1988). But ASEAN made good progress on financial and sectoral cooperation. Chatterjee (1990, 73) argues, for example, that the ASEAN swap agreement was a major achievement. In addition, the ability to speak in unison on extraregional economic matters was of particular value. For instance, Lee Kuan Yew (2000, 332–33), the founder and the first prime minister of Singapore, underscores the benefits accrued to the members from forming a unified bargaining position vis-à-vis economically powerful countries, such as Japan and Australia.[28]

As I argued in the presentation of the theoretical framework in chapter 2, the expanded scope allowed for greater issue linkage and reinforced the habit of cooperation. As Jorgensen-Dahl (1982, 176–77) points out, "A slowly growing perception of mutual economic dependence partially brought about by the participation in ASEAN . . . has produced a heightened awareness that, in terms of the stated goals of ASEAN, threats and the use of force are highly destructive methods of diplomacy."[29] In short, during this period, greater economic scope has increased the benefits provided by ASEAN, which, in turn, increased the opportunity cost of conflict. At the same time, keeping in mind this mechanism's still limited scope and, in some instances, sluggish implementation, its pacifying effect was likely to be modest.

Turning to high-level officials, their recurrent interaction was especially instrumental in cementing mutual trust and cordiality among the members of ASEAN. Partly due to the need for political coordination related to the situation in Indochina and partly due to the growing economic scope, foreign and finance ministers met with an ever-growing frequency. This evolving practice of face-to-face consultations resulted in better appreciation of each other's perspectives and greater solidarity (Castro 1981; Jorgensen-Dahl 1982, 235; Leifer 1989, 157). Moreover, while some outstanding issues during this period remained in the domain of bilateral diplomacy, the multilateral setting provided by ASEAN proved to be more instrumental in advancing greater understanding and goodwill.

Bilateral consultations, such as the 1980 meeting between the Malaysian and Indonesian leaders, made the other ASEAN members suspicious and increased regional tensions (Indorf 1984, 77). In addition, the call for bilateral negotiations on particular issues could be mistakenly viewed as a sign of weakness and vulnerability. Yet the regional and informal setting provided by ASEAN facilitated the resolution of bilateral disputes by keeping the channels of communication open when bilateral channels were strained (Jorgensen-Dahl 1982, 235). In addition, the multilateral forum advanced a spirit of accommodation. As Jorgensen-Dahl (1982, 235–36) explains, "More than the bilateral, the multilateral setting served to discourage extreme behavior, modify extravagant demands, and inspire compromise. Moreover, because of its 'transparency,' the multilateral setting probably offers fewer opportunities for disruptive negotiating tactics such as playing one party against another."

Finally, the growing rapport among top ASEAN officials was conducive to third-party mediation. The so-called Herzog Affair of 1986 illustrates this process. A visit of the Israeli president to Singapore resulted in mounting tensions between Malaysia and Singapore (Leifer 1989, 144–47; Tan 2001, 39–44). In this context, Suharto visited the two states in an attempt to mediate between them (Jetly 2003). Tan (2001, 43–44) argues that his involvement "indicated the disquiet felt by Indonesia's government over the deterioration in Singapore-Malaysia relations and its potentially negative consequences for ASEAN unity." His visit, in turn, helped to highlight the importance of the organization and the opportunity costs involved in these bilateral tensions (Kivimäki 2001, 14). This point was not lost on the two governments, which restored cordial diplomatic relationships shortly after Suharto's visit (Leifer 1989, 146; Tan 2001, 44). This incident further underscores the pacifying effect of regular meetings among high-level officials and the manners by which a mediator can utilize the gains from cooperation as leverage during negotiations. In other words, the conflict management and the opportunity cost mechanisms reinforced each other to discourage intra-ASEAN aggression.

1992–97: The Early Post–Cold War Period

The end of the Vietnamese occupation of Cambodia in 1989 and the 1992 Singapore summit are considered to be the next milestones in the evolution of ASEAN (Narine 2002). In the eyes of most observers, the subsequent five years established ASEAN as a durable and successful organization (Collins 2003b, 140; Khong 1997, 335–37). For example, Henderson (1999, 9–10) asserts, "ASEAN emerged from the Cold War as that region's pre-eminent institution. Despite doubts about the capacity of the child of the Cold War to adjust to new strategic circumstances, the early results were positive, even dramatic." Indeed, during this time, the members of ASEAN greatly expanded their cooperation. The 1992 ASEAN Free Trade Area (AFTA) significantly expanded intraregional trade liberalization. The ambitious plans were followed by an impressive, albeit imperfect, implementation (Hund 2002; Nesadurai 2003). Important agreements on the free movement of services and the ASEAN Investment Area were also signed in the next several years (Narine 2002, 128–31; Nesadurai 2003). In addition, several subregional "growth triangles" that formed in the early 1990s promoted market-oriented industrial cooperation.[30]

From an institutional perspective, ASEAN expanded the regional secretariat and its powers. The rank of the secretary-general was upgraded from ambassadorial to ministerial level, the mandate of the secretariat was expanded to include the initiation of ASEAN activities, and recruitment of staff was allowed to be made through an open selection process rather than through appointments by member governments. As a result, it "assumed more political independence internally and externally" (Hund 2002, 114). Even so, the authority of the secretariat remained limited (Hund 2002, 115;

Severino 2007, 420–21). In addition, for the first time, ASEAN instituted a DSM for matters related to the execution of and compliance with the AFTA agreement. This mechanism included binding third-party arbitration by an ad hoc panel to be composed of either the ASEAN Economic Ministers or the participants of the Senior Economic Officials Meeting (SEOM) (Hund 2002, 108–9). The 1990s also saw further increase in the number of committees and meetings at all levels. Most important, the organization institutionalized the practice of recurrent summits. Heads of state met every three years since 1992 and annually since 1995 (Davidson 2003, 21–27). Overall, during the early post–Cold War era, ASEAN enjoyed a sharp increase in the levels of its economic scope, independence, and regional institutionalization more broadly.

The ASEAN members also experienced increasing bilateral tensions in the first half of the 1990s. Territorial disputes that were dormant throughout the two preceding decades began to surface in these years (Ganesan 1999, 14–15).[31] The most visible disputes were between Malaysia and Singapore, Malaysia and Indonesia, and Malaysia and Thailand (Amer 1998; Ganesan 1999; Tan 2000).[32] Some of these disputes have led to inflammatory rhetoric as well as militarized incidents. Notable examples involve the Indonesian-Malaysian dispute over the Sipadan and Ligitan islands (Haller-Trost 1995, 30–31; Mak 2009) and the Malaysian-Singaporean dispute over the Pedra Branca islets (Kivimäki 2001, 10; Tan 2000, 23). In addition, the accession of Vietnam to ASEAN in 1995 "imported" a number of conflicts into the organization. These include bilateral disputes with Thailand and the Philippines. Nonetheless, in all these conflicts, aggression was contained and further escalation was prevented (Amer 1998).

ASEAN restrained these bilateral tensions in at least two distinct ways. First, the ASEAN members valued the accomplishments of the organization and were worried that such conflicts would undermine them. Beyond international prestige, ASEAN provided a range of benefits that were derived from its substantive activities and their associated benefits. In other words, with increasing regional institutionalization, the opportunity cost of conflict has become very high. As a Thai official noted in 1997, "ASEAN has matured to the point where we recognize our mutual benefits, and these outweigh bilateral problems" (Visser 1997).[33]

Although it is difficult to pin down the specific activities that contributed to peace,[34] one feature that attracted the attention of policymakers and scholars alike is the newly formed "growth triangles." Consistent with the theoretical expectations, such industrial zones create economic interdependence in border areas that are sometimes the subject of bilateral disagreements. Aggressive foreign policy in these areas can thus jeopardize these benefits (Acharya 2001, 144; Collins 2003b, 118; Dosch 2003, 161; Dosch 2007). In contrast to previous periods, the signing of AFTA provided a comprehensive framework for intraregional trade liberalization. The implementation of AFTA was accompanied by a modest increase of intraregional trade. The share of intraregional trade in the total trade increased from about 20 percent in the early 1990s to 23 percent in the middle 1990s (Ganesan 1994, 462; Mahani 2002, 1266–67; Stubbs 2000, 313). In light of the gradual implementation of the AFTA provisions, member states could also reasonably have expected future gains from trade.

A second manner by which ASEAN facilitated intraregional peace is the now-established habit of formal and informal communication between high-level officials. These increasing contacts and the growing awareness of each other's problems and interests were instrumental in playing down intraregional frictions. As Ganesan (1994, 460) points out, the bilateral tensions of the early 1990s have been stabilized "by familiarity among the political and bureaucratic elite." In addition, top-level ASEAN meetings served as an informal forum to mitigate bilateral tensions (Caballero-Anthony 1998, 60–61). One news report notes that "border disputes which have arisen between Indonesia and Malaysia, and between Malaysia and Thailand, were quietly defused in the multilateral ASEAN context when to do so amidst bilateral formality might well have been much more difficult" (*South China Morning Post*, August 4, 1991). These developments and the growing confidence of regional leaders in the so-called ASEAN Way led some observers to argue that the organization represents a sort of security community, in which intramural violence is no longer possible (Acharya 1998, 218–19; Tuan 1996, 71).[35] In line with the theoretical framework presented in chapter 2, frequent meetings among top-level officials promoted peace through the mechanisms of information, conflict management, and socialization.

There is little evidence to suggest that either the regional secretariat or the DSM facilitated peace within ASEAN. Despite the increased capacity of the secretariat, its staff had to attend to ever-growing administrative matters (Hund 2002; Ravenhill 2008; Severino 2007). More broadly, while it is undeniable that lower-level regional interconnectedness sharply increased in the post–Cold War era, its effect on conflict seems weak. As Acharya

(2001, 131) explains, "Invocation of the 'ASEAN spirit' has been a factor in moderating and diffusing these controversies [bilateral disputes] but it has been effective only at the highest political level. At the grassroots, concerns about 'ASEANness' has mattered little."[36] Furthermore, while the formal status of the secretary-general was enhanced, its role remained limited and apolitical (Hund 2002, 115). There is thus no indication that the secretariat mitigated bilateral conflicts between the organization's members.

As of 2012, the ASEAN DSM remains unused and untested. Since its inception in the middle 1990s, not one member has filed a complaint against another member (Ravenhill 2008, 480). This is not because conflicts related to AFTA have been absent. Rather, as the decade unfolded, serious disputes with respect to the liberalization of agricultural and automotive products emerged (Nesadurai 2003, 155–58; Yoshimatsu 2006). ASEAN governments preferred to manage these disagreements through less legalistic channels, such as diplomatic consultations and negotiations, which often took place during the ASEAN ministerial meetings (Khong and Nesadurai 2007, 53).[37] Nesadurai (2003, 166) explains that ASEAN officials were worried "that invoking the DSM could jeopardize political relationships in ASEAN." This logic offers support to the argument, discussed in chapter 2, that legalization can sometimes undermine the effectiveness of international institutions. Given that the DSM had no role in the adjudication of economic disputes, it is inconceivable that it was instrumental in preventing the escalation of these disputes. In short, the growing independence of ASEAN during the 1990s appears to have had little impact on regional conflict.

As pointed out earlier, ASEAN is not only an economic but also a political organization. One should entertain the possibility that the latter aspect was also instrumental in reducing violent conflict. Indeed, during the post–Cold War era, the organization ascertained its security role in two manners. First, members reaffirmed their commitment to the TAC principles, including the peaceful resolution of bilateral disputes, and encouraged non-ASEAN countries to accede this treaty. Nonetheless, a regional mechanism for conflict resolution remained elusive during this period. The ASEAN members preferred to tackle their disputes either bilaterally or through informal ASEAN meetings. In instances in which they were not able to iron out their differences in these manners, they turned to extraregional bodies, such as the International Court of Justice (Ganesan 1994, 461; Leifer 1999, 26). For instance, after Indonesia and Malaysia failed to resolve their territorial dispute with respect to the Sipadan and Ligitan islands, the former proposed to submit it to the High Council. Malaysia refused, however, and the dispute was eventually submitted to the ICJ (Acharya 2001, 132; Haller-Trost 1995, 31–32; Jacob 1996).

Second, in 1993, the organization initiated the ASEAN Regional Forum (ARF). This body endeavors to facilitate confidence-building measures (CBMs) between the ASEAN members and extraregional actors, most notably China, as well as between the ASEAN members themselves. It was meant to proceed in three stages: CBMs (mainly information exchange and informal discussions), preventive diplomacy, and conflict resolution. Thus far, it has moved forward only on the first stage (Collins 2003b, 177; Khong and Nesadurai 2007; Tan 2000, 50). It is noteworthy that under Chinese pressure, the increasingly volatile tensions with respect to the Spratly Islands have been kept off the agenda of the ARF (Collins 2003b, 195–97; Narine 2002, 106). The ARF may still contribute to the stability of the broader East Asian region, but its part in the management of intra-ASEAN disputes appears minor.

Overall, it seems that the increasing level of regional institutionalization was instrumental in mitigating the growing bilateral tensions of the early 1990s. Meetings and consultations of high-level officials and expanded scope played important roles in this respect. Security cooperation and the higher level of institutional independence were not important factors in preventing intraregional aggression. Even more than previous periods, the opportunity cost mechanism operated as a significant restraint on armed conflict. The mechanisms of information, conflict management, and socialization were also at work, but primarily among top-level policymakers.

1997–2010: The Asian Financial Crisis and Its Aftermath

Beginning in 1997, ASEAN faced several challenges, the most important of which were the Asian financial crisis and the admission of three new members: Cambodia, Laos, and Myanmar (Burma). Other problems included domestic instability in Indonesia, the Philippines, Thailand, and Cambodia, as well as terrorism and regional haze (Collins 2003a; Narine 2002, 170–76).[38] The failure of ASEAN to respond adequately to the financial crisis and other tribulations tarnished the reputation of the organization and led some observers to discard the organization and declare its untimely death (Collins 2003a; Jones and Smith 2002; Narine 2008, 421; Rüland 2003; Webber 2003, 135). Nonetheless, ASEAN continued to expand its scope and cooperation during these years, and "to the surprise of many commentators," it "appeared to emerge somewhat strengthened by [the financial crisis]" (Ravenhill 2008, 470).

In 2002, the original members of ASEAN completed the elimination or reduction of tariffs required by the AFTA agreements (Khong and Nesadurai 2007). The 1998 Hanoi Plan of Action provided for additional liberalization in the areas of trade in services and foreign investment (Ravenhill 2008). Subsequent agreements led to the initiation of the ASEAN Economic Community (AEC), which calls for the free movement of goods, services, investment, and skilled labor (but not a customs union) by 2015 (Khong and Nesadurai 2007; Ravenhill 2008; Yoshimatsu 2006). This ambitious plan is still in its early stages. ASEAN also continued to coordinate external economic policies, most notably by signing framework agreements with China, South Korea, and India.[39] Finally, the organization fostered sectoral harmonization (Yoshimatsu 2006); expanded its involvement in regional development projects (Dosch 2007; Yoshimatsu 2006); established a development bank; created the ASEAN Surveillance Process, which aims to avoid future financial disruptions (Mahani 2002; Narine 2002, 161–64; Tay 2001); and revamped its currency swap agreements (Narine 2008). It appears, then, that the economic scope of ASEAN has continued to expand in the first decade of the twenty-first century.

Similar trends are evident with respect to ASEAN's institutions. The members' top officials convened repeatedly throughout this period in formal ASEAN meetings. A new forum, dubbed the "ASEAN foreign ministers' retreat," was established in 1999 to facilitate informal discussion of regional problems (Collins 2003a, 141). Another newly established body is the ASEAN Troika, which comprises the foreign ministers of the present, past, and future chairs of the ASEAN Standing Committee. This ad hoc body was created in order to tackle urgent political matters (Hund 2002; Narine 2002). The AEC further strengthens the ASEAN secretariat and DSM. The power of the secretariat was expanded to include a legal unit, to provide consultation services during economic disputes, and to collect information with respect to the rate of compliance of member states with AEC-related agreements (Hund 2002; Yoshimatsu 2006). The new DSM protocol (signed in 2004) establishes an appellate body made of independent professional experts and procedures for surveillance of compliance with and implementation of the ruling (Ravenhill 2008; Yoshimatsu 2006). Decisions made by the appellate body are not binding, however, as SEOM retains the power to reject them. Thus, ASEAN has become more independent, albeit incrementally, in the decade that followed the Asian financial crisis.

From 1997 to 2011, the number and intensity of militarized disputes between ASEAN members remained high. Many of these conflicts involved at least one new member. These include a 1999 maritime dispute between Vietnam and the Philippines as well as border clashes between Thailand and Myanmar in 2001 and between Thailand and Cambodia from 2008 to 2011. The Thailand-Myanmar dispute resulted in 50 to 100 battle deaths (Collins 2003b, 100; Haacke 2003, 210–11). The spat between Thailand and Cambodia, which erupted several times over a three-year period, left tens of military personnel and civilians dead, hundreds wounded, and tens of thousands displaced (Haywood 2011). These two disputes are the most severe militarized incidents since the Konfrontasi. Some of these disputes were not altogether new but registered as intra-ASEAN conflicts only after the expansion of membership. From this perspective, the organization had "imported" these conflicts (Acharya 2001; Amer 1998, 45–47; Narine 2002, 119–20). Other armed conflicts erupted from tensions between the founding members of ASEAN. Two prominent examples include the 1999 mobilization of forces by Malaysia and the Philippines in the South China Sea and the 2005 military standoff between Indonesia and Malaysia over the Ambalat area (Mak 2009).

The high level of institutionalization achieved by ASEAN during this period has allowed the organization to absorb some of the bilateral tensions between its members. Even though intraregional conflicts surfaced rather frequently, one could imagine a much greater level of hostility, considering the acute challenges its members faced in this turbulent period (Leifer 1999, 37). From this perspective, the benefits provided by ASEAN have continued to restrain aggression and escalation of disputes (Tan 2001, 74). For example, despite mounting tensions between Indonesia and Malaysia over Ambalat, senior officials on both sides ruled out the use of military force. They pointed to mutual membership in ASEAN as a moderating force (Emmerson 2005, 175). Some analysts point out that the commercial interdependence facilitated by AFTA was very instrumental in this respect. Lim (2009, 122), for example, argues that "AFTA's non-binding and non-punitive nature arguably promotes the mitigation of potential conflict, while at the same time pushing towards lower tariffs to raise the level of intraregional trade, thereby creating more interdependence and linkages as a way to cement better ties within ASEAN."

Others emphasize the pacifying effect of growth areas, such as the Greater Mekong Subregion. As Dosch (2007, 126–27) explains, "Cooperation in the Mekong basin is primarily concerned with minimizing potential conflicts over a common resource [water]; the scheme works as a multidimensional confidence-building measure."[40] Similarly, Caballero-Anthony (1998, 55) argues that the Sabah dispute remains dormant due to the ever-improving relationship between Malaysia and the Philippines, which was "strengthened further by the deepening economic linkages stimulated by the establishment of the East ASEAN Growth Area that covers the Philippine province of Mindanao and its neighboring localities in Malaysia, Indonesia, and Brunei."

The frequent meetings among high-level officials also continued to play an important role in keeping Southeast Asia largely peaceful. In the aftermath of the first foreign ministers' retreat, the Singaporean foreign minister stated that "whatever bilateral disputes there have been, the foreign ministers . . . have been able to keep up the cooperation" (*Jakarta Post*, July 23, 1999). The frequent contact between top government officials was useful in preventing the escalation of open conflicts. During the 2008 dispute between Thailand and Cambodia, for example, the Indonesian president and the Indonesian and Malaysian foreign ministers helped restrain both sides and prevented risky escalation (Japan Economic Newswire, July 22, 2008). Similarly, in the aftermath of an April 2011 flare-up, Indonesian and other ASEAN diplomats engaged in intense mediation efforts between Thailand and Cambodia, promoting a plan to dispatch Indonesian observers to the disputed area.[41] Notably, the breakthrough in the negotiations took place on the sidelines of the ASEAN summit via informal discussions (Nazeer 2011). While the fate of this proposal and its effectiveness (if implemented) remains to be seen, it does indicate that face-to-face meetings among high-level officials remain an essential instrument of conflict management in the region (Haywood 2011).

At the same time, the effectiveness of such informal mediation appears to be diminishing in recent years, mainly due to the gradual expansion of ASEAN. The admission of new members that are different from the original members in terms of recent historical experience, as well as economic and political development, weakened the cohesion and mutual understanding at the highest levels (Binh and Duong 2001, 196; Jones and Smith 2002; Narine 2002, 1211). For example, during the 2001 militarized dispute between Thailand and Myanmar, "it was evident that neither [side] wished for third-party intervention and the [ASEAN] Troika was convened" (Collins 2003a, 142). Furthermore, the recurring escalation of the Thai-Cambodian border dispute raises some doubts about the efficacy of this informal approach (Sukma 2008).

The growing heterogeneity of ASEAN strengthened the calls to move beyond the "ASEAN Way," to use a more formal mechanism of dispute resolution, and to allow the secretariat a greater role in this process (Acharya 2001, 156; Hund 2002). As one regional observer argues, "Pluralism . . . is making it hard for Asean officials to knit together the much-vaunted regional consensus. Now more than ever, Asean needs to build a framework for dispute resolution that will allow the collective security of the region to trump domestic politics and nationalist breast-beating" (Vatikiotis 2008). Nonetheless, the members of ASEAN have continued to reject the use of such mechanisms to resolve their differences. During both the Indonesian-Malaysian dispute over Ambalat and the ongoing dispute between Thailand and Cambodia, attempts to refer the incident to the elusive High Council or to the organization's secretary-general were rebuffed by the disputants (Choong 2008; Vatikiotis 2009). Despite the growing independence of the secretariat, this body and its top officials continue to perform administrative tasks and have little authority with respect to political matters (Severino 2007). Similarly, the economic DSM remains untested, and a formal mechanism to resolve political disputes is yet to be realized.

On the whole, the ASEAN region has experienced some significant changes since 1997. Not least among them are the financial crisis and its domestic ramifications in a number of key countries, the growing membership of ASEAN, and the growing influence of China in the wider region. Despite these changes, ASEAN remains instrumental in keeping peace and stability in this region. As in previous periods, functional cooperation on a variety of issues has increased the opportunity cost of violent conflict. Despite some setbacks and challenges, it appears that ASEAN remains a viable economic organization that provides valuable benefits to its members and prevents the escalation of bilateral disputes.

Similarly, regular meetings at the highest level foster mutual trust among top officials and serve as a forum of informal discussion and mediation when disagreements surface. For more than four decades, this arrangement has been at the heart of regional peace in Southeast Asia. The admission of new members and new leadership of some of the old ASEAN members appear to have made these meetings less comfortable and to have reduced their effectiveness in recent years. Nonetheless, meetings among high-level officials have been instrumental in creating new bonds between this new generation of policymakers and in building long-term mutual trust. The greater independence of ASEAN, epitomized in a more powerful secretariat and a more legalized framework for dispute resolution, did not make a noticeable contribution to regional peace. These findings offer additional support to the theoretical framework and the statistical evidence reported in previous chapters.

The Effect of Conflict on Southeast Asian Regional Institutionalization

Previous chapters underscore the endogenous nature of international institutions. Thus, to have a complete understanding of the link between armed conflict and regional organizations, it is important to reverse the causal arrow and to account for alternative explanations. Taking up reversed causality first, the theoretical discussion indicates that the expectations with respect to the effect of conflict on institutionalized cooperation depend on one's perspective. Some scholars believe that such cooperation facilitates peaceful resolution of conflict. This, in turn, ought to generate demand for international institutions. Others who emphasize constraints on long-term cooperation argue that REOs thrive only when peace and amity are already well established. Therefore, conflict, suspicion, and animosity are likely to thwart the provision of international institutions.

The results of the statistical analysis regarding the effect of conflict on regional institutions are mixed. They show that both logics can be at work in manners that are more complex and nuanced than either perspective suggests. The ASEAN case study allows one to take a closer look at the implications of armed disputes for the evolution of regional institutions. The historical analysis indicates that there were some time periods in which the demand-side logic motivated the building of such institutions, some periods when the supply-side logic weakened them, and still other periods in which conflict was not an important determinant of regional institutionalization. The narrative begins to identify the conditions under which conflict affects REOs and the manners by which it does so. The first part of this section examines this nexus from the early 1960s to the late 1980s, and the second part examines it during the 1990s and 2000s.

The Cold War Era

The rise and fall of regional organizations in the middle 1960s is intimately related to the highly antagonistic atmosphere of this period. Most clearly, Maphilindo was formed to facilitate the resolution of disputes between Malaya, on the one hand, and Indonesia and the Philippines, on the other (Fifield 1979, 4–5; Solidum 1974, 29). This organization failed to bridge the differences between its members and actually accentuated their disagreements and mutual distrust (Caballero-Anthony 1998, 44). As soon as Malaya became independent and Indonesia set in motion the Konfrontasi, this organization collapsed (Fifield 1979, 6; Leifer 1989, 19; Solidum 1974, 54).

Similarly, ASA was negatively affected by the Malaysia-Philippine dispute over Sabah. Consistent with the supply-side logic, the conflict between the two countries produced animosity and suspicion, which, in turn, undermined regional cooperation and led to the suspension of top-level meetings (Jorgensen-Dahl 1982, 24; Leifer 1989, 34). President Macapagal of the Philippines, for example, said to his foreign secretary, "You've got to go slow on this ASA thing; our foreign policy effort has to focus on North Borneo [Sabah], and everything else must take a back seat" (Gordon 1966, 25–26; see also Jorgensen-Dahl 1982, 196). Indeed, the breakdown of diplomatic relations between the two parties brought ASA to a halt in 1963 (Gordon 1966). Antolik (1990, 14–15) summarizes these early experiences as follows: "Neither association, ASA or Maphilindo, was able to mute nationalistic interests, and both were destroyed by inter-state rivalries that involved irredentism, challenges to others' legitimacy, interference in others' internal affairs, and ultimately Sukarno's war to crush Malaysia."

Conflict played an important role in the formation of ASEAN as well. On the one hand, the cessation of hostilities opened the door for renewed efforts to form a regional organization in Southeast Asia. This was reflected in the revival of ASA in 1966 and the formation of ASEAN a year later. It appears, then, that an initial level of peace, stability, and convergence in the political orientation of member governments provided the foundations needed for sustainable functional and economic cooperation (R. Irvine 1982, 11; Leifer 1999, 26–27; Solingen 1999). On the other hand, during these early days, peace was very fragile and by no means assured. In line with the demand-side logic, policymakers pressed on with ASEAN exactly because they believed that it would strengthen the embryonic goodwill among the would-be members and keep the peace (Amer 1998). Indeed, one of the main goals of ASEAN was to prevent future bilateral hostilities between the members of the organization (Antolik 1990, 155; Leifer 1989, 2; Severino 2006, 162–64). Thus, the events surrounding the formation of ASEAN demonstrate that conflict provided incentives and, at the same time, constrained institutionalized functional cooperation. In this particular instance, peace was required to get ASEAN under way, but this organization was created to cement this fragile peace.

The vulnerability of regional peace was evident shortly after the birth of ASEAN. As discussed earlier, the Sabah dispute of the late 1960s put ASEAN to its first test. Here again, political conflict proved to be an impediment to cooperation. Because of the spat, Malaysia and the Philippines severed their diplomatic relations, and Malaysia, insisting that ASEAN and the Sabah conflict were closely linked, refused to participate in ASEAN meetings until the Philippines withdrew its claim to Sabah (M. L. Brown 1994, 109). This brought ASEAN's activities to a halt for more than a year. Jorgensen-Dahl (1982, 208) argues, "But whilst ASEAN exercised some positive influence on the course of the dispute, the major flow of effects clearly went in the opposite direction. For eight months the organization was completely moribund and on several occasions its final demise seemed merely a matter of time."[42] This episode corroborates the perspective that violent conflict operates as an impediment to regional cooperation.

The fading of the Sabah conflict was followed by several years of reconciliation, which, in turn, paved the way for further regional institutionalization (Ganesan 1995, 212; D. Irvine 1982, 37–38). The lack of conflict during this period operated as a background condition and does not account for the timing of ASEAN's increase in regional institutionalization, which began in earnest in 1976. The main drivers of this institutional progression were the 1972 UN report mentioned earlier, which gave ASEAN a sense of direction; the rise of economic protectionism across the globe (D. Irvine 1982, 38–39; Jorgensen-Dahl 1982, 112–13); and, most important, the unfolding events in Indochina. Vietnam's 1978 invasion of Cambodia, which lasted for more than a decade, preoccupied the members of ASEAN during this time. In particular, ASEAN members deepened their habit of informal coordination and created a diplomatic community (Leifer 1989). Their main goal was to end the Vietnamese occupation, which they perceived as a serious threat to regional stability. Intraregional bilateral tensions persisted during these years but had a modest negative effect on institutional developments.[43] Thus, during the late 1970s and the early 1980s, intra-ASEAN conflicts had a secondary effect on the development of the organization, with events external to the organization playing a primary role.

The Post–Cold War Era

The end of the Cold War and the Vietnamese presence in Cambodia shifted the focus back to intraregional politics. As discussed earlier, the number and severity of armed disputes in the early 1990s was on the rise. Nonetheless, these conflicts did not get in the way of regional cooperation and integration. Rather, ASEAN's scope of economic activity and institutional framework were deepened and expanded. Thus, after 25 years of gradual progress, ASEAN was robust enough to withstand occasional discord between its members. Bilateral tensions did not undermine the general trust between the members of ASEAN and the confidence they had in the organization itself (Caballero-Anthony 1998, 57; Ganesan 1995, 220). Even the expansion of ASEAN in the second half of the 1990s and the related conflicts it had to manage did not hinder the organization's development. In contrast to the supply-side logic, higher levels of violent conflict were accompanied by thriving regional cooperation.

On the demand side, the initial phase of post–Cold War institutionalization was driven by extraregional events, such as the formation of important trade blocs (especially the EU and NAFTA), the need to attract foreign capital, and the rising Chinese economic and military power (Narine 1998a; Nesadurai 2003; Ravenhill 1995, 854–55). The expansion of membership and some of the institutional changes that accompanied this process emerged from the need to deal with potential aggression. One of the main rationales for bringing Vietnam and the other new members into ASEAN was precisely to prevent political disputes from escalating into armed ones (Amer 1998, 45–46; Tuan 1996, 72–73). As Vietnam's then deputy foreign minister said, "Vietnam is joining ASEAN in order to . . . promote peace, stability, and cooperation in the region."[44] Moreover, the addition of new members and the attempts to deal with the challenges presented by their inclusion led to further institutional development. This is reflected by more formal and informal meetings at all levels, the formation of subregional growth areas (e.g., the Greater Mekong Subregion),[45] and compensation mechanisms designed to accommodate the newly admitted and poorer members (Denoon and Colbert 1998/99, 509). Hence, historical animosity and the threat of future violence and instability were important motivations for the expansion of ASEAN, in terms of membership, economic scope, and institutions.

Turning to the post-1997 period, ASEAN was mostly affected by developments beyond the control of its members. Initially, the organization suffered a serious blow from the financial crisis and then attempted to deal with its domestic, regional, and global ripples. More recently, the organization endeavored to grapple with changing economic and political conditions in the wider region, especially the ever-growing Chinese influence (Narine 2008). As in the precrisis period, bilateral tensions did not play a major role in determining the level of regional institutionalization. A number of serious incidents—such as the 2001 armed conflict between Thailand and Myanmar, the ongoing tensions between Indonesia and Malaysia over Ambalat, and the territorial dispute between Thailand and Cambodia—did not have a visible negative effect on regional cooperation. As the foreign minister of Singapore explained, "Within ASEAN, some of us have disputes or quarrels. On that we agreed just as we have managed the differences in the past it should not impede ASEAN cooperation" (*Jakarta Post,* July 23, 1999). Considering the significance of bilateral disputes, the gains made by ASEAN were by no means a foregone conclusion. Actually, early in this period, some observers argued that these bilateral tensions were likely to take their toll on regional cooperation (Ganesan 1999; Tan 2000). As this book goes to press, these gloomy forecasts have not yet materialized.

On the demand side, intraregional disputes did not play a major role in the evolution of ASEAN. Nonetheless, as pointed out earlier, these conflicts and the growing diversity of the organization's membership drew attention to the limits of using the ASEAN Way in conflict management. This resulted in calls for more formal mechanisms of dispute resolution (economic as well as political). ASEAN responded by strengthening its secretariat and economic DSM and by recommitting to a legalized mechanism of political dispute resolution. At the time of this writing, these mechanisms remain largely on paper and contribute little to regional peace, partly because member governments are reluctant to use them (as discussed earlier). This is consistent with the statistical findings, which point to the positive effect of militarized disputes on institutional independence even though the latter does not appear to promote peace.

On the whole, the effect of armed disputes on institutionalized cooperation in Southeast Asia varies across time. The perspective that expects animosity to constrain violence but peace to facilitate regional cooperation and integration is supported by the early experience in the region. This logic is less compelling with respect to more recent developments. Even though several bilateral disputes reared their head, member states remained committed to regional cooperation and continued to deepen and expand ASEAN. This observation suggests that the negative effect of conflict on REOs is more pronounced when and where these organizations are weakly institutionalized. To the extent that member states manage to institutionalize the organization, however, interstate violence is not as detrimental to regional cooperation.

The view that underscores the need to form institutions when the risk of armed conflict is high bears out in a number of episodes. The belief that regional cooperation is essential for regional peace inspired the formation of ASA, Maphilindo, and, most significantly, ASEAN. This logic also played an important role in the post–Cold War era, especially with respect to the organization's newly admitted members and their relationships with existing ones. Here, it appears that the number of members and their heterogeneity shaped the demand for regional institutions (Martin 1994). In particular, the increasing diversity of ASEAN members called for cooperation in new areas and for a more independent organization. Finally, the narrative indicates that intraregional conflict and peace sometimes play a secondary role in the evolution of REOs, which is consistent with the statistical findings. It also highlights the significance of external events that are not easily captured in a cross-regional analysis. In the case of ASEAN, Vietnam's occupation of Cambodia and the 1997 financial crisis stand out as two events that had a notable effect on the organization.

Alternative Explanations to the Southeast Asian Peace

Regional institutions and conflict not only affect each other but are also influenced by and impinge on other domestic and international factors. To the extent that these factors generate both phenomena, one runs the risk of attributing regional institutions a spurious or exaggerated pacifying effect. To alleviate these concerns, I consider alternative accounts for the relative peace that characterized Southeast Asian international relations in the late twentieth century and early twenty-first century.

Explanations that emphasize power politics do not offer a compelling account for the enduring stability in the regions. The view that states come together in response to a common external threat carried some weight in the 1980s, when the members of ASEAN were able to forge a united front against Vietnam (Leifer 1989). It does not easily square with the sustained regional unity in the 1990s, following the stabilization of Indochina and the termination of Cold War rivalries (Narine 1998b; Kivimäki 2008). The experience of ASEAN also defies the notion that regions where power distribution is skewed are more peaceful than regions where capabilities are distributed more equally. Power in ASEAN is relatively balanced, as indicated by its low ratio of power concentration.[46] While Indonesia is the most powerful country in the region, it does not enjoy substantial advantage over its neighbors. Its lower level of economic development compared with other ASEAN members also detracts from its aspiration for regional domination. Thus, Indonesia is better understood as a *primus inter pares* rather than a hegemon that manages regional security matters. As I conjectured in the previous chapter, ASEAN institutions appear to satisfy a need to promote regional order in the absence of an unmistakable dominant power.

Two explanations associated with the liberal perspective do not sit well with the historical record. The democratic peace thesis is not applicable to the region (Khong and Nesadurai 2007, 48; Kivimäki 2001; Peou 2002, 121–22). Most members, such as Singapore, Vietnam, and Malaysia, are stable nondemocracies. Others, such as Thailand, the Philippines, and Indonesia, have experimented with democratization with uneven degrees of success. This process did not contribute to regional peace, and in the short term, it pushed in the other direction. Democratic transitions have increased domestic instability in some members and resulted in more frequent turnovers of high-level officials in others (Leifer 1999; Webber 2003). This, in turn, weakened the vaunted cohesion among ASEAN senior officials (Narine 2002). To the extent that democracy will take stronger hold in the region, its impact may become more positive and pronounced in the future.

Similarly, the intensity of intraregional trade is rather low and remained at a constant level that hovered around 20 percent of total regional trade from the 1960s to the 2000s. Kivimäki (2001) shows that intraregional trade in the ASEAN region was actually higher during the Konfrontasi than in the 1970s and 1980s. The share of intraregional trade has gradually increased in the 1990s and early 2000s, to reach 25 percent in the middle 2000s (Ozeki 2007). Nevertheless, the commercial ties of ASEAN members with extraregional economies—such as the United States, the EU, and, most recently,

China—are much more extensive than intra-ASEAN ties (Solingen 1999). It appears unlikely, then, that trade flows, in and of themselves, have transformed members' assessments of the costs and benefits of armed disputes.

Two domestic and closely intertwined factors were more instrumental in promoting regional peace. First, the economic and political orientation of member governments converged around a set of policies that emphasized close relationships with the West, state-led capitalism, and integration into the world economy (Haftel 2010; Solingen 1999; Stubbs 2000). These internationalist coalitions emphasized domestic stability and economic development and worked to suppress military competition (Solingen 1999). There is little doubt that this shared perspective restrained aggressive instincts in the region. Second, the focus on economic development produced the anticipated results: the original members of ASEAN benefited from significant and uninterrupted levels of economic growth from the 1970s to the 1990s.[47] Consistent with the statistical results and theories that underscore the pacifying effect of economic development (Gratzke 2007; McDonald 2007, 2009; Mousseau 2000), both governments and a growing middle class were loath to forgo economic prosperity for short-term political gains (Kivimäki 2008; Solingen 1999). Importantly, ASEAN was part and parcel of this approach. The organization was deliberately created and designed to advance economic development. While it was not the only instrument by which governments promoted economic well-being in the region, the functional cooperation facilitated by this REO (detailed earlier) made an important contribution to the attainment of this goal. In this respect, ASEAN reflected the preferences of its members and, at the same time, had a genuine impact on their relationships.

The final alternative explanation emanates from the quantitative analysis presented in the preceding chapter, which points to domestic strife as a key constraint on regional institutionalization and as a significant stimulator of interstate armed conflict. The ASEAN record with respect to this link is mixed and corresponds to the statistical results only to a degree. ASEAN members certainly suffered from numerous episodes of domestic unrest in the second half of the twentieth century. This included, for example, violent communist opposition in Malaysia and Thailand and ethnic insurgency in Indonesia and the Philippines. At least until the middle 1990s, there is little evidence that domestic instability spiraled into interstate armed disputes or hampered regional cooperation through ASEAN (Jorgensen-Dahl 1982). Actually, one important objective of ASEAN was to contain domestic opposition and violence. It promoted this goal in two complementary manners. First, it adopted the principle of noninterference and sanctified national borders, which, in turn, reduced the potential spillover of domestic unrest (Huxley 1990; Leifer 1989). Second, by promoting economic growth and prosperity, ASEAN intended to reduce the appeal of communist ideology and separatism in the region (Frost 1990, 7–8; Yew 2000, 330).

Domestic strife played a more prominent role in regional politics in the decade that followed the 1997 financial crisis. Indonesia's crisis with respect to the demand of East Timor for independence and the ongoing political struggle in Thailand and some of the new member states, especially Myanmar and Cambodia, detracted from these countries' ability and willingness to devote resources to ASEAN. It also created a rift between member states that wanted the organization to play a greater role in these conflicts and those that insisted on sticking to the principle of nonintervention (Haacke 2003; Narine 2002, 168–69). This debate had a greater impact on political, rather than economic, cooperation, however. In addition, domestic conflicts remained largely contained within national borders and did not spark interstate violence.[48] On the whole, domestic strife appears to have created demand for regional institutions that were designed to suppress it. In recent years, domestic instability wields some moderate constraints on institutionalized cooperation. These mixed findings do not correspond to the strong relationships between domestic strife, interstate conflict, and regional institutionalization identified in previous chapters. They thus call for further research of this nexus.

Taken together, the discussion of alternative explanations indicates that the effect of ASEAN on matters of regional security is real. The pacifying effect of regional institutionalization does not appear to be an artifact of any of the factors examined in this section. This does not mean, of course, that highly institutionalized REOs are a panacea. The path to peace is multifaceted, and no individual variable is likely to capture this complex dynamic. The discussion suggests that regional institutions sometimes substitute for and sometimes complement important sources of peace. In the ASEAN case, hegemony and democracy exemplify the substitutive role, and regional affinity and economic development illustrate the complementary role. This observation casts additional light on the manners by which international institutions interact with other factors and shows that they are both affected by and have an impact on their members' interests and interaction.

ASEAN and Regional Order Reconsidered

The historical analysis reported in this chapter bears on the recent theoretical debate with respect to the link between ASEAN and Southeast Asian security. The two main contenders in this debate are the realist and the constructivist schools of thought (Eaton and Stubbs 2006; Peou 2002). The former perspective argues that ASEAN had little impact on regional peace and stability, which were largely determined by external pressures and balance-of-power politics. It also points to the marginal contribution of formal security institutions to regional order in Southeast Asia (Ganesan 1995; Jones and Smith 2002; Leifer 1999). The latter perspective advances the possibility that ASEAN represents a security community with shared norms and identity. According to this view, intraregional war in the region has become very unlikely, because ASEAN has transformed the region and produced a "we feeling" among its member states (Acharya 2001; Busse 1999; Kivimäki 2008; Tuan 1996). A more instrumental institutionalist approach was largely dismissed either because "neoliberalism avoids dealing with security concerns" (Narine 1998b, 41) or because commercial interdependence appears weak (Peou 2002). For example, Kivimäki (2001, 2008) rejects the opportunity cost mechanism because intraregional trade (as a percentage of total regional trade) was higher before than after the formation of ASEAN.

This chapter demonstrates that the realist and constructivist accounts miss some important aspects of regional politics in Southeast Asia, mainly because they do not pay sufficient attention to the mechanisms by which REOs affect conflict.[49] The preceding narrative concurs with the critics of ASEAN who assert that formal institutions of dispute resolution were largely ineffective, but it shows that this is only one manner by which regional organizations can potentially mitigate conflict. In the ASEAN case, other mechanisms, largely overlooked by ASEAN skeptics, were more effective. In their turn, constructivists exaggerate the degree to which ASEAN members have developed a common identity and shared values. Moreover, as this chapter details, territorial and other disputes are still rampant in the region, and violent means are still considered legitimate in resolving them. The claim that ASEAN is tantamount to a security community is therefore, at the very least, premature. This chapter also indicates that the reasons for the rejection of the opportunity cost mechanism are not convincing. Theoretical and empirical considerations underscore the notion that international trade is only one component—and not necessarily the most important one—of economic interdependence. In ASEAN, a common bargaining position and development projects, for example, have rendered armed conflict less attractive. Thus, even though intraregional trade remained largely unchanged, economic interdependence did rise with the institutionalization of ASEAN.

The debate between realists and constructivists is limiting from a practical perspective as well. The efforts to determine whether ASEAN is a security community sidestepped an equally important question: given that the possibility of violent conflict in Southeast Asia is a fact of life, in what ways has ASEAN reduced the probability and severity of such conflicts? Specifying the alternative causal mechanisms by which regional institutionalization mitigates conflict and differentiating between them reveals that both camps get some aspects of the story right but miss others. This chapter fills some important gaps in this debate and indicates that REOs are best understood as a product of their members' preferences, which nonetheless shape their interactions in meaningful and enduring manners.

Looking ahead, it appears that prospects of continued peace and stability are likely to be enhanced by the deepening of economic and functional cooperation among the ASEAN 10 and by maintaining the tradition of frequent meetings at the highest level. The latter is especially important in light of growing membership, greater diversity, and the generational shift in the region. Despite the many calls to create new and use existing formal mechanisms of dispute resolution, these institutions appear less effective in managing Southeast Asian security. I return to this point in the concluding chapter.

Conclusion

This chapter provides an in-depth analysis of institutionalized cooperation and conflict in Southeast Asia. Taking advantage of the lengthy experience of this region in building regional institutions and managing bilateral disputes as well as the substantial variation on these phenomena, it evaluated in a specific historical context the hypotheses laid out in chapter 2. This narrative offers important insights into the relationships between regional institutions and violent conflict. The findings with respect to the effect of REOs on conflict largely confirm the statistical results. They indicate that these organizations mitigate conflict and that their pacifying effect grows as their level of institutionalization grows. Evidently, ASEAN was more effective in mitigating conflict than its predecessors, ASA and Maphilindo, and was especially instrumental in the post–Cold War era, when it was highly institutionalized.

The evidence indicates that some institutional features are conducive to peace and that others are not. In particular, over the years, regular meetings of foreign ministers and heads of state helped build trust and a shared perspective among these policymakers. These meetings also provided a forum for the management of bilateral disputes in an informal and relaxed manner, known as the ASEAN Way. In addition, the scope of economic activity brought numerous benefits to the member states and increased the opportunity cost of violence. This was especially apparent in the 1990s, with the formation of AFTA and the creation of growth triangles in border areas. In comparison, institutional independence and formal mechanisms of dispute resolution had little impact on peace and stability in Southeast Asia. Even when the ASEAN secretariat became more autonomous and when a more legalized DSM was created, these features had little impact on regional reconciliation. Similarly, despite the widely held view of ASEAN as a security institution, features designed to directly address regional security, such as the High Council and the ASEAN Regional Forum, played a minor role in the peaceful management of intra-ASEAN disputes.

The narrative also begins to untangle the mechanisms by which regional institutions mitigate conflict. The opportunity cost mechanism appears to have a secondary effect during the Cold War. Even when economic interdependence was thin and fragile, however, governments developed some expectations of future benefits, which were incorporated into their foreign policy calculations. This mechanism increased in effectiveness in the 1990s, in tandem with the growing economic ties among the members of ASEAN. Rather than managing actual crises, it often promoted peace by preventing members from engaging in conflict in the first place (Kivimäki 2008, 437). The information mechanism was also important. In some instances, such as the Sabah dispute, the willingness to forgo the benefits associated with ASEAN was used to signal the seriousness of member states during disputes. More important, the exchange of believable information that took place during top-level meetings was an essential ingredient of regional peace. As emphasized in chapter 2, the recurrence of these meetings, their formats, and the composition of the individuals attending them have created favorable conditions for the operation of this mechanism.

The conflict management mechanism functioned in several instances and prevented dangerous escalation of brewing disputes. In line with the theoretical framework, it was most effective at the highest level and mostly through informal mediation. Here, third-party leaders, such as Suharto, had a stake in preventing the intensification of conflict, even though they were not necessarily indifferent to the nature of the deal. It also appears that the conflict management mechanism is most effective when it is combined with other mechanisms, such as the opportunity cost mechanism. The neutrality of the regional secretariat did not render the secretary-general an attractive mediator, perhaps because this body was more concerned with the fate of ASEAN than with the interests of the disputants.

Similarly, the more legalized nature of formal DSMs did not make them effective adjudication bodies. Instead, member states preferred to manage their disagreements informally or, in a small number of cases, via extraregional bodies. This observation reinforces the claim that more legalization and formality are not always conducive to smoother interaction, especially when they do not correspond to states' preferences on this matter. Finally, the socialization mechanism promoted peace by creating a sense of common interests and by cementing mutual trust and habits of cooperation. This mechanism had operated almost exclusively at the elite level, however. Lower-level officials and the mass public remained on the sidelines of this process. This divergence suggests that a more nuanced theorization of this mechanism is warranted.

Reversing the causal arrow, it appears that the effect of conflict on regional cooperation and integration is complex and depends on the circumstances. In some periods, such as the late 1960s and the late 1990s, it resulted in calls for the creation or expansion of such institutions. Policymakers deemed REOs instrumental in keeping aggression in check and invested in them precisely for this reason. In other times, such as the 1970s and 1980s, intraregional conflict was not an important determinant of the evolution of regional institutions, which were driven by other factors. Likewise, several serious bilateral disputes during the 1990s and 2000s did not slow down the pace of regional cooperation. In still other periods, such as the early 1960s, conflict did hamper the building of regional institutions. The consideration of alternative explanations to the level of regional conflict indicates that they do not challenge the conclusion that regional institutionalization promoted peace in Southeast Asia. It also points to a number of ways by which ASEAN interacted with some of these factors to shape regional security dynamics.

Taken as a whole, these observations shed light on the multifaceted relationships between armed disputes and regional cooperation and point to the possibility of a mutually reinforcing feedback loop between these two variables (Russett and Oneal 2001, 212). The pre-ASEAN period exemplifies a vicious cycle in which intense bilateral tensions created hostility and distrust, which undermined attempts to promote regional cooperation. In turn, existing international organizations could have done little to neutralize these tensions. In contrast, regional reconciliation in the second half of the 1960s provided a window of opportunity to form a meaningful REO and to gradually institutionalize it. In the 1990s, ASEAN, now highly institutionalized, was successful in defusing a growing number of intraregional differences, which, in turn, facilitated still higher levels of regional institutionalization. This virtuous cycle remained intact in the face of new and sometimes unexpected challenges, such as the inclusion of new members and a severe financial crisis. This observation indicates that violent conflict is more detrimental to international cooperation when the latter is still nascent and that conflict is not as damaging when cooperation is more mature. Put somewhat differently, one might argue that REOs may not be the most effective device to create peace in regions where conflict is rampant. Nevertheless, given a modicum of peace, they are instrumental in maintaining and cementing it over the long haul (Kivimäki 2008, 437).

In summary, the experience of ASEAN and its predecessors largely substantiates the theoretical framework and corroborates the results of the quantitative analysis. The historical narrative shows that regional institutionalization had a noticeable pacifying effect in Southeast Asia. These findings further substantiate the view that REOs can have an independent effect on matters of national security. That only some institutional features facilitated intraregional peace points to the need to pay greater attention to the casual mechanisms underlying the effect of international institutions on conflict and to clearly specify the manners by and conditions under which they reduce aggression.

CHAPTER 7

Conclusion: Regional Organizations and Orders into the Twenty-first Century

The new wave of economic regionalism is central to the contemporary global economy. Today, most of the industrial and less developed states in the world are members of at least one regional economic organization. Governments that formed these institutions envisioned them as vehicles not only of economic prosperity but also of regional cohesion and peace. This aspiration has become ever more pronounced with the demise of Cold War rivalries and the growing autonomy of regions around the world. In some parts of the world, such as Europe and Southeast Asia, these hopes have come to fruition as REOs proved effective in keeping aggression in check. In others, however, the promise of these institutions has remained unfulfilled.

The objective of this book has been to account for the divergence in the ability of regional institutions to craft peace among their members. The picture that emerges from the previous chapters is encouraging: with appropriate design and implementation, REOs are instrumental in mitigating interstate conflict and make a meaningful contribution to regional peace. This chapter revisits the argument and the empirical findings, reflects on their theoretical and practical implications, and considers avenues for future research.

Theorizing REOs and Conflict

In chapter 2, I presented several causal mechanisms linking regional institutions to armed disputes. Thinking about conflict as a bargaining process in which states may use either force or peaceful means to get what they want, I considered the manners by which REOs can mitigate violence. The first mechanism calls attention to the economic gains afforded by the organization and to the risk of forgoing them if conflict breaks out. Using the extensive research on the link between economic interdependence and peace, I argued that institutionalized cooperation increases the opportunity cost of armed conflict and, in turn, has a moderating effect on members' foreign policy. The second mechanism pertains to the role of information during bargaining and highlights the ability of REOs to foster honest communication between the opponents. As recent research shows, the exchange of such information reduces the risk of miscalculation and conflict escalation. The third mechanism involves conflict management, which potentially expands the bargaining space and renders disputed issues more divisible and tractable. Here, the conventional view holds that the neutrality of international organizations makes them effective mediators or arbitrators. But several recent studies indicate that greater impartiality and legalization may actually undercut conflict management efforts. Finally, I considered the socialization mechanism, which goes beyond the rationalist framework and relaxes the assumption of fixed interests. The logic of socialization suggests that REOs facilitate the convergence of interests among their members, especially in the long haul.

One key insight of this theoretical discussion is that the effect of these causal processes is continuous rather than binary; that is, it is not the case that these mechanisms either function or do not. Instead, they may operate in full steam, have only a weak impact, or function somewhere in between. For example, the opportunity cost mechanism depends on the degree of economic interdependence (or future expectations thereof), which could be low, medium, or high. Similarly, the conflict management mechanism hinges on the neutrality of international organizations, which, in turn, depends on their independence. The independence of international organizations can also take different values along a continuum. This observation indicates that the assumption that international organizations are homogenous and that their effect on conflict is uniform, an assumption commonly made in extant research, stands in the way of a more comprehensive understanding of this nexus (Mansfield and Pevehouse 2000; Russett and Oneal 2001). Relaxing this assumption, I argued, offers new insights into the manner by which REOs affect conflict. In particular, it suggests that more institutionalized organizations should be successful in fostering regional peace.

In a second central theoretical contribution, I argued that the efficacy of the four causal mechanisms depends not only on the level of institutionalization but also on the functions and structure of the organization. Accordingly, I identified a number of specific design features that are commonly included in REOs and that may mitigate armed disputes. Specifically, emphasizing the benefits of economic interdependence and issue linkage, I coupled the mechanisms of opportunity cost and information with the REO's scope of economic activity. Tapping into recent studies on diplomacy, which were not considered in this context to date, I then linked the mechanisms of information, conflict management, and socialization to regular meetings of high-level officials. Furthermore, I argued that in order for these mechanisms to work, these design features require implementation: functional cooperation dampens violence only to the extent that words are translated into deeds, and high-level diplomacy is much more effective when top officials meet in person.

Extending research on mediation and legalization in world politics, I connected the information and conflict management mechanisms to corporate bureaucracy and DSMs. Disentangling these causal processes and linking them to particular institutional features allowed me to derive several hypotheses with respect to the effect of REOs on armed disputes. They were also instrumental in considering counterarguments to these hypotheses. In particular, taking stock of recent developments in research on mediation suggests that the widely held assumption that the neutrality of REOs renders them effective intermediaries may be unwarranted. This observation casts doubt on the hypothesized pacifying effect of regional bureaucracy and DSMs.

Finally, I discussed the endogenous nature of REOs. Like other international institutions, they are created and designed by states and thus reflect their prior relationships and mutual interests. A book that attributes a causal effect to these organizations must therefore guard against the possibility that they are only a window dressing behind which are more fundamental forces. I argued that the real issue is not whether REOs are affected by their members' interests but, rather, the specific substance of these interests. I showed that two competing logics offer different answers to this question, each emphasizing different dynamics.

One view underscores the obstacles to international cooperation in an anarchical environment. It maintains that relationships between states that engage in fierce security competition and rivalry are plagued by mutual suspicion, which, in turn, hampers institutionalized cooperation (Grieco 1993; Jervis 1999; Mearsheimer 1994/95). Accordingly, any apparent association between institutionalized cooperation and peace does not mean that the former caused the latter. Instead, it is more plausible either that amity is conducive to regional institutionalization or that affinity and mutual trust produce both phenomena (Gowa 1994; Solingen 1998). Thus, REOs are expected to thrive in regions where peace is already well established but to remain weak in war-prone regions. This perspective suggests that the pacifying effect of REOs is rather limited.

The alternative view highlights the role of institutions as problem solvers. It asserts that to the extent that states believe that regional institutions facilitate cooperation and peace, they will invest in these organizations precisely where interests diverge, conflict is rampant, or tensions are high (Fortna 2004; Martin 1994; Wallander and Keohane 1999). From this point of view, REOs help states reduce antagonism and build lasting trusting relationships. They are therefore likely to be institutionalized in war-prone regions, where they are most needed. This view has considerable faith in the ability of international institutions to shape regional security dynamics.

The discussion in this book indicates that both perspectives are theoretically plausible. The former emphasizes supply-side dynamics, and the latter emphasizes demand-side dynamics. Both may be at work simultaneously. I concluded that there is no a priori reason to believe that one logic will always override the other and that the best way to tackle this issue is empirical.

Data and Findings

To test the hypotheses developed in chapter 2, I employed quantitative as well as qualitative analyses. Chapter 3 laid out the groundwork for the statistical analysis by defining and operationalizing several key variables related to the scope and institutions of regional organizations. As pointed out in that chapter, much of the extant empirical research treats regional organizations as uniform and takes little notice of their design. It also takes into account only the stated objectives and organs of REOs and assumes away the implementation of signed agreements. The variables created for this study begin to address this lacuna by including the specific functions and structure of regional institutions as well as the degree to which member states actually follow up on their obligations. With these variables in hand, I produced a data set that includes detailed information on 25 REOs formed in most parts of the world during the 1980s and 1990s. This data set reveals a great deal of variation in the design of regional institutions both across regions and across time. It also exposes substantial disparity in the ability of REOs to realize their agreements, with an especially wide gap between the two in a number of organizations in the developing world.

Chapter 4 reported the results of the statistical analysis with respect to the effect of the aggregate measure of regional institutionalization on armed disputes. Including a host of control variables and using different model specifications, I found strong support for the hypothesized relationships: higher levels of institutionalized cooperation are associated with fewer interstate armed disputes. This effect holds only for the measure that accounts for the degree of implementation, however. REOs that embrace far-reaching plans that remain on paper do not promote peace. These findings indicate that variation in regional institutions has important repercussions for regional security and that the implementation of signed agreements is crucial in this respect. Thus, action speaks louder than words.

The large-N qualitative analysis presented in chapter 4 offers additional support for this hypothesis. In it, I divided the 25 REOs into several groups with a similar baseline risk of conflict, which is the number of intraregional conflicts expected based on the values of all the independent variables *except* the variable of interest (Fortna 2004). Holding all else (largely) equal, I then conducted a within-group comparison of the level of implemented regional institutionalization. This analysis showed that regions with more institutionalized organizations, such as WAEMU and ANCOM, have experienced fewer armed disputes compared to similar regions that have less institutionalized REOs, such as ECCAS and the CACM. This contrast was especially visible in regions with intermediate levels of conflict. This finding corroborates the argument made in this book that regional institutions can contribute to peace in conflict-prone regions.

This analysis has also begun to identify the limits of these institutional effects. It suggested that REOs are less effective in regions where interstate violence is especially intense, such as South Asia and the Horn of Africa. In these regions, it appears, hostility runs too deep to allow for meaningful economic cooperation. This, in turn, prevents organizations in these "zones of war" from promoting peace and goodwill. The early history of regional cooperation in Southeast Asia offers additional evidence to this conclusion.

As described in the previous chapter, attempts to form two international organizations, ASA and Maphilindo, crumbled in the face of severe diplomatic and, at times, violent crises between Malaysia, on the one hand, and the Philippines and Indonesia, on the other. As a result, the pacifying effect of these organizations ranged from limited (for ASA) to nil (for Maphilindo). Only the cessation of hostilities brought a modicum of stability to the region and provided favorable conditions for the formation of the more resilient ASEAN. Operating in a still hostile but more manageable environment, ASEAN has proved effective in maintaining and consolidating regional amity.

Chapter 5 moved beyond aggregate measures and tested the pacifying effect of specific design features. The results, which revealed that not all design features are equally effective in reducing armed conflict, underscored the notion that the consequences of regional institutions for conflict are determined not only by the broader level of cooperation but also by the specific features of which these organizations are composed. In line with hypothesis 1 in chapter 2, wider scope of economic activity, when implemented, results in fewer militarized disputes. This finding, which is robust to the inclusion of alternative explanations and to several model specifications, indicates that as member states become more economically intertwined, they are less likely to resolve their differences militarily. It also highlights the importance of a variety of economic issue areas (not just trade) and of the need to carry out signed agreements when conceptualizing economic interdependence.

The ASEAN case study in chapter 6 corroborates these findings. The economic benefits provided by the organization had a significant moderating effect on intraregional interactions, especially in the 1990s and 2000s, when economic cooperation had become deeper and more wide-ranging. Notably, many of the gains emanated not from the elimination of trade barriers but, rather, from cooperation in other issue areas, such as foreign investment and development projects. The experience of ASEAN sheds some light on the causal mechanisms purported to link interdependence and conflict. For the most part, economic interdependence dissuaded governments from engaging in aggressive behavior in the first place, as liberals have argued for at least two centuries (Crescenzi 2005; Polachek 1980; Russett and Oneal 2001). This observation is also consistent with the stronger pacifying effect of economic scope on less severe MIDs, reported in chapter 5. In line with the more recent rationalist logic (Morrow 1999, 2003),

ASEAN members occasionally exploited their economic ties to communicate during political crises, instead of taking more extreme measures.

The statistical results provided strong support for the hypothesis that regular meetings of high-level officials reduce the number of armed conflicts. This variable had a significant pacifying effect, both statistically and substantively. This finding indicates that recurrent top-level meetings in a regional setup make substantial contribution to interstate peace. Contrary to the widely held view of such meetings as ineffective, wasteful, and even counterproductive, the analysis showed that they play a vital role in the dynamics of regional politics, even if it is not always visible. Again, the evolution of ASEAN substantiates this conclusion. The annual meeting of ASEAN foreign ministers and, later, the annual summits were at the heart of regional diplomacy since the inception of this organization.

Consistent with the causal mechanisms identified in chapter 2, these meetings have fostered the exchange of credible information and helped build trust among top government officials. During times of bilateral tensions they often functioned as an instrument of conflict management and de-escalation when officials from third countries engaged in informal mediation behind the scenes. The significance of such dynamics is reflected by the robust effect of these meetings on the most violent MIDs. Finally, the repeated interaction of the same individuals—sometimes for serious discussions and negotiations and sometimes for golf playing or karaoke singing—created strong bonds and a sense of cohesion among this small group of policymakers. As argued in chapter 2, such meetings are especially conducive to peace building.

The hypotheses that pertain to the independence of regional institutions were not supported by the statistical analysis. Neither more independent regional bureaucracies nor more legalized DSMs appeared to decrease armed conflict between member states. Their meager moderating effect challenges the institutionalist faith in these bodies and the conventional view that the neutrality of these bodies makes them effective tools of conflict management. It corroborates the opposing view, which highlights the limitations of impartial mediators and excessively legalized DSMs.

Once more, the ASEAN case study is in step with the statistical findings. Since its formation in the late 1970s, that organization's secretariat was rather weak, and its operation left little mark on regional politics. Even when it became larger and more independent, it was continually sidelined by member states on issues of regional security. Similarly, a DSM that was formed in the middle 1990s and became more legalized in the 2000s remained largely untested and did little to resolve economic disputes, much less political ones. Moreover, formal bodies that were specifically designed to deal with security affairs, like the High Council and the Troika, also stood idle or had a minor effect on such matters. These findings suggest that greater institutional independence does not set in motion the mechanisms of conflict management, information, and socialization that are commonly alleged to be associated with this design feature.

Like the theoretical framework, the empirical analysis devoted a great deal of attention to the possibility of reversed causality and endogeneity. Chapter 5's investigation of the determinants and specific design features of regional institutionalization emphasized the effect of armed disputes on the level of institutionalized cooperation. If REOs thrive where peace is already well established but are anemic where conflict is rampant, such disputes should dampen regional institutionalization. The statistical results do not support this contention. With the exception of DSMs, which appeared to *increase* in legalization as the number of disputes mounted, conflict did not affect regional institutions in a systematic manner, either negatively or positively. The finding that greater violence is associated with more legalized DSMs corroborates the perspective that governments that anticipate disagreements are more inclined to invest in dispute resolution instruments.

The view that points to conflict as a constraint on cooperation did not bear out in the historical analysis of the ASEAN region either. Chapter 6 showed that the effect of conflict on regional cooperation was not uniform. In some periods, the demand-side logic and the supply-side logic were at work simultaneously. In the early 1960s, the latter dominated the former, but in the 1990s, the opposite was true. In other times, such as the 1980s, interstate conflict was not a primary driver of regional institutionalization. Echoing the statistical findings, times of intense conflict have increased pressure to institute and utilize dispute settlement bodies, exemplified by Maphilindo in the early 1960s and the High Council in the 2000s.

The examination of the sources of variation across REOs, conducted in parts of chapters 5 and 6, provides a more complete picture of the relationships between regional institutionalization, conflict, and other domestic and international factors. The analysis shows, as one might expect, that the institutional structure of REOs is endogenous in the sense that it is affected by their members' interests and interactions. Regional institutions are shaped by a mix of incentives, such as high levels of international trade, and constraints, such as power preponderance, faced by their members. In most cases, however, the variables that impinge on regional institutionalization do not affect conflict or push it in the opposite direction. These findings alleviate concerns that the relationships between these two phenomena are spurious.

Of particular importance, regional affinity was found to contribute to the institutionalization of REOs but did not appear to contribute to peace. This does not mean that mutual political concerns do not matter, of course. Rather, it bolsters the need to specify these interests more precisely and to consider their implications more carefully. The ASEAN experience shows, for example, that a shared political orientation among the political elite in the region (and a blend of common and conflicting interests) was conducive to both regional cooperation and peace. In short, REO members have common as well as divergent interests that have significant bearings on their relationships. This does not prevent international institutions from affecting these dynamics in real and meaningful ways.

The only variable that exerts a strong negative effect on institutionalized regional cooperation and peace is domestic strife. This finding points to the possibility that domestic political stability is an important prerequisite to the emergence of prosperous zones of peace. Interestingly, though, the effect of domestic unrest on regional politics in the ASEAN region was rather varied. Especially in the early years, it actually advanced, rather than hampered, institutional building. The implications of domestic unrest for regional cooperation and conflict appear significant but still tentative. This caveat notwithstanding, the quantitative and qualitative analyses indicated that the effect of regional institutions on conflict is genuine, considerable, and not an artifact of other, more fundamental factors. They began to untangle the multifaceted nature of regional politics and the manners by which REOs fit into these complex dynamics, both as a cause and an effect.

Theoretical Implications

This book has several broad theoretical implications. The picture that emerges from previous chapters provides a fresh perspective on the role of international institutions in world politics. It shows that the tired debate between realists and institutionalists on whether such institutions matter is too crude and obscures the nuanced and contingent manners by which they affect state behavior. Taken as a whole, the findings indicate that the realists' outright dismissal of international institutions as trivial is unfounded. There is ample evidence that REOs are not mere reflections of preexisting power relationships and that they can promote regional peace and stability independent of their members.

The book offers general, but not unconditional, support for the institutionalist perspective. Joining a small but growing body of research that investigates the consequences of institutional design for conflict (Bearce and Omori 2005; Boehmer, Gartzke, and Nordstrom 2004; Fortna 2004; Hansen, Mitchell, and Nemeth 2008), this book shows that the structure and functions of regional institutions affect their ability to promote peace. It shows that economic scope and top-level diplomacy promote peace but that regional secretariats and DSMs do not. This finding underscores the need to bring institutional variation to the center of the analysis (Acharya and Johnston 2007; Koremenos 2005; Koremenos, Lipson, and Snidal 2001). The book also highlights the benefits of moving beyond institutional design and taking into account the implementation of signed agreements. While this institutional dimension is not easily conceptualized and measured, neglecting it is likely to hamper a complete understanding of the ways by which international institutions affect and are affected by their members. Finally, this book reveals that even if regional institutions are designed well and implemented, their value is not without limits. It appears, in particular, that REOs are less effective in regions where violent conflict is especially intense.

These contingent effects indicate that both realists and institutionalists capture some aspects of the dynamic relationships between states and institutions but miss others. The evolution of regional institutions is endogenous to the domestic structure and interests of their members as well as the ties among them. Nonetheless, such institutions tend to be "sticky" and have meaningful consequences for international politics (Keohane and Martin 1995). As a consequence, regions where relationships are highly antagonistic are likely to discourage the emergence of an institutionalized REO, thereby leading to a vicious cycle of more conflict and less cooperation. In contrast, REOs have better prospects in regions where interactions are more amicable, thereby resulting in a virtuous cycle of more cooperation and fewer armed disputes. In this respect, regional institutions are particularly useful in reinforcing an existing but tenuous peace.

This study is concerned with not only the conditions under which institutions mitigate conflict but also with the manners by which they do so. Chapter 2 put a magnifying glass on the causal mechanisms believed to produce their salutary effects. The discussion uncovered assumptions and pointed to logical quandaries that often go unnoticed in extant research. The role of neutrality in conflict management and the issue of ad hoc versus repeated top-level meetings illustrate the analytical benefits of this discussion. Linking these causal mechanisms to specific design features offers additional insights on the manners by which they operate. The conflict management and information mechanisms, for example, appear to operate rather effectively at the highest levels but remain dormant at lower levels of interaction. Similarly, constructivists, who frequently argue that international institutions socialize their members, stop short of specifying how this process comes about. This book suggests that socialization is manifested mostly among top-level officials. There is little evidence of socialization among bureaucrats and the mass public. From this perspective, the emphasis of constructivists on security communities and broad social transformations may miss the sphere in which the socialization process is most significant.

These observations shed new light on the concept of institutional independence. The study of international institutions often comes with a normative appreciation (either implicit or explicit) to their neutrality and autonomy. A careful application of insights from the mediation literature indicates that these characteristics can sometimes be detrimental to the goals of the institution. In contrast, the more partial and politically driven top-level meetings are more likely to succeed in mitigating regional conflict. This means not that institutional independence does not matter but, rather, that it matters in different ways and under certain conditions. The corporate secretariat and DSM may still facilitate cooperation on economic and social issues. Thus, when thinking about independence, one should be mindful of the varying degrees of neutrality, autonomy, and delegation within international organizations. In addition to comparing independence across organizations, it is important to compare the independence of different features inside them and consider their implications.

This study advances several bodies of literature discussed in previous chapters. It contributes in a number of ways to the debate on the link between interdependence and peace. It shows that the conceptualization of interdependence in terms of trade flows is too narrow and misses much of the cross-border economic interaction that takes place in the contemporary era (Fawn 2009). Recognizing the multidimensional nature of economic interdependence is likely to improve the scholarly understanding of the manners by which economic relations affect security affairs (Gartzke 2003; Rosecrance and Thompson 2003). Second, much of the extant research examines only dyadic relationships and overlooks multilateral interactions. This study shows that economic interdependence cannot always be reduced to bilateral relations. Frequently, functional cooperation takes place in a broader regional context. Taken together, these two points suggest that extant research underestimates the degree of economic interdependence. This observation is especially relevant for research that examines the more recent era of globalization, in which economic cooperation and integration is becoming ever more complex.

This study also supports the contention, made by recent studies, that employing cross-regional analysis is useful to grasp recent developments in world politics (Buzan and Wæver 2003; Gleditsch 2002; Kacowicz 1998; Lake and Morgan 1997; Solingen 1998). It is apparent that regional dynamics capture a great deal of international interactions and thus require greater scholarly attention. It is also clear that interstate relations vary substantially from one region to another. While in-depth studies of one or two regions may illuminate the specific circumstances of these cases, comparative analyses can situate individual cases in a broader context and offer new appreciation to the relationships uncovered in these cases.

The ASEAN case study nicely illustrates this point. Numerous observers are puzzled by the reputation of this organization as successful and effective (see chapter 6). Judging ASEAN on its own right or against European integration, such analysts accentuate the areas where progress is stalled and where accomplishments fall short of the European model. The more comprehensive assessment conducted in this book reconciles this seeming contradiction. ASEAN certainly suffers from weaknesses, and the rhetoric of its member governments is not always matched with practice. Nevertheless, comparing this organization not only to the EU but also to several REOs in Asia, Africa, and the Americas shows that ASEAN is one of the most advanced and effective organizations in the developing world.

Practical Implications

This book offers important lessons for policymakers who sit at the negotiation table and design regional organizations as well as to the individuals who or bodies that advise them on such matters. The empirical analysis indicates that member states ought to consider a variety of issue areas of functional cooperation, which goes beyond the elimination of trade barriers. From this point of view, the recent wave of regionalism—which broadens the agendas of many regional institutions to include a range of economic issues—appears to be a step in the right direction. In addition, implementation of agreed-on cooperation is essential. Considering the frequently wide gap between institutional design and implementation, if policymakers hope to promote intraregional peace through economic activities, rhetoric and practice should match more closely.

REOs should also institute regular meetings among top-level policymakers. Despite the commonly held view of such meetings as costly and futile "talk shops," this book points to the ways by which such repeated conferences promote peaceful coexistence. The design of these organizations should include frequent summitries and meetings among top-level ministers. Members should ensure that these meetings actually take place, providing officials the opportunity to meet face-to-face, and that they are planned in advance. Such planning should allow for casual interaction among officials, alongside the more formal agenda. Upholding these meetings is especially desirable during times in which bilateral tensions surface or when regional politics are in flux. Under these circumstances, this study shows, the management of territorial and other difficult conflicts is best handled by high-level government officials. It also appears that a wide scope of economic activity bolsters the ability of top government officials to manage regional conflict: it allows them to use it as leverage during negotiations and, in turn, to expand the range of bargaining solutions. The empirical association between these two design features is encouraging in this respect.

Design features that contribute to the independence of REOs should not be expected to play a major role in the management of violent conflict. Regional bureaucrats may be instrumental in facilitating cooperation on economic and social issues but are not well positioned to mediate in bilateral conflicts (Gutner and Thompson 2010, 243). Efforts to do so are likely to prove unsuccessful and might distract the staff from their core missions. Similar lessons can be drawn with respect to regional DSMs. It is apparent that these bodies are not well suited to address bilateral political conflict, partly because such conflicts are beyond their mandate.

Even if they do have jurisdiction over security matters, however, this study indicates that greater legalization is not necessarily advantageous. In particular, when there is a mismatch between the legal power of these mechanisms and inclination of member states to yield to their authority, these institutions are likely to remain inactive or ineffective. Considering the frequent calls to strengthen these legal bodies in order to manage interstate conflict, this is not a trivial point. As discussed in chapter 6, with the growing friction among ASEAN members, some experts recommended that they be tackled with stronger DSMs (Hund 2002; Severino 2006; Vatikiotis 2009). This book corroborates the opposing perspective, which casts doubt on the ability of these institutions to promote cordiality in the region (Eaton and Stubbs 2006). Greater legalization is likely to prove effective only to the extent that governments are willing to make use of the services provided by regional DSMs.

Finally, the conditional relationships between peace and REOs indicate that some regions are more likely than others to benefit from regional institutions. The findings show that in parts of the world where conflict is especially intense, forming an economic organization may be premature. Thus, it is doubtful that security relations in regions such as the Middle East, South Asia, and the Balkans would benefit from the formation of REOs. There, such organizations are likely to remain weakly institutionalized and ineffective. Governments in these regions should devote their time and energy to terminating hostilities and normalizing their relationships. Only after greater stability is achieved should states turn their attention to regional cooperation through institutions. Regional institutions should be promoted in regions where a transformation from zones of conflict to zones of peace is under way. In these regions, REOs can promote goodwill and reinforce the nascent peace. Regions that fit this description include, for example, Central America, Eastern Europe, East Asia, and Southern Africa. Advancing regional institutions in these regions is likely to yield considerable peace dividends.

Future Research

This book leaves a number of unanswered questions, thereby opening up exciting new directions for inquiry. Additional attention to the causal mechanisms by which regional institutions affect conflict and to the specific manners by which they do so is one promising avenue of future research. Chapter 2 pointed to recent works that aspire to reconcile the purported pacifying effect of economic interdependence with the rationalist framework of war. According to them, governments threaten to cut their economic ties to demonstrate their resolve during crises (Morrow 1999; Stein 2003). The ASEAN case study offers some, but by no means overwhelming, support for the behavior anticipated by this model. Perhaps these threats are made tacitly rather than overtly, or perhaps governments prefer to demonstrate their resolve in other ways. Further empirical analysis of the link between economic statecraft and crisis bargaining may shed light on this question.

A second causal mechanism that could benefit from greater consideration is socialization. This book shows that this is an important manner by which institutions alter the dynamics by which their members interact. By making a distinction between high- and low-level officials and between ad hoc and serial meetings, it also begins to identify the conditions under which socialization is most effective. The empirical analysis identifies additional factors that can possibly shape the socialization process. These include the number of members in the institution, initial cultural affinity, and domestic political institutions. In ASEAN, greater democratization in some of its members during the 1990s and 2000s may have sowed the seeds of a Southeast Asian civil society (Nesadurai 2009), but it also resulted in greater turnover of leadership, thereby undermining the cohesion at the highest level. A more nuanced understanding of international socialization and how it evolves in different settings is likely to offer fresh insights into the role of institutions in world politics.

From an empirical perspective, this study is only a first step in unpacking the relationship between REOs and conflict. As discussed in previous chapters, systematic conceptualization and measurement of variation across these organizations is still underdeveloped. This reality presents scholars with a difficult choice between large data sets that capture this variation only roughly (if at all) and data sets that provide a more nuanced depiction of this variation but have a more limited spatial and temporal coverage. Refining and coming to scholarly agreement on measurements of regional institutionalization as well as expanding existing data sets will allow researchers to avoid this trade-off and reach firmer conclusions regarding the implications of institutional variation for international relations.

In addition, generalization of the findings beyond regional economic organizations requires caution. In particular, it is possible that their economic mandate restricts the ability of the secretariat and DSM to manage armed conflict. Similar features that are embedded in security organizations may be more effective in this respect (Boehmer, Gartzke, and Nordstrom 2004; Hansen, Mitchell, and Nemeth 2008; Shannon 2009). A broader sample of international organizations that accounts for institutional design as well as implementation may cast additional light on the effect of these institutions on conflict. Additionally, a growing number of organizations combine economic and security aspects. This book emphasizes the functional and economic dimensions and touched on security cooperation only briefly, mainly in the context of ASEAN. A more thorough typology and analysis of security institutions that are embedded in economic organizations is a promising avenue of future research.

The empirical findings point to several factors that affect regional politics in important ways, but a detailed analysis of the manners by which they interact with REOs and conflict is beyond the scope of this study. In particular, this book concentrates on international factors and considers domestic factors only as competing explanations to or factors conditioning the former. The analysis suggests that domestic politics have significant repercussions for international conflict and cooperation. The statistical results indicate that civil wars are strongly associated with both less economic cooperation and more interstate violence. The evidence regarding the link between domestic conflict and regional politics in the ASEAN case is mixed. In some periods, like in the aftermath of the 1997 financial crisis, domestic crises undermined regional cooperation and accentuated the differences between the members of the organization. In contrast, one of the primary objectives of ASEAN in its initial phase was to restrain domestic oppositions and prevent the spillover of intrastate struggles. Thus, like interstate conflict, civil wars may sometimes create demands for international institutions. The relationships between domestic conflicts and international institutions remain understudied and poorly understood. The growing frequency and severity of civil wars underscores the need to more fully explore this nexus.

Another internal factor that requires greater attention is regime type. This study focuses on international organizations and commercial ties, the second and third legs of the Kantian tripod of requirements for peace (Russett and Oneal 2001). The first and most studied leg, democracy, is here considered much less extensively. Surprisingly, the findings do not corroborate the widely held view that more democratic regions facilitate greater economic cooperation and are less war-prone. Some suggestive evidence points to political stability as more important than the degree of democracy to international conflict. Consistent with the argument made by Mansfield and Snyder (2002), regions that are going through democratic transitions tend to be less stable and peaceful. The manners by which domestic institutions interact with both regional institutions and conflict, especially in the developing world, require greater scholarly attention.

This final chapter has considered the broader lessons of this study. Revisiting the theoretical framework and the empirical findings, it underscores the central message of this book: if designed properly and implemented, regional institutions are capable of crafting a sustainable peace among their members. Their ability to mitigate conflict is genuine as well as considerable. This chapter also points to the ways by which this study advances the understanding of international politics more broadly, and it draws this study's implications for policymakers who engage in institutional building. Lastly, this chapter points to questions raised in this book that scholars ought to examine more fully.

Notwithstanding these remaining issues, this book lays theoretical and empirical foundations to the study of the relationships between regional institutions and violent conflict. Given the growing clout of emerging regional powers and the potential destabilizing effect of their ascendance, a good grasp of the manners by which REOs can assist with the management of security matters is expected to become increasingly valuable in years and decades to come.

NOTES

Chapter 1

1. The COMESA treaty can be found at http://comesa3.comesa.int/attach ments/article/94/110829_COMESA_Treaty_EN.pdf (accessed October 12, 2011).

2. Less institutionalized arrangements, such as bilateral preferential trade agreements (PTAs), are excluded from this group of organizations. For a more detailed discussion of the definition of REOs and criteria for inclusion or exclusion of different types of arrangements, see chapter 3.

3. Implementation is thus related to but distinct from compliance. The former is usually a key step toward the latter but is neither a necessary nor a sufficient condition for it (Raustiala and Slaughter 2002, 539; Simmons 1998; Underdal 1998). For example, governments may sometimes comply with international agreements without signing them. Implementation is also different from effectiveness and performance, which refer to the relative success of an institution in obtaining its stated goals (Acharya and Johnston 2007, 24–25; Gutner and Thompson 2010; Raustiala and Slaughter 2002; Victor, Raustiala, and Skolnikoff 1998). A central objective of this study is to evaluate the relationships between implementation and effectiveness.

4. An expanded data set contains observations up to 2007 (Haftel 2011). The analysis in this book excludes the 2000s because, at the time of writing, the most recent data on militarized interstate disputes, which is used to measure conflict, ended in 2001.

5. These are the 24 indicators subsumed by the scope of economic activity and regular meetings of high-level officials. Regarding regional bureaucracy and DSMs, I make a distinction between an agreement to form these institutions and their actual establishment.

6. For a useful discussion of these approaches, see Caporaso 1998 and Mattli 1999.

7. Chapter 2 provides a more thorough discussion of security communities, socialization, and peace.

8. The other two legs in the "Kantian tripod" are democracy and economic interdependence. For an overview of these topics, see Mansfield and Pollins 2003 and Russett and Oneal 2001.

Chapter 2

1. Research that builds on this framework is voluminous; see Reiter 2003 for a useful review. Specific studies that pertain to the argument developed in this book are discussed subsequently.

2. See also Powell 2006.

3. Levy (2002) points out that if governments are risk acceptant and if the expected outcome of military confrontation is sufficiently rewarding, rational states may still go to war.

4. See also Moravcsik 1998, 91–94. Eilstrup-Sangiovanni and Verdier (2005) and Eilstrup-Sangiovanni (2008) consider the pacifying role of regional institutions only from the perspective of credible commitments and overlook other mechanisms examined herein. They make a convincing case for the value of European integration as a vehicle of peace, by pointing to the efficiency gains and exit costs it generated. This claim is more consistent with the opportunity cost mechanism than the credible commitment mechanism, however.

5. For studies that challenge this general view, see Barbieri 2002 and Waltz 1970. Other works argue that the pacifying effect of economic interdependence is restricted to the post–World War II era and, in particular, that extensive commerce did not prevent World War I (Copeland 1996; Levy and Ali 1998; McDonald 2009; Ripsman and Blanchard 1996/97). This book examines interdependence and conflict in the late twentieth century and does not speak directly to this debate.

6. Speech before the National Geographic Society, Washington, DC, June 11, 1998.

7. Gruber (2000) points out that members sometimes derive lower net benefits from international institutions than they had in a previous, institution-free environment. Still, given the reality of an REO, this uninstitutionalized setting becomes a hypothetical counterfactual rather than a real option. Examples of states that left REOs after they determined that the costs outweigh the benefits include Chile, which left the Andean Pact in 1976, and Honduras, which suspended its membership in the Central American Common Market in 1970 (only to rejoin in 1990).

8. Similar tensions dogged the Latin American Free Trade Association (Bulmer-Thomas 1997).

9. This well-known distinction was introduced by Keohane and Nye (2001). For a more recent discussion, see Crescenzi 2005, 27–29.

10. Some instances of border cooperation, such as those in the Andean, European, and ASEAN regions, are designed especially to produce interdependence and to constrain aggressive instincts (Diez, Albert, and Stetter 2008; Simmons 2005a).

11. The main alternative to this model is a society-based pluralist model, which assumes that the government act on behalf organized economic interests. This model poses fewer difficulties to the opportunity cost argument (Press-Barnathan 2009; Simmons 2003, 37–38). Thus, the more demanding model is considered.

12. The distinction is not clear-cut, however. Morrow (2003, 90) points out that the informational story "sounds much like the traditional argument," and Polachek

and Xiang (2010) argue that the signaling model works only if one assumes that the loss of interdependence is costly.

13. I thus adopt a broad definition of diplomacy that includes not only professional diplomats but also policymakers that engage in foreign affairs (Jönsson 2002, 213). The diplomatic roles of political leaders, in general, and summitry, in particular, have greatly increased in recent decades (Jönsson 2002, 216; Melissen 2003).

14. See also Bearce 2003 and Gilady and Russett 2002.

15. See Bearce 2003 for a more detailed description of the pacifying role of GCC, as well as ECOWAS, summits.

16. *Economist,* January 6, 2004.

17. The role of regional bureaucracy as a potential mediating body is discussed in detail later in this chapter. Of course, REOs are not the only bodies that can serve as mediators. A variety of other organizations, states, or individuals may serve in this capacity, sometimes in tandem with the REO. Also, not all mediation attempts sponsored by REOs have been successful (however success is defined). Even in such instances, they played a moderating role. For example, in the dispute between Guyana and Suriname previously mentioned, CARICOM's mediation efforts fell short, and the dispute was handed over to the International Court of Justice. Nonetheless, the regional meeting facilitated communication between the two countries and prevented escalation of the crisis.

18. In a more recent example, the president of Liberia used summits of the Mano River Union to mediate a territorial dispute between the two other members, Sierra Leone and Guinea (BBC, April 30, 2007).

19. Quoted in Berridge 2002, 170.

20. Presumably, the role of these professionals resembles that of the Nepalese guides for Himalayan mountaineers.

21. For an extensive discussion of these concepts and how they are linked, see Abbott and Snidal 1998 and Haftel and Thompson 2006. The concept of independence is closely related to two other terms used by other scholars. These include centralization (Koremenos, Lipson, and Snidal 2001) and structure (Boehmer, Gartzke, and Nordstrom 2004). Chapter 3 expands on the choice of terminology.

22. The literature on mediation is voluminous. For a summary of extant research and more detailed definitions, see, for example, Bercovitch 1997; Gilady and Russett 2002; and Touval and Zartman 2001.

23. See also Boehmer, Gartzke, and Nordstrom 2004 and Mitchell and Hensel 2007.

24. As Gelpi (1999, 116) explains, the favored disputant is more likely to compromise because it trusts that the mediator will not ask for concessions that undermine important interests of the disputant (and, by extension, of the mediator). The less favored disputant may benefit from the power of the mediator over its opponent, but only up to a point.

25. Both studies cited in the text examine states and overlook other types of mediators, including international organizations.

26. See also Beltramino 2005, 192.

27. See also Dunn 1996, 251, and Melissen 2003, 14.

28. For further discussion of ASEAN as a security community, see chapter 6.

29. I thank an anonymous reviewer for elucidating this point.

30. See also Koremenos, Lipson, and Snidal 2001, 785.

31. The possibility of such a virtuous circle is not unique to the relationships between regional institutionalization and conflict. For example, democratizing states are more likely to join IGOs (Mansfield and Pevehouse 2006), while IGOs are instrumental in committing their members to democratic regimes (Pevehouse 2005). In a logic that parallels the discussion here, IGOs promote democracy by making it costly for governments to renege on their commitment to democracy.

Chapter 3

1. For a comprehensive review of security regionalism, see Mansfield and Solingen 2010.

2. See Mansfield and Pevehouse 2000; Page 2000b; Pevehouse, Nordstrom, and Warnke 2004; Smith 2000; and Union of International Associations 2000.

3. One notable exception is EU research, in which scholars have collected and analyzed national-level data on implementation of and compliance with the organization's regulations. The complex and multifaceted implementation process in the EU (Garrett and Weingast 1993, 191–94) attests to the difficulty in evaluating implementation systematically. For a review of research that examines the implementation of EU rules and the challenges it faces, see Treib 2008.

4. Arguably, collecting data on compliance is even thornier. As Simmons (2010, 284) points out with respect to trade law, "Accumulating a convincing data set on compliance with treaty law in this area would be a mind-boggling endeavor, even if one were to focus only on the WTO and set aside the large number of regional agreements governing trade relationships."

5. On the importance of this issue for the CACM, the Mano River Union, and the EU, see Bulmer-Thomas 1998, 320; Sesay 1990, 80; and Swann 1996, 61–68, respectively.

6. This REO was WAEMU's precursor.

7. These sectors are business, communications, construction, distribution, education, environment, finance, health and social services, tourism, recreation, and transportation.

8. REOs that have a monetary union are assumed to coordinate their monetary and exchange rate policies.

9. Another dimension, frequently considered in the study of international organizations, is voting rules. Scholars distinguish between those that make decisions by consensus and those that make them with a majority vote (Acharya and Johnston 2007; Haftel and Thompson 2006; Koremenos, Lipson, and Snidal 2001). Even though this is an important aspect of control and independence, it lacks variation with respect to the organizations examined in this study. With the exception of the

EU, all REOs make decisions by consensus. This aspect is therefore excluded from the analysis.

10. Other observers conceptualized this dimension as institutional authority (Grieco 1997, 169–70) and commitment institutions (Mattli 1999, 54).

11. ASEAN governments, for example, resisted the creation of a permanent APEC secretariat due to fears of lost sovereignty. Some ministers even complained about secretariat officials being connected by e-mail, arguing that it reflected too much "institutionalization" (Funabashi 1995, 139).

12. This categorization of functions builds on Jacobson 1984.

13. This is different from utilization. DSMs may be operational but underutilized. As discussed in chapter 2, the design of DSMs may affect their utilization and effectiveness (Posner and Yoo 2005).

14. A five-year interval, as oppose to four- or seven-year intervals, is conventional in studies that do not use an annual setup. See, for example, Mansfield 1994 and Singer, Bremer, and Stuckey 1972 .

15. http://www.efta.int/free-trade/free-trade-agreements.aspx (accessed February 3, 2011).

16. http://www.aseansec.org/4920.htm (accessed February 1, 2011).

17. I verified and updated Smith's coding. I coded cases that are excluded from his study according to his own criteria, with the same sources referred to herein. The IMF's *Directory of Economic, Commodity, and Development Organizations* can be found at http://www.imf.org/external/np/sec/decdo/contents.htm.

18. http://www.caricom.org/jsp/single_market/free_movement.jsp?menu= csme (accessed February 9, 2011).

19. http://www.comunidadandina.org/ingles/sociolaboral/migration.htm (accessed February 9, 2011).

20. The secondary sources used in the coding are too numerous to cite in full here. Haftel 2004b provides a more extensive list of these studies.

21. See also Bourenane 2002; Chanthunya 2001; and Poku 2001.

22. For similar assessments, see Page 2000b, 214, and Sánchez Sánchez 2009, 170–71.

23. For each REO, the value represents the average across the different time points. Even though the level of institutionalization changes over time, most REOs remain in the same category.

24. This gap reflects, in part, failed attempts by developing countries to "import" European agreements and institutions to their own regions. Langhammer and Hiemenz (1990, 2) label this the "fallacy of transposition."

25. Newly formed REOs have low levels of regional institutionalization that may lead to an artificially low average. It is thus more informative to compare the same group of organizations across time.

26. Most, but not all, REOs have experienced increasing institutionalization. Some organizations, such as SACU and LAIA, showed little dynamism, and others, such as the Mano River Union and CEPGL, have experienced declining levels of institutionalization.

27. This wave is sometimes dubbed as the "new" or "open" regionalism.

28. The implementation ratio ranges from 0, if none of the planned indicators are realized, to 1, if all the designed indicators are implemented. The interpretation of this statistic requires some caution. The score of some of the shallowest REOs, such as LAIA and the Bangkok Agreement, is very high not because they accomplished a great deal but, rather, because their stated goals are very limited. This is consistent with the idea that compliance is high when the required deviation from the status quo is low (Downs, Rocke, and Barsoom 1996).

29. The first group includes the EU, EFTA, and NAFTA and is heavily influenced by the EU. Average levels of implemented regional institutionalization for the developed world, Latin America, Africa, and Asia are 13.1, 8.3, 5.6, and 5.3, respectively.

30. Average implementation ratios for the developed world, Asia, Latin America, and Africa are 0.87, 0.65, 0.56, and 0.40, respectively.

31. Specifically, I divided economic scope into two components. The trade-related component includes the indicators related to trade in goods, common external tariff, and trade in services. The second component includes the remaining 15 indicators.

32. R^2 is about 0.57 and 0.61 for the implemented and designed indicators, respectively.

33. Many REOs have a nonbinding DSM. See Smith 2000.

Chapter 4

1. A panel setup refers to data sets that are cross-sectionally dominated. My data set contains 25 sections (REOs) and up to four time points.

2. The random effects specification is preferable to the fixed effects specification only insofar as it is consistent. A Hausman test indicates that the coefficients in the random effects models are not systematically different from the ones in the fixed effects models and are thus indeed consistent. Nevertheless, I also ran negative binomial models with clustered standard errors rather than random effects. This did not change the results in a meaningful manner.

3. The quality of these models depends, however, on the "instrument" used to replace the original variable. A good instrument is highly correlated with the original variable but not with the error term. In many areas of social science—and political science is no exception—good instruments are few and far between.

4. Specifically, the dependent variable is aggregated as follows: 1982–86, 1987–91, 1992–96, 1997–2001.

5. Only three full-scale wars between REO members are recorded during this time period. These are the war between India and Pakistan in 1999, the war between Ethiopia and Eritrea from 1998 to 2000, and the war that has revolved around the Democratic Republic of Congo from 1998 to 2000. The latter is counted multiple times because it involved several countries that are members in a number of REOs.

6. I tested for a fourth conflict variable, the number of regional MIDs weighted by the number of members. Using a panel-corrected standard error specification

and dropping the variable *members* from the model, I found that the results reported in this chapter remain intact. They are available from the author on request.

7. Trade data for SACU are not available and most likely do not exist (Page 2000b, 117).

8. The body of literature on this issue is voluminous. For a concise statement of the theory and findings, see Russett and Oneal 2001.

9. This data set does not provide information on microstates (population less than one million). Such states are not included in the calculation of regional measures. All members of the OECS are microstates; thus, values for this organization are missing.

10. This threshold follows the conventional practice in the definition of mature democracies.

11. Mansfield and Snyder examine changes in regime type rather than their absolute values.

12. A minor armed conflict involves at least 25 battle-related deaths per year and fewer than 1,000 battle-related deaths during the course of the conflict. An intermediate conflict involves at least 25 but less than 1,000 battle-related deaths per year and an accumulated total of at least 1,000 battle-related deaths during the course of the conflict. Like in the COW data set, a war involves at least 1,000 battle-related deaths per year.

13. Internationalized internal disputes are excluded in order to minimize the possibility of overlap with the dependent variable.

14. The globally weighted measure of alliance portfolio is used. Data is obtained from the EUGene software (Bennett and Stam 2000).

15. For two good reviews of these contending perspectives, see Miller 2001 and Stein and Lobell 1997.

16. An alternative way to capture the effect of global politics on regional conflict is to consider the structure of the international system. A categorical variable that scores 0 for the Cold War period and 1 for the post–Cold War period was included to account for this possibility. It was statistically insignificant, did not change the findings, and is reported elsewhere (Haftel 2007).

17. Consistent with the COW project, Lemke identifies five great powers: the United States, China, the Soviet Union, Great Britain, and France. According to Lemke (2002, 150–51), the United States can intervene in all regions of the world; China in Southeast Asia; Great Britain, France, and the Soviet Union in North Africa, West Africa, and the northern part of South America; and the Soviet Union in the southern part of South America. Lemke does not code Central America and North America, Western Europe, and Central Asia. Based on Lemke's criteria and on personal communication with him, I assume that the United States, Great Britain, France, and the Soviet Union can intervene in Europe and the Americas and that the United States and the Soviet Union can intervene in Central Asia. Our operationalization of specific regions often diverges. To the extent that any great power can interfere in at least two members of an REO, I consider the REO vulnerable to intervention by this great power.

18. In practice, it varies from 1 to 4. The United States can project its power in all corners of the globe, and no region is vulnerable to all great powers' intervention.

19. Following the conventional practice, a border is defined as either a boundary of land or a water separation of less than 150 miles (Russett and Oneal 2001).

20. For one possible explanation for the weaker effect of regional institutionalization on MIDs that involve the use of force, see chapter 5.

21. I also tested the pacifying effect of the difference in regime types, measured as the standard deviation on the average Polity score for the REO. The estimate was positive but statistically insignificant.

22. The Bangkok Agreement is an exception to this pattern.

23. A third example is ASEAN, discussed in great detail in chapter 6.

24. The rivalries are between Peru and Ecuador and between Venezuela and Colombia. Peru and Colombia, in particular, suffer from persistent domestic unrest.

25. The most recent incident occurred between Mali and Niger in 1994.

Chapter 5

1. For a similar approach to this issue, see Fortna 2004; Mansfield and Pevehouse 2000; and Russett and Oneal 2001.

2. Summary statistics and bivariate correlations between the control variables are reported in previous chapters.

3. These models are equivalent to the basic model presented in chapter 4. Additional robustness checks that parallel those presented in that chapter were conducted for the models reported here. They produced very similar results and are not reported here.

4. As discussed in chapter 3, the trade-related variable includes indicators 1–9, and the nontrade variable includes indicators 10–24 (in table 3.2). The results on these variables are not reported here.

5. Nevertheless, some social dynamics such as shaming and group pressure (Johnston 2001) may still be at work.

6. Also, recall that the correlation between regular meetings of high-level officials and REO independence is positive. Presumably, governments increase their oversight as they delegate more power to the organization. In this respect, independence should be compared not only across international organizations but also across different features within them.

7. The five-year aggregations are 1977–81, 1982–86, 1987–91, and 1992–96.

8. Using the absolute number of disputes or normalizing them by the number of borders does not change the picture that emerges from the analysis.

9. For a more detailed discussion of this nexus, see Haftel 2011.

10. Interestingly, several recent studies cast doubt on this logic and question its empirical validity (Acharya and Johnston 2007; Grieco 1997; Kahler 1995). These studies do not offer a systematic empirical evaluation of the link between trade flows and the organizations that regulate them, however.

11. Substituting the Polity regional average with the variable *democracy dummy* does not change the results.

12. This conclusion echoes a recent study by Boehmer and Nordstrom (2008), who find that the effect of armed disputes on shared membership in IGOs is rather weak. They reason that opponents "form or join IGOs to escape conflict while other IGOs may be a function of peace" (296).

13. The effect of this variable on high-level meetings and regional bureaucracy is also negative but is statistically insignificant in most models.

14. The large coefficients reflect a limited variation on this variable, rather than a sizable substantive effect.

Chapter 6

1. ASEAN was formed in 1967 by Indonesia, Malaysia, the Philippines, Singapore, and Thailand. Brunei joined in 1984, Vietnam joined in 1995, Myanmar (Burma) and Laos joined in 1997, and Cambodia joined in 1999. References herein to the "ASEAN region" are to the members of ASEAN before and after its formation.

2. The purpose of theory testing can be contrasted with theory building, which commonly precedes and is used to generate quantitative models. Ideally, one would use several cases to test the theory. As Lieberman (2005, 441) points out, however, given time and resource constraints, "more energy ought to be devoted to identifying and analyzing causal process observations within cases, rather than to providing thinner insights about more cases."

3. That is why they do not pose a major obstacle for the quantitative analysis.

4. Such statements should be interpreted with caution. On the one hand, they are the most direct reflection of actors' motivations and intentions. On the other hand, policymakers tend to make statements that serve political purposes, rather than historical accuracy.

5. For historical background and detailed accounts of this dispute, see Gordon 1966 and Jorgensen-Dahl 1982.

6. All five MIDs in this period are related to this conflict. It resulted in about 700 battle deaths on both sides (Lyon 1969, 188).

7. The members of ASA were Thailand, Malaya/Malaysia, and the Philippines.

8. The members of Maphilindo were Indonesia, Malaya/Malaysia, and the Philippines.

9. On earlier attempts to form organizations that included states from outside the region, such as the Southeast Asia Treaty Organization, see Jorgensen-Dahl 1982, 9–10.

10. Gordon (1966, 186) points out, "No doubt this is not what observers generally look for when evaluating international organizations for regional cooperation, nor was this ASA's primary purpose. Yet, one of the functions of an organization is to provide—intentionally or not—a rubric for the settlement of disputes among its participants."

11. The first article of the Bangkok Declaration states that the aims of ASEAN shall be "to accelerate the economic growth, social progress and cultural develop-

ment in the region through joint endeavors in the spirit of equality and partnership in order to strengthen the foundation for a prosperous and peaceful community of South East Asian nations" (cited in Davidson 2003, 171).

12. These projects pertained mainly to sectoral cooperation and excluded trade liberalization. For a list of such projects and their implementation, see Solidum 1974, 153–55. For a critical evaluation of these projects, see Indorf 1975, 45–46.

13. The 1971 declaration of Southeast Asia as a "zone of peace, freedom, and neutrality" is an oft-cited early attempt to address issues of regional security. This declaration did not have any practical implications and is not considered as a meaningful instance of cooperation (R. Irvine 1982, 27–29; Leifer 1989, 56–59).

14. See also R. Irvine 1982; Jorgensen-Dahl 1982, 48–49; Khong 1997, 326–35.

15. In one incident, dated April 1968, several Malaysian warships and jet fighters crossed into Philippine territory (M. L. Brown 1994, 102; Caballero-Anthony 1998, 54).

16. Quoted in Leifer 1989, 35.

17. This does not mean that the process was always smooth. As one might expect, the movement from aspirations to concrete plans resulted in disagreements and tough negotiations over the general framework of economic cooperation as well as specific programs. Despite these differences, high-level officials were able to reach consensus and carve out a roadmap for economic cooperation in a number of areas (Castro 1981; Suriyamongkol 1988).

18. This observation is echoed by numerous other area experts. See, for example, Antolik 1990, 91; Indorf 1984, 85; Leifer 1999, 28; Severino 2006; Sopiee 1986, 227.

19. Quoted in R. Irvine 1982, 22.

20. Modern Southeast Asian leaders borrowed these two concepts from customs practiced in traditional Malay societies. As Jorgensen-Dahl points out (1982, 167), however, "the claims to uniqueness occasionally made on behalf of musjawarah are largely exaggerated."

21. For similar views, see Frost 1990; Jorgensen-Dahl 1982, 51–52; and Narine 2002.

22. This agreement included a restricted list of products. Ravenhill (1995, 853) notes, "ASEAN members offered preferential tariffs on products that either were not produced or not traded in the region, the most notorious examples being the Philippines' inclusion of snowplow equipment and Indonesia's listing of nuclear power plants in their tariff offers." Nonetheless, this agreement was gradually expanded. One early study observes, "The progress achieved has belied the cynics who have all along expected ASEAN economic co-operation to break down at the point where words have to be translated into deeds" (Rieger 1985, 25).

23. For charts of the organizational structures before and after the Bali summit, see Narine 2002, 17–18. On the limitations of this secretariat, see Indorf 1984, 68; D. Irvine 1982, 56; and Leifer 1989, 26–27.

24. As I discuss later in this chapter, however, this mechanism—known as the High Council—was never implemented.

25. See, for example, Huxley 1990; Indorf 1984; and Leifer 1989.

26. Quoted in M. L. Brown 1994, 105. It turns out, however, that this statement did not lay to rest the Philippines' claim to Sabah.

27. Leifer (1995, 135) comments, "The fact is that those dispute settlement provisions have laid dormant, not even on the table, but tucked away in a drawer. It would seem that the drawer has been locked and the key has been thrown away." See also Collins 2003b, 135; Davidson 2003, 142–43; and Tan 2000, 46.

28. See also Chatterjee 1990 and Kurus 1993, 823.

29. See also Castro 1981.

30. These "growth triangles" are industrial zones established on interstate borders and utilize resources from the neighboring states. For example, in the most successful initiative—the Singapore-Johor-Riau (SIJORI) triangle—Singapore contributes capital and infrastructure, and Indonesia and Malaysia provide labor and land. While these initiatives are outside the ASEAN formal framework, they are generally considered to be an important part of regional economic cooperation (Dosch 2007; Tongzon 1998, 84–96; Weatherbee 1995).

31. The causes of these rising tensions are a matter of debate. Ganesan (1999, 15) argues that the end of the Cold War and the Vietnamese decline prompted these developments. Others emphasize the principles that were adopted in the 1982 UN Conference on the Law of the Sea and the increased pressure on the dwindling maritime resources in the region. These developments resulted in a growing number of maritime territorial disputes (Acharya 2001, 130; Collins 2003b, 192–93; Denoon and Colbert 1998/99, 506; Mak 2009).

32. It is also noteworthy that an intensified arms race took place during these years (Collins 2003b, 95–97; Huxley 1990).

33. See also Kivimäki 2001, 13.

34. Policymakers are rarely explicit about such links.

35. Even during these euphoric times, other observers pointed out that ASEAN falls short of a security community (Ganesan 1994; Huxley 1996).

36. See also Emmerson 2005.

37. In some instances, the disputes were resolved by revising the agreements in a manner that accommodated the noncomplying member (Nesadurai 2003).

38. The haze resulted from burning forests in Indonesia. It spread throughout the region and caused a serious public health crisis.

39. At the same time, ASEAN members have begun to conclude bilateral FTAs with important extraregional countries, such as Japan, Australia, and the United States. These agreements weaken ASEAN's ability to act in unison vis-à-vis third countries (Ravenhill 2008).

40. See also Lim 2009, 123–25.

41. At Cambodia's request, the dispute was brought to the UN Security Council in February 2011 and to the ICJ in April 2011. Both bodies delegated this matter back to ASEAN, reaffirming its central role in the management of conflicts in the region (Haywood 2011).

42. The Philippine foreign minister Narciso Ramos complained, "ASEAN is in great difficulty. Unless we do something quickly, ASEAN may fall apart. Certainly we are able to do nothing about things like an ASEAN common market until we settle these disputes" (quoted in M. L. Brown 1994, 110).

43. For example, Leifer (1989, 25) reports that "a third meeting [between the leaders of ASEAN] was long delayed partly because of continuing differences between Malaysia and the Philippines over Sabah." Yet the Herzog Affair did not leave a noticeable impression on regional cooperation.

44. Quoted in Goodman 1996, 593.

45. For example, Thailand, Cambodia, Laos, and Vietnam formed the Mekong River Commission in 1995 and the Mekong Basin Development Cooperation in 1996 (Dosch 2007, 118).

46. ASEAN's score ranges from 0.27 to 0.36, with an average of 0.31. Compare this to the average of 0.43 for the entire sample.

47. Most members suffered a setback in the aftermath of the 1997 financial crisis but recovered in a matter of several years.

48. The Thai-Cambodian dispute, which appears to be fueled by domestic instability in both countries (Haywood 2011), is perhaps an exception to this general rule.

49. For a broader critique of these approaches, see Nesadurai 2009.

REFERENCES

Abbott, Kenneth W., and Duncan Snidal. 1998. "Why States Act through Formal International Organizations." *Journal of Conflict Resolution* 42:3–32.

Abbott, Kenneth, and Duncan Snidal. 2000. "Hard and Soft Law in International Governance." *International Organization* 54:421–56.

Acharya, Amitav. 1998. "Collective Identity and Conflict Management in Southeast Asia." In *Security Communities in Comparative Perspective*, edited by Emanuel Adler and Michael N. Barnett, 198–227. Cambridge: Cambridge University Press.

Acharya, Amitav. 2000. *The Quest for Identity: International Relations of Southeast Asia.* Singapore: Oxford University Press.

Acharya, Amitav. 2001. *Constructing a Security Community in Southeast Asia: ASEAN and the Problem of Regional Order.* London: Routledge.

Acharya, Amitav. 2007. "The Emerging Regional Architecture of World Politics." *World Politics* 59:629–52.

Acharya, Amitav, and Alastair Iain Johnston, eds. 2007. *Crafting Cooperation: Regional International Institutions in Comparative Perspective.* Cambridge: Cambridge University Press.

Adler, Emanuel, and Michael N. Barnett, eds. 1998. *Security Communities in Comparative Perspective.* Cambridge: Cambridge University Press.

African Development Bank. 2000. *African Development Report 2000: Regional Integration in Africa.* Oxford: Oxford University Press.

Agence France Presse. 1996. "Andean Community to Speed Up Integration Process." March 11.

Agence France Presse. 2006. "ECOWAS Urges 'Maximum Restraint' in Benin-Burkina Border Crisis." January 31.

Aggarwal, Vinod K. 1998. *Institutional Design for a Complex World: Bargaining, Linkages, and Nesting.* Ithaca: Cornell University Press.

Aggarwal, Vinod K., and Min Gyo Koo, eds. 2008. *Asia's New Institutional Architecture: Evolving Structures for Managing Trade, Financial, and Security Relations.* Berlin: Springer.

Alford, Peter. 1999. "Talks Aim to Soothe Border Tensions." *Australian,* February 12.

Amer, Ramses. 1998. "Expanding ASEAN's Conflict Management Framework in Southeast Asia: The Border Dispute Dimension." *Asian Journal of Political Science* 6:33–56.

Antolik, Michael. 1990. *ASEAN and the Diplomacy of Accommodation*. New York: M. E. Sharpe.

Axelrod, Robert, and Robert O. Keohane. 1986. "Achieving Cooperation under Anarchy: Strategies and Institutions." In *Cooperation under Anarchy*, edited by Kenneth A. Oye, 226–54. Princeton: Princeton University Press.

Aydin, Aysegul. 2010. "The Deterrent Effects of Economic Integration." *Journal of Peace Research* 47:523–33.

Baccini, Leonardo. Forthcoming. "Democratization and Trade Policy: An Empirical Analysis of Developing Countries." *European Journal of International Relations*.

Bach, Daniel C. 1990. "Francophone Regional Organizations and ECOWAS." In *West African Regional Cooperation and Development*, edited by Julius Emeka Okolo and Stephen Wright, 53–66. Boulder: Westview.

Bach, Daniel C. 1997. "Institutional Crisis and the Search for New Models." In *Regional Integration and Cooperation in West Africa: A Multidimensional Perspective*, edited by Real Lavergne, 77–101. Ottawa: Africa World Press and International Development Research Centre.

Baier, Scott L., and Jeffrey H. Bergstrand. 2007. "Do Free Trade Agreements Actually Increase Members' International Trade?" *Journal of International Economics* 71:72–95.

Balassa, Bela. 1961. *The Theory of Economic Integration*. Homewood, IL: Richard D. Irwin.

Barbieri, Katherine. 2002. *The Liberal Illusion: Does Trade Promote Peace?* Ann Arbor: University of Michigan Press.

Barnett, Michael, and F. Gregory Gause III. 1998. "Caravans in Opposite Directions: Society, State, and the Development of a Community in the Gulf Cooperation Council." In *Security Communities*, edited by Emanuel Adler and Michael Barnett, 161–97. Cambridge: Cambridge University Press.

BBC. 1986. *British Broadcasting Corporation Worldwide Monitoring*. "ANAD Communiqué on Meeting on Burkina Faso-Mali Dispute and Ceasefire." January 1.

BBC. 1999. *British Broadcasting Corporation Summary of World Broadcasts*. "Andean Community Gives Venezuela 30 Days to Lift Ban on Colombian Trucks." July 20.

BBC. 2000a. *British Broadcasting Corporation Worldwide Monitoring*. "Guyana Wants Caribbean Community to Impose Sanctions Against Suriname." June 21.

BBC. 2000b. *British Broadcasting Corporation Summary of World Broadcasts*. "Minister Seeks to Ease Tension with Venezuela on Cargo Transhipment." November 4.

BBC. 2004. *British Broadcasting Corporation Monitoring Latin America*. "CARICOM Confident Barbados-Trinidad Fishing Dispute will be Settled Amicably." February 13.

BBC. 2005. *British Broadcasting Corporation Worldwide Monitoring*. "Algerian Minister Says Morocco's Boycott of Maghreb Summit Unjustified." May 25.

BBC. 2007. *British Broadcasting Corporation Monitoring Africa*. "Subregional Body to Discuss Guinea-Sierra Leone Border Conflict." April 30.

Bearce, David H. 2003. "Grasping the Commercial Institutional Peace." *International Studies Quarterly* 47:347–70.

Bearce, David H., and Stacy Bondanella. 2007. "Intergovernmental Organizations, Socialization, and Member-State Interest Convergence." *International Organization* 61:703–33.

Bearce, David H., and Sawa Omori. 2005. "How Do Commercial Institutions Promote Peace?" *Journal of Peace Research* 42:659–78.

Beltramino, Juan Carlos M. 2005. "The Building of Mercosur: A Continuous Negotiation Process." In *Peace versus Justice: Negotiating Forward- and Backward-Looking Outcomes,* edited by I. William Zartman and Victor Kremenyuk, 177–97. Lanham, MD: Rowman and Littlefield.

Bennett, D. Scott, and Allan Stam. 2000. "*EUGene:* A Conceptual Manual." *International Interactions* 26:179–204.

Bercovitch, Jacob. 1997. "Mediation in International Conflict: An Overview." In *Peacemaking in International Conflict: Methods and Techniques,* edited by I. William Zartman and J. Lewis Rasmusen, 125–53. Washington, DC: United States Institute of Peace.

Bercovitch, Jacob, and Allison Houston. 1996. "The Study of International Mediation: Theoretical Issues and Empirical Evidence." In *Resolving International Conflicts: The Theory and Practice of Mediation,* edited by Jacob Bercovitch, 11–35. Boulder: Lynne Rienner.

Berridge, G. R. 2002. *Diplomacy: Theory and Practice.* 2nd ed. New York: Palgrave Macmillan.

Best, Edward. 1991. "Latin American Integration in the 1990s: Redefinition amid Uncertainty." *International Review of Administrative Sciences* 57:611–40.

Binh, Nguyen Phuong, and Luan Thuy Duong. 2001. "Expectations and Experiences of the New Members: A Vietnamese Perspective." In *Reinventing ASEAN,* edited by Simon S. C. Tay, Jesus P. Estanislao, and Hadi Soesastro, 185–205. Singapore: Institute of Southeast Asian Studies.

Boehmer, Charles, Erik Gartzke, and Tim Nordstrom. 2004. "Do Intergovernmental Organizations Promote Peace?" *World Politics* 57:1–38.

Boehmer, Charles, and Tim Nordstrom. 2008. "Intergovernmental Organization Membership: Examining Political Community and the Attributes of International Organizations." *International Interactions* 34:282–309.

Bourenane, Naceur. 2002. "Regional Integration in Africa: Status and Perspectives." In *Regional Integration in Africa,* edited by Jorge Braga de Macedo and Omar Kabbaj, 17–46. Paris: Organization for Economic Cooperation and Development.

Bouzas, Roberto, and Hernan Soltz. 2001. "Institutions and Regional Integration: The Case of Mercosur." In *Regional Integration in Latin America and the Caribbean: The Political Economy of Open Regionalism,* edited by Victor Bulmer-Thomas, 95–118. London: Institute of Latin American Studies.

Brown, Michael E. 1996. "The Causes and Regional Dimensions of Internal Conflict." In *The International Dimensions of Internal Conflict,* edited by Michael E. Brown, 571–601. Cambridge, MA: MIT Press.

Brown, M. Leann. 1994. *Developing Countries and Regional Economic Cooperation.* Westport, CT: Praeger.

Bueno de Mesquita, Bruce. 1981. *The War Trap.* New Haven: Yale University Press.

Bulmer-Thomas, Victor. 1997. "Regional Integration in Latin America since 1985: Open Regionalism and Globalisation." In *Economic Integration Worldwide,* edited by Ali M. El-Agraa, 253–77. New York: St. Martin's Press.

Bulmer-Thomas, Victor. 1998. "The Central American Common Market: From Closed to Open Regionalism." *World Development* 26:313–22.

Bulmer-Thomas, Victor, Rudolfo Cerdas, Eugenia Gallarado, and Michael Seligson. 1992. *Central American Integration: Report for the Commission of the European Community.* Miami: University of Miami North-South Center.

Busse, Nikolas. 1999. "Constructivism and Southeast Asian Security." *Pacific Review* 12:39–60.

Büthe, Tim, and Helen V. Milner. 2008. "The Politics of Foreign Direct Investment into Developing Countries: Increasing FDI through International Trade Agreements?" *American Journal of Political Science* 52:741–62.

Buzan, Barry. 1991. *People, State, and Fear: An Agenda for International Security Studies in the Post–Cold Era.* 2nd ed. London: Harvester Wheatsheaf.

Buzan, Barry, and Ole Wæver. 2003. *Regions and Powers: The Structure of International Security.* Cambridge: Cambridge University Press.

Caballero-Anthony, Melli. 1998. "Mechanisms of Dispute Settlement: The ASEAN Experience." *Contemporary Southeast Asia* 20:38–67.

Caporaso, James. 1998. "Regional Integration Theory: Understanding Our Past and Anticipating the Future." In *Supranational Governance: The Institutionalization of the European Union,* edited by Wayne Sandholtz and Alec Stone Sweet, 334–51. New York: Oxford University Press.

Castro, Amado A. 1981. "Economic Cooperation and the Development of an ASEAN Culture." In *ASEAN: Identity, Development, and Culture,* edited by R. P. Anand and Purification Valera-Quisumbing, 226–44. Quezon City, Philippines: University of the Philippines Law Center and the East-West Center Culture Learning Institute.

Chanthunya, Charles L. 2001. "The COMESA Free Trade Area: Concept, Challenges, and Opportunities." In *The Free Trade Area of the Common Market for Eastern and Southern Africa,* edited by Victor Murinde, 13–29. Aldershot: Ashgate.

Chatterjee, Srikanta. 1990. "ASEAN Economic Co-operation in the 1980s and the 1990s." In *ASEAN into the 1990s,* edited by Alison Broinowski, 58–82. London: Macmillan.

Checkel, Jeffrey T. 2005. "International Institutions and Socialization in Europe: Introduction and Framework." *International Organization* 59:801–26.

Checkel, Jeffrey T. 2007. "Social Mechanisms and Regional Cooperation: Are Europe and the EU Really All That Different?" In *Crafting Cooperation: Regional International Institutions in Comparative Perspective,* edited by Amitav Acharya and Alastair Iain Johnston, 221–43. Cambridge: Cambridge University Press.

Choi, Young Jong, and James A. Caporaso. 2002. "Comparative Regional Integration." In *Handbook of International Relations,* edited by Walter Carlsnaes, Thomas Risse, and Beth A. Simmons, 480–99. London: Sage.

Choong, William. 2008. "Asean Needs to Find Ways to Resolve Disputes, Say Experts." *Straits Time* (Singapore), July 24.

Cobden, Richard. 1868. *Political Writings.* Vol. 1. New York: D. Appleton.

Coelho, Tulio, and Ana Luiza Ferreira. 2004. "Legal Developments Brazil." *Legal Week Global,* February 27.

Cohen, Benjamin J. 1997. "The Political Economy of Currency Regions." In *The Political Economy of Regionalism,* edited by Edward D. Mansfield and Helen V. Milner, 50–76. New York: Columbia University Press.

Collins, Alan. 2003a. "ASEAN: Challenges from Within and Without." In *Asia-Pacific Economic and Security Cooperation: New Regional Agendas,* edited by Christopher M. Dent, 136–51. New York: Palgrave Macmillan.

Collins, Alan. 2003b. *Security and Southeast Asia: Domestic, Regional, and Global Issues.* Boulder: Lynne Rienner.

Common Market of Eastern and Southern Africa. 2005. *COMESA Annual Report 2005.* Lusaka: COMESA Secretariat.

Copeland, Dale C. 1996. "Economic Interdependence and War: A Theory of Trade Expectations." *International Security* 20:5–41.

Coppedge, Michael. 1999. "Thickening Thin Concepts and Theories: Combining Large N and Small in Comparative Politics." *Comparative Politics* 31:465–76.

Crescenzi, Mark J. C. 2005. *Economic Interdependence and Conflict in World Politics.* Lanham, MD: Lexington Books.

Dassel, Kurt, and Eric Reinhardt. 1999. "Domestic Strife and the Initiation of Violence at Home and Abroad." *American Journal of Political Science* 43:56–85.

Davidson, Paul J. 2003. *ASEAN: The Evolving Legal Framework for Economic Cooperation.* Singapore: Times Academic.

Davies, Graeme A. M. 2002. "Domestic Strife and the Initiation of International Conflicts: A Directed Dyad Analysis, 1950–1982." *Journal of Conflict Resolution* 46:672–92.

Davis, Christina L. 2004. "International Institutions and Issue Linkage: Building Support for Agricultural Trade Liberalization." *American Political Science Review* 98:153–69.

de la Torre, Augusto, and Margaret R. Kelly. 1992. *Regional Trade Arrangements.* Occasional Paper 93. Washington: International Monetary Fund.

Denoon, David B. H., and Evelyn Colbert. 1998/99. "Challenges for the Association of Southeast Asian Nations (ASEAN)." *Pacific Affairs* 71:505–23.

Deutsch, Karl W., Sidney A. Burrell, Robert A. Kann, Maurice Lee Jr., Martin Lichterman, Raymond E. Lindgern, Francis L. Loewenheim, and Richard W. Van Wagenen. 1957. *Political Community in the North Atlantic Area.* Princeton: Princeton University Press.

Diez, Thomas, Mathias Albert, and Stephen Stetter. 2008. *The European Union and Border Conflicts: The Power of Integration and Association.* Cambridge: Cambridge University Press.

Domínguez, Jorge I. 2007. "International Cooperation in Latin America: The Design of Regional Institutions by Slow Accretion." In *Crafting Cooperation: Regional International Institutions in Comparative Perspective*, edited by Amitav Acharya and Alastair Iain Johnston, 83–128. Cambridge: Cambridge University Press.

Domke, William K. 1988. *War and the Changing Global System*. New Haven: Yale University Press.

Dorussen, Han, and Hugh Ward. 2008. "Intergovernmental Organizations and the Kantian Peace." *Journal of Conflict Resolution* 52:189–212.

Dorussen, Han, and Hugh Ward. 2010. "Trade Networks and the Kantian Peace." *Journal of Peace Research* 47:29–42.

Dosch, Jörn. 2003. "Sub-Regional Co-operation in the Mekong Valley: Implications for Regional Security." In *Asia-Pacific Economic and Security Cooperation: New Regional Agendas,* edited by Christopher M. Dent, 152–66. New York: Palgrave Macmillan.

Dosch, Jörn. 2007. *The Changing Dynamics of Southeast Asian Politics*. Boulder: Lynne Rienner.

Downs, George W., David M. Rocke, and Peter M. Barsoom. 1996. "Is the Good News about Compliance Good News about Cooperation?" *International Organization* 50:379–406.

Dunn, David H. 1996. "How Useful Is Summitry?" In *Diplomacy at the Highest Level: The Evolution of International Summitry,* edited by David H. Dunn, 249–68. New York: Macmillan.

Eaton, Sarah, and Richard Stubbs. 2006. "Is ASEAN Powerful? Neorealist versus Constructivist Approaches to Power in Southeast Asia." *Pacific Review* 19:135–55.

ECO (Economic Cooperation Organization). 2000. *Annual Economic Report 2000*. Tehran: ECO Secretariat.

Economic Commission for Africa. 2004. *Assessing Regional Integration in Africa*. Addis Ababa: Economic Commission for Africa.

Eilstrup-Sangiovanni, Mette. 2008. "Uneven Power and the Pursuit of Peace: How Regional Power Transitions Motivate Integration." *Comparative European Politics* 6:102–42.

The Economist. 2004. "Back to Playing Cricket." January 6.

Eilstrup-Sangiovanni, Mette, and Daniel Verdier. 2005. "European Integration as a Solution to War." *European Journal of International Relations* 11:99–135.

El-Agraa, Ali M., and Shelton M. A. Nicholls. 1997. "The Caribbean Community and Common Market." In *Economic Integration Worldwide,* edited by Ali M. El-Agraa, 278–96. New York: St. Martin's.

Emmerson, Donald K. 2005. "Security, Community, and Democracy in Southeast Asia: Analyzing ASEAN." *Japanese Journal of Political Science* 6:165–85.

Ero, Comfort, Waheguru Pal Singh Sidhu, and Augustine Toure. 2001. *Toward a Pax West Africana: Building Peace in a Troubled Sub-region*. Report on the IPA-ECOWAS seminar in Abuja, Nigeria, September 27–29, 2001. New York: International Peace Academy.

Fawn, Rick. 2009. "'Regions' and Their Study: Wherefrom, What For, and Where To?" *Review of International Studies* 35:5–34.

Fearon, James D. 1995. "Rationalist Explanations for War." *International Organization* 49:379–414.

Feld, Werner J., Robert S. Jordan, and Leon Hurwitz. 1994. *International Organizations: A Comparative Approach.* 3rd ed. Westport, CT: Praeger.

Fifield, Russell H. 1979. *National and Regional Interests in ASEAN: Competition and Co-operation in International Politics.* Occasional Paper 57. Singapore: Institute of Southeast Asian Studies.

Foroutan, Faezeh. 1993. "Regional Integration in Sub-Saharan Africa: Past Experience and Future Prospects." In *New Dimensions in Regional Integration,* edited by Jaime de Melo and Arvind Panagariya, 234–71. New York: Cambridge University Press.

Foroutan, Faezeh. 1998. "Does Membership in a Regional Preferential Trade Arrangement Make a Country More or Less Protectionist?" *World Economy* 21:305–35.

Fortna, Virginia P. 2004. *Peace Time: Cease-Fire Agreements and the Durability of Peace.* Princeton: Princeton University Press.

Frankel, Jeffery A. 1997. *Regional Trading Blocs in the World Economic System.* Washington, DC: Institute for International Economics.

Frost, Frank. 1990. "ASEAN since 1967: Origins, Evolution, and Recent Developments." In *ASEAN into the 1990s,* edited by Alison Broinowski, 1–31. London: Macmillan.

Funabashi, Yoichi. 1995. *Asia Pacific Fusion: Japan's Role in APEC.* Washington, DC: Institute for International Economics.

Gale, Bruce. 2009. "Playing Hardball." *Straits Time* (Singapore), July 4.

Ganesan, N. 1994. "Taking Stock of Post–Cold War Developments in ASEAN." *Security Dialogue* 25:457–68.

Ganesan, N. 1995. "Rethinking ASEAN as a Security Community in Southeast Asia." *Asian Affairs: An American Review* 21:210–26.

Ganesan, N. 1999. *Bilateral Tensions in Post–Cold War ASEAN.* Singapore: Institute of Southeast Asian Studies.

Garrett, Geoffrey, and Barry R. Weingast. 1993. "Ideas, Interests, and Institutions: Constructing the European Community's Internal Market." In *Ideas and Foreign Policy: Beliefs, Institutions, and Political Change,* edited by Judith Goldstein and Robert O. Keohane, 173–206. Ithaca: Cornell University Press.

Gartzke, Erik. 2003. "The Classical Liberals Were Just Lucky: A Few Thoughts about Interdependence and Peace." In *Economic Interdependence and International Conflict: New Perspectives on an Enduring Debate,* edited by Edward D. Mansfield and Brian M. Pollins, 96–110. Ann Arbor: University of Michigan Press.

Gartzke, Erik. 2006. *The Affinity of Nations Index, 1946–2002.* Version 4.0. http://dss.ucsd.edu/~egartzke/htmlpages/data.html (accessed October 21, 2011).

Gartzke, Erik. 2007. "The Capitalist Peace." *American Journal of Political Science* 51:166–91.

Gartzke, Erik, Quan Li, and Charles Boehmer. 2001. "Investing in the Peace: Economic Interdependence and International Conflict." *International Organization* 55:391–438.

Gelpi, Christopher. 1999. "Alliances as Instruments of Intra-Allies Control." In *Imperfect Unions: Security Institutions over Time and Space,* edited by Helga Haftendorn, Robert O. Keohane, and Celeste Wallander, 107–39. Oxford: Oxford University Press.

Genna, Gaspare M. 2008. "Power Preponderance, Institutional Homogeneity, and the Likelihood of Regional Integration." In *Regional Integration Fifty Years after the Treaty of Rome: The EU, Asia, Africa, and the Americas,* edited by Joaquin Roy and Roberto Dominguez, 19–34. Coral Gables, FL: Jean Monnet Chair of the University of Miami and Miami-Florida European Union Center of Excellence.

George, Alexander L., and Andrew Bennett. 2005. *Case Studies and Theory Development in the Social Sciences.* Cambridge, MA: MIT Press.

Gerring, John. 2004. "What Is a Case Study and What Is It Good for?" *American Political Science Review* 98:341–54.

Ghosn, Faten, Glenn Palmer, and Stuart A. Bremer. 2004. "The MID3 Data Set: Procedures, Coding Rules, and Description." *Conflict Management and Peace Science* 21:133–54.

Gilady, Lilach, and Bruce Russett. 2002. "Peacemaking and Conflict Resolution." In *Handbook of International Relations,* edited by Walter Carlsnaes, Thomas Risse, and Beth A. Simmons, 392–408. London: Sage.

Gilpin, Robert. 1981. *War and Change in World Politics.* Cambridge: Cambridge University Press.

Girvan, Norman. 2008. "'Learning to Integrate': The Experience of Monitoring the CARICOM Single Market and Economy." In *Governing Regional Integration for Development: Monitoring Experiences, Methods, and Prospects,* edited by Philippe De Lombaerde, Antoni Estevadeordal, and Kati Souninen, 31–56. Aldershot: Ashgate.

Glaser, Charles L. 1994/95. "Realists as Optimists: Cooperation as Self-Help." *International Security* 19:50–90.

Gleditsch, Kristian S. 2002. *All International Politics Is Local: The Diffusion of Conflict, Integration, and Democratization.* Ann Arbor: University of Michigan Press.

Gleditsch, Nils P., and Havard Hegre. 1997. "Peace and Democracy: Three Levels of Analysis." *Journal of Conflict Resolution* 41:283–310.

Gleditsch, Nils Peter, Peter Wallensteen, Mikael Eriksson, Margareta Sollenberg, and Harvard Strand. 2002. "Armed Conflict 1946–2001: A New Dataset." *Journal of Peace Research* 39:615–37.

Goldstein, Andrea, and Njuguna S. Ndung'u. 2001. "New Forms of Co-operation and Integration in Emerging Africa: Regional Integration Experience in the Eastern African Region." Technical Paper 171, OECD Development Centre, Paris.

Goldstein, Judith, and Joanne Gowa. 2002. "US National Power and the Post-War Trading Regime." *World Trade Review* 1:153–70.

Goodman, Allan E. 1996. "Vietnam and ASEAN: Who Would Have Thought It Possible?" *Asian Survey* 36:592–600.

Gordon, Bernard K. 1966. *The Dimensions of Conflict in Southeast Asia.* New Jersey: Prentice Hall.

Gortzak, Yoav, Yoram Z. Haftel, and Kevin Sweeney. 2005. "Offense-Defense Theory: An Empirical Assessment." *Journal of Conflict Resolution* 49:67–89.

Gowa, Joanne. 1994. *Allies, Adversaries, and International Trade.* Princeton: Princeton University Press.

Gowa, Joanne, and Edward D. Mansfield. 1993. "Power Politics and International Trade." *American Political Science Review* 87:408–20.

Grieco, Joseph M. 1988. "Realist Theory and the Problem of International Cooperation: Analysis with an Amended Prisoners' Dilemma Model." *Journal of Politics* 50:600–624.

Grieco, Joseph M. 1993. "Anarchy and the Limits of Cooperation: A Realist Critique of the Newest Liberal Institutionalism." In *Neorealism and Neoliberalism: The Contemporary Debate,* edited by David A. Baldwin, 116–40. New York: Columbia University Press.

Grieco, Joseph M. 1997. "Systemic Sources of Variation in Regional Institutionalization in Western Europe, East Asia, and the Americas." In *The Political Economy of Regionalism,* edited by Edward D. Mansfield and Helen V. Milner, 164–87. New York: Columbia University Press.

Gruber, Lloyd. 2000. *Ruling the World: Power Politics and the Rise of Supranational Institutions.* Princeton: Princeton University Press.

Gutierrez, Estrella. 1997. "Andean Community: Last Ditch Effort to Keep Peru In." *Inter Press Services,* April 25.

Gutner, Tamar, and Alexander Thompson. 2010. "The Politics of IO Performance: A Framework." *Review of International Organizations* 5:227–48.

Haacke, Jürgen. 2003. *ASEAN's Diplomatic and Security Culture: Origins, Development, and Prospect.* London: RoutledgeCurzon.

Haas, Ernest B. 1964. *Beyond the Nation-State.* Stanford: Stanford University Press.

Haas, Ernest B. 1966. "International Integration and the Universal Process." In *International Political Communities: An Anthology,* 93–130. New York: Anchor Books.

Haftel, Yoram Z. 2004a. "From the Outside Looking In: The Effect of Trading Blocs on Trade Disputes in the GATT/WTO." *International Studies Quarterly* 48:121–42.

Haftel, Yoram Z. 2004b. "Violent Conflict and Regional Institutionalization: A Virtuous Circle?" PhD diss., Ohio State University.

Haftel, Yoram Z. 2007. "Designing for Peace: Regional Integration Arrangements, Institutional Variation, and Militarized Inter-state Disputes." *International Organization* 61:217–37.

Haftel, Yoram Z. 2010. "Conflict, Regional Cooperation, and Foreign Capital: Indonesian Foreign Policy and the Formation of ASEAN." *Foreign Policy Analysis* 6:87–106.

Haftel, Yoram Z. 2011. "Commerce and Institutions: Trade, Scope, and the Design of Regional Economic Organizations." Paper presented at the annual convention of the International Studies Association, Montreal, Canada, March 15–18.

Haftel, Yoram Z., and Alexander Thompson. 2006. "The Independence of International Organizations: Concept and Applications." *Journal of Conflict Resolution* 50:253–75.

Haggard, Stephan. 1997. "Regionalism in Asia and the Americas." In *The Political Economy of Regionalism,* edited by Edward D. Mansfield and Helen V. Milner, 20–49. New York: Columbia University Press.

Haller-Trost, R. 1995. *The Territorial Dispute between Indonesia and Malaysia over Pulau Sipadan and Pulau Ligitan in the Celebes Sea: A Study in International Law.* Boundary and Territory Briefings 2, no. 2. Durham: International Boundaries Research Unit, University of Durham.

Hansen, Holley, Sara McLaughlin Mitchell, and Stephen C. Nemeth. 2008. "IO Mediation of Inter-state Conflicts: Moving Beyond the Global vs. Regional Dichotomy." *Journal of Conflict Resolution* 52:295–325.

Hawkins, Darren G., David A. Lake, Daniel L. Nielson, and Michael J. Tierney. 2006. "Delegation under Anarchy: States, International Organizations, and the Principal-Agent Theory." In *Delegation and Agency in International Organizations,* edited by Darren G. Hawkins, David A. Lake, Daniel L. Nielson, and Michael J. Tierney, 3–38. Cambridge: Cambridge University Press.

Haywood, Holly. 2011. "Examining ASEAN Capacity in the Context of the Thai-Cambodian Border Dispute." *NTS Alert.* September (issue 1). Singapore: RSIS Centre for Non-Traditional Security (NTS) Studies for NTS-Asia.

Henderson, Jeannie. 1999. *Reassessing ASEAN.* Adelphi Paper 328. London: International Institute for Strategic Studies.

Heston, Alan, Robert Summers, and Bettina Aten. 2002. *Penn World Table.* Version 6.1. Philadelphia: Center for International Comparisons at the University of Pennsylvania.

Hettne, Bjorn. 1999. "Rethinking the 'New Regionalism' in the Context of Globalization." In *Globalism and the New Regionalism,* edited by Bjorn Hettne, Andras Inotai, and Osvaldo Sunkel, 1–24. London: MacMillan.

Hicks, Raymond, and Soo Yeon Kim. 2010. "Credible Commitments through RTAs and Their Effects on Trade: A Study of Asia's Reciprocal Trade Agreements." Paper presented at the Workshop on the Politics of Trade Agreements: Theory, Measurement, and Empirical Applications, Princeton, NJ, April 30–May 1.

Hooghe, Liesbet. 2005. "Several Roads Lead to International Norms, but Few via International Socialization: A Case Study of the European Commission." *International Organization* 59:861–98.

Hufbauer, Gary C., and Jeffrey J. Schott. 1994. *Western Hemisphere Economic Integration.* Washington, DC: Institute for International Economics.

Hund, Markus. 2002. "From 'Neighbourhood Watch Group' to Community?" *Australian Journal of International Affairs* 56:99–122.

Hurrell, Andrew. 1998. "An Emerging Security Community in South America." In *Security Communities in Comparative Perspective,* edited by Emanuel Adler and Michael N. Barnett, 228–64. Cambridge: Cambridge University Press.

Hurrell, Andrew. 2001. "The Politics of Regional Integration in Mercosur." In *Regional Integration in Latin America and the Caribbean: The Political Economy of Open Regionalism,* edited by Victor Bulmer-Thomas, 194–211. London: Institute of Latin American Studies.

Huth, Paul K. 1997. "Reputations and Deterrence: A Theoretical and Empirical Assessment." *Security Studies* 7:72–99.

Huxley, Tim. 1990. "ASEAN Security Co-operation: Past, Present, and Future." In *ASEAN into the 1990s,* edited by Alison Broinowski, 83–111. London: Macmillan.

Huxley, Tim. 1996. "Southeast Asia in the Study of International Relations: The Rise and Decline of a Region." *Pacific Review* 9:199–228.

Ikenberry, John G. 2001. *After Victory: Institutions, Strategic Restraint, and the Rebuilding of Order after Major Wars.* Princeton: Princeton University Press.

IMF (International Monetary Fund). 1994. *International Trade Policies: The Uruguay Round and Beyond.* Vol. 2. Washington, DC: IMF.

Indorf, Hans H. 1975. *ASEAN: Problems and Prospects.* Singapore: Institute of Southeast Asian Studies.

Indorf, Hans H. 1984. *Impediments to Regionalism in Southeast Asia: Bilateral Constraints among ASEAN Member States.* Singapore: Institute of Southeast Asian Studies.

Institute for the Integration of Latin America and the Caribbean (INTAL). 2000. *Central American Report No. 1.* Buenos Aires: INTAL.

Irvine, David. 1982. "Making Haste Less Slowly: ASEAN from 1975." In *Understanding ASEAN,* edited by Alison Broinowski, 37–75. New York: St. Martin's.

Irvine, Roger. 1982. "The Formative Years of ASEAN, 1967–1975." In *Understanding ASEAN,* edited by Alison Broinowski, 8–36. New York: St. Martin's.

Jacob, Paul. 1996. "Suharto to Meet Mahathir on Sipadan Dispute." *Straits Time* (Singapore), September 23.

Jacobson, Harold K. 1984. *Networks of Interdependence: International Organizations and the Global Political System.* 2nd ed. New York: Alfred A. Knopf.

Jaggers, Keith, and Ted R. Gurr. 1995. "Tracking Democracy's Third Wave with the Polity III Data." *Journal of Peace Research* 32:469–82.

Jakarta Post. 1999. "ASEAN Pledges Solidarity and Unity in Spite of Rows." July 23.

Japan Economic Newswire. 2008. "ASEAN Ministers Meet to Offer Mediation on Thailand-Cambodia Dispute." July 22.

Jenkins, Carolyn. 2001. "New Forms of Co-operation and Integration in Emerging Africa: Integration and Co-operation in Southern Africa." Technical Paper 172, OECD Development Centre, Paris.

Jervis, Robert. 1999. "Realism, Neoliberalism, and Cooperation." *International Security* 24:42–63.

Jetly, Rajshree. 2003. "Conflict Management Strategies in ASEAN: Perspectives for SAARC." *Pacific Review* 16:53–76.

Johnston, Alastair Iain. 2001. "Treating International Institutions as Social Environments." *International Studies Quarterly* 45:487–515.

Jones, Daniel M., Stuart A. Bremer, and J. David Singer. 1996. "Militarized Interstate Disputes, 1816–1992: Rationale, Coding Rules, and Empirical Patterns." *Conflict Management and Peace Science* 15:459–82.

Jones, David M., and Michael L. R. Smith. 2002. "ASEAN's Imitation Community." *Orbis* 46:93–109.

Jorgensen-Dahl, Arnfinn. 1982. *Regional Organization and Order in South-East Asia.* Hong Kong: Macmillan.

Jönsson, Christer. 2002. "Diplomacy, Bargaining, and Negotiation." In *Handbook of International Relations,* edited by Walter Carlsnaes, Thomas Risse, and Beth A. Simmons, 213–34. London: Sage.

Kacowicz, Arie M. 1998. *Zones of Peace in the Third World: South America and West Africa in Comparative Perspective.* Albany: State University of New York Press.

Kahler, Miles. 1995. *International Institutions and the Political Economy of Integration.* Washington, DC: Brookings Institution Press.

Kahler, Miles. 2000. "Conclusion: The Causes and Consequences of Legalization." *International Organization* 54:661–83.

Katzenstein, Peter J. 1997. "Introduction: Asian Regionalism in Comparative Perspective." In *Network Power: Japan and Asia,* edited by Peter J. Katzenstein and Takashi Shiraishi, 1–44. Ithaca: Cornell University Press.

Katzenstein, Peter J. 2005. *World of Regions: Asia and Europe in the American Imperium.* Ithaca: Cornell University Press.

Kelegama, Saman. 2001. "Bangkok Agreement and BIMSTEC: Crawling Regional Economic Groupings in Asia." *Journal of Asian Economics* 12:105–21.

Keohane, Robert O. 1984. *After Hegemony: Cooperation and Discord in the World Political Economy.* Princeton: Princeton University Press.

Keohane, Robert O., and Lisa L. Martin. 1995. "The Promise of Institutionalist Theory." *International Security* 20:39–51.

Keohane, Robert O., Andrew Moravcsik, and Anne-Marie Slaughter. 2000. "Legalized Dispute Resolution: Inter-state and Transnational." *International Organization* 54:457–88.

Keohane, Robert O., and Joseph S. Nye. 2001. *Power and Interdependence.* 3rd ed. New York: Longman.

Keshk, Omar M. G., Brian M. Pollins, and Rafael Reuveny. 2004. "Trade Still Follows the Flag: The Primacy of Politics in a Simultaneous Model of Interdependence and Armed Conflict." *Journal of Politics* 66:1155–179.

Khandelwal, Padamja. 2004. "COMESA and SADC: Prospects and Challenges for Regional Trade Integration." Working Paper 04/227, International Monetary Fund, Washington, DC.

Khong, Yuen Foong. 1997. "ASEAN and the Southeast Asian Security Complex." In *Regional Orders: Building Security in a New World,* edited by David A. Lake and Patrick M. Morgan, 318–39. University Park: Pennsylvania State University Press.

Khong, Yuen Foong, and Helen E. S. Nesadurai. 2007. "Hanging Together, Institutional Design and Cooperation in Southeast Asia: AFTA and the ARF." In *Crafting Cooperation: Regional International Institutions in Global Politics,* edited by

Amitav Acharya and Alastair Iain Johnstone, 32–82. Cambridge: Cambridge University Press.

Kivimäki, Timo. 2001. "The Long Peace of ASEAN." *Journal of Peace Research* 38:5–25.

Kivimäki, Timo. 2008. "Power, Interest, or Culture: Is There a Paradigm That Explains ASEAN's Political Role Best?" *Pacific Review* 21:431–50.

Kono, Daniel Y. 2007a. "Making Anarchy Work: International Legal Institutions and Trade Cooperation." *Journal of Politics* 69:746–59.

Kono, Daniel Y. 2007b. "When Do Trade Blocs Trade?" *International Studies Quarterly* 51:165–81.

Koremenos, Barbara. 2005. "Contracting around International Uncertainty." *American Political Science Review* 99:549–65.

Koremenos, Barbara, Charles Lipson, and Duncan Snidal. 2001. "The Rational Design of International Institutions." *International Organization* 55:761–99.

Kurus, Bilson. 1993. "Understanding ASEAN: Benefits and Raison d'Etre." *Asian Survey* 33:819–31.

Kydd, Andrew H. 2003. "Which Side Are You On? Bias, Credibility, and Mediation." *American Journal of Political Science* 47:597–611.

Kydd, Andrew H. 2005. *Trust and Mistrust in International Relations.* Princeton: Princeton University Press.

Kydd, Andrew H. 2006. "When Can Mediators Build Trust?" *American Political Science Review* 100:449–62.

Lake, David A. 1997. "Regional Security Complexes: A Systems Approach." In *Regional Orders: Building Security in a New World,* edited by David A. Lake and Patrick M. Morgan, 45–67. University Park: Pennsylvania State University Press.

Lake, David A. 1999. *Entangling Relations: American Foreign Policy and Its Century.* Princeton: Princeton University Press.

Lake, David A., and Patrick M. Morgan, eds. 1997. *Regional Orders: Building Security in a New World.* University Park: Pennsylvania State University Press.

Langhammer, Rolf J., and Ulrich Hiemenz. 1990. *Regional Integration among Developing Countries: Opportunities, Obstacles, and Options.* Kieler Studien 232. Tubingen: Mohr.

Laursen, Finn. 2003. "International Regimes or Would-Be Polities? Some Concluding Questions and Remarks." In *Comparative Regional Integration: Theoretical Perspectives,* edited by Finn Laursen, 283–93. Aldershot: Ashgate.

Legrenzi, Matteo. 2003. "The Long Road Ahead: Economic Integration in the Gulf States." *Cooperation South Journal* (United Nations Development Programme), 33–45.

Leifer, Michael. 1989. *ASEAN and the Security of South-East Asia.* London: Routledge.

Leifer, Michael. 1995. "ASEAN as a Model of a Security Community?" In *ASEAN in a Changed Regional and International Political Economy,* edited by Hadi Soesastro, 129–42. Jakarta: Centre for Strategic and International Studies.

Leifer, Michael. 1999. "The ASEAN Peace Process: A Category Mistake." *Pacific Review* 12:25–38.

Lemke, Douglas. 2002. *Regions of War and Peace*. Cambridge: Cambridge University Press.

Levy, Jack S. 2002. "War and Peace." In *Handbook of International Relations*, edited by Walter Carlsnaes, Thomas Risse, and Beth A. Simmons, 350–68. London: Sage.

Levy, Jack S., and Salvatore Ali. 1998. "From Commercial Competition to Strategic Rivalry to War: The Evolution of the Anglo-Dutch Rivalry, 1609–1652." In *The Dynamics of Enduring Rivalries*, edited by Paul Diehl, 29–63. Urbana: University of Illinois Press.

Lewis, Jeffrey. 2000. "The Method of Community in EU Decision-Making and Administrative Rivalry in the Council's Infrastructure." *Journal of European Public Policy* 7:261–89.

Lieberman, Evan S. 2005. "Nested Analysis as a Mixed-Method Strategy for Comparative Research." *American Political Science Review* 99:435–52.

Lim, Hank. 2009. "Regional Trade Agreements and Conflict: The Case of Southeast Asia." In *Regional Trade Integration and Conflict Resolution*, edited by Shaheen Rafi Khan, 102–29. London: Routledge.

Long, J. Scott. 1997. *Regression Models for Categorical and Limited Dependent Variables*. Thousand Oaks, CA: Sage.

Long, J. Scott, and Jeremy Freese. 2006. *Regression Models for Categorical Outcomes Using Stata*. 2nd ed. College Station, TX: Stata Press.

Long, Simon. 2010. "A Sea of Trouble." In "The World in 2011," edited by Daniel Franklin, special edition, *Economist*, 65.

Lyon, Peter. 1969. *War and Peace in South-East Asia*. London: Oxford University Press.

Mace, Gordon. 1994. "The Andean Integration System, 1968–1985." In *The Political Economy of Regional Cooperation: Comparative Case Studies*, edited by W. Andrew Axline, 34–71. Madison: Fairleigh Dickinson University Press.

Mahani, Zainal-Abidin. 2002. "ASEAN Integration: At Risk of Going in Different Directions." *World Economy* 25:1263–77.

Majone, Giandomenico. 2001. "Two Logics of Delegation: Agency and Fiduciary Relations in EU Governance." *European Union Politics* 2:103–22.

Mak, J. N. 2009. "Sovereignty and the Problem of Maritime Cooperation in the South China Sea." In *Security and International Politics in the South China Sea: Towards a Cooperative Management Regime*, edited by Sam Bateman and Ralf Emmers, 110–27. London: Routledge.

Mansfield, Edward D. 1994. *Power, Trade, and War*. Princeton: Princeton University Press.

Mansfield, Edward D. 2003. "Preferential Peace: Why Preferential Trade Arrangements Inhibit Inter-state Conflict." In *Economic Interdependence and International Conflict: New Perspectives on an Enduring Debate*, edited by Edward D. Mansfield and Brian M. Pollins, 222–36. Ann Arbor: University of Michigan Press.

Mansfield, Edward D., and Helen V. Milner. 1999. "The New Wave of Regionalism." *International Organization* 53:529–627.

Mansfield, Edward D., Helen V. Milner, and Jon C. Pevehouse. 2008. "Democracy, Veto Players, and the Depth of Regional Integration." *World Economy* 31:67–96.

Mansfield, Edward D., Helen V. Milner, and B. Peter Rosendorff. 2002. "Why Democracies Cooperate More: Electoral Control and International Trade Agreements." *International Organization* 56:477–513.

Mansfield, Edward D., and Jon C. Pevehouse. 2000. "Trade Blocs, Trade Flows, and International Conflict." *International Organization* 54:775–808.

Mansfield, Edward D., and Jon C. Pevehouse. 2006. "Democratization and International Organizations." *International Organization* 60:137–67.

Mansfield, Edward D., Jon C. Pevehouse, and David H. Bearce. 1999/2000. "Preferential Trading Arrangements and Military Disputes." *Security Studies* 9:96–118.

Mansfield, Edward D., and Brian M. Pollins, eds. 2003. *Economic Interdependence and International Conflict: New Perspectives on an Enduring Debates.* Ann Arbor: University of Michigan Press.

Mansfield, Edward D., and Eric Reinhardt. 2003. "Multilateral Determinants of Regionalism: The Effects of GATT/WTO on the Formation of Preferential Trading Arrangements." *International Organization* 57:829–62.

Mansfield, Edward D., and Eric Reinhardt. 2008. "International Institutions and the Volatility of International Trade." *International Organization* 62:621–52.

Mansfield, Edward D., and Jack Snyder. 1995. "Democratization and the Danger of War." *International Security* 20:5–38.

Mansfield, Edward D., and Jack Snyder. 2002. "Democratic Transitions, Institutional Strength, and War." *International Organization* 56:297–337.

Mansfield Edward D., and Etel Solingen. 2010. "Regionalism." *Annual Review of Political Science* 13:145–64.

Marshall, Monty G., Ted Robert Gurr, and Keith Jaggers. 2010. *Polity IV Project: Political Regime Characteristics and Transitions, 1800–2009: Dataset Users' Manual.* Vienna, VA: Center for Systemic Peace.

Martin, Lisa L. 1994. "Heterogeneity, Linkage, and Commons Problems." *Journal of Theoretical Politics* 6:473–93.

Martin, Lisa L. 2000. *Democratic Commitments: Legislatures and International Cooperation.* Princeton: Princeton University Press.

Martin, Lisa L., and Beth A. Simmons. 1998. "Theories and Empirical Studies of International Institutions." *International Organization* 52:729–57.

Mattli, Walter. 1999. *The Logic of Regional Integration: Europe and Beyond.* Cambridge: Cambridge University Press.

McDonald, Patrick J. 2007. "The Purse Strings of Peace." *American Journal of Political Science* 51:569–82.

McDonald, Patrick J. 2009. "The Invisible Hand of Peace: Capitalism, the War Machine, and International Relations Theory." Cambridge: Cambridge University Press.

Mearsheimer, John J. 1990. "Back to the Future: Instability in Europe after the Cold War." *International Security* 15:5–56.

Mearsheimer, John J. 1994/95. "The False Promise of International Institutions." *International Security* 19:5–49.

Melissen, Jan. 2003. "Summit Diplomacy Coming of Age." Discussion Papers in Diplomacy 86. The Hague: Netherlands Institute of International Relations Clingendael.

Mendoza, Miguel R. 1999. "Dealing with Latin America's New Regionalism." In *Trade Rules in the Making: Challenges in Regional and Multilateral Negotiations,* edited by Miguel Rodriguez Mendoza, Patrick Low, and Barbara Kotschwar, 81–105. Washington, DC: Organization of American States and Brookings Institution Press.

Miller, Benjamin. 2001. "Hot War, Cold Peace: International-Regional Synthesis." In *War in a Changing World,* edited by Zeev Maoz and Azar Gat, 93–141. Ann Arbor: University of Michigan Press.

Mitchell, Sara McLaughlin, and Paul R. Hensel. 2007. "International Institutions and Compliance with Agreements." *American Journal of Political Science* 51:721–37.

Mitrany, David. 1946. *A Working Peace System: An Argument for the Functional Development of International Organization.* London: Oxford University Press.

Mitzen, Jennifer. 2005. "Reading Habermas in Anarchy: Multilateral Diplomacy and Global Public Spheres." *American Political Science Review* 99:401–17.

Moravcsik, Andrew. 1998. *The Choice for Europe: Social Purpose and State Power from Messina to Maastricht.* Ithaca: Cornell University Press.

Morrow, James D. 1994. "Modeling the Forms of International Cooperation: Distribution versus Information." *International Organizations* 48:387–423.

Morrow, James D. 1999. "How Could Trade Affect Conflict?" *Journal of Peace Research* 36:481–89.

Morrow, James D. 2003. "Assessing the Role of Trade as a Source of Costly Signals." In *Economic Interdependence and International Conflict: New Perspectives on an Enduring Debate,* edited by Edward D. Mansfield and Brian M. Pollins, 89–95. Ann Arbor: University of Michigan Press.

Mortimer, Robert A. 1999. "The Arab Maghreb Union: Myth and Reality." In *State, Society, and Economic Transformation in the 1990s,* edited by Yahia H. Zoubir, 177–91.Gainesville: University Press of Florida.

Mousseau, Michael. 2000. "Market Prosperity, Democratic Consolidation, and Democratic Peace." *Journal of Conflict Resolution* 44:472–507.

Mytelka, Lynn K. 1973. "The Salience of Gains in Third-World Integrative Systems." *World Politics* 25:236–50.

Narine, Shaun. 1998a. "ASEAN and the Management of Regional Security." *Pacific Affairs* 72:195–214.

Narine, Shaun. 1998b. "Institutional Theory and Southeast Asia: The Case of ASEAN." *World Affairs* 161:33–47.

Narine, Shaun. 2002. *Explaining ASEAN: Regionalism in Southeast Asia.* Boulder: Lynne Rienner.

Narine, Shaun. 2008. "Forty Years of ASEAN: A Historical Review." *Pacific Review* 21:411–29.

Nazeer, Zubaidah. 2011. "Border Spat: 'Package Solution' Mooted; Thailand, Cambodia to Consider Approach Where Steps are Taken at Same Time to Resolve Crisis." *Straits Time* (Singapore), May 10.

Nesadurai, Helen E. S. 2003. *Globalisation, Domestic Politics, and Regionalism: The ASEAN Free Trade Area.* London: Routledge.

Nesadurai, Helen E. S. 2009. "ASEAN and Regional Governance after the Cold War: From Regional Order to Regional Community?" *Pacific Review* 22:91–118.

Nicholls, Shelton, Anthony Birchwood, Philip Colthrust, and Earl Boodoo. 2000. "The State of the Prospects for Deepening and Widening of Caribbean Integration." *World Economy* 23:1161–98.

Nicholls, Shelton, Garnett Samuel, Philip Colthrust, and Earl Boodoo. 2001. "Open Regionalism and Institutional Developments among the Smaller Integration Schemes of CARICOM, the Andean Community and the Central American Common Market." In *Regional Integration in Latin America and the Caribbean: The Political Economy of Open Regionalism,* edited by Victor Bulmer-Thomas, 141–64. London: Institute of Latin American Studies.

North, Douglass. 1990. *Institutions, Institutional Change, and Economic Performance.* New York: Cambridge University Press.

North, Douglass, and Barry Weingast. 1989. "Constitutions and Commitment: The Evolution of Institutions Governing Public Choice in 17th-Century England." *Journal of Economic History* 49:803–32.

Ntumba, Luaba Lumu. 1997. "Institutional Similarities and Differences: ECOWAS, CEEAC, and PTA." In *Regional Integration and Cooperation in West Africa: A Multidimensional Perspective,* edited by Real Lavergne, 303–20. Ottawa: Africa World Press and International Development Research Centre.

Nye, Joseph S. 1971. *Peace in Parts: Integration and Conflict in Regional Organization.* Boston: Little, Brown.

OECD (Organization for Economic Cooperation and Development). 1993. *Regional Integration and Developing Countries.* Paris: OECD.

Oneal, John R., and Bruce M. Russett. 1999. "The Kantian Peace: The Pacific Benefits of Democracy, Interdependence, and International Organizations, 1885–1992." *World Politics* 52:1–37.

Osava, Mario. 2008. "Latin America: Mill Conflict Continues to Delay Integration." *Inter Press Services,* January 3.

Osman, Salim. 2009. "Anger over Ambalat, Runaway Wife; Territorial Feud, Abuse Claim against Kelantan Prince Stir Nationalism." *Straits Time* (Singapore), June 4.*Panafrican News Agency.* 2001. "Sub-Regional Integration Runs out of Inspiration." February 24.

Ostrom, Elinor, and James M. Walker. 1991. "Communication in a Commons: Cooperation without External Enforcement." In *Laboratory Research in Political Economy,* edited by Thomas R. Palfrey, 287–322. Ann Arbor: University of Michigan Press.

Oye, Kenneth A. 1986. "Explaining Cooperation under Anarchy: Hypotheses and Strategies." In *Cooperation under Anarchy,* edited by Kenneth A. Oye, 1–24. Princeton: Princeton University Press.

Ozeki, Hiromichi. 2007. "Development of De Facto Economic Integration in East Asian Trade." In *Deepening Economic Integration: The ASEAN Economic Community and Beyond,* edited by Hadi Soesastro, 24–44. Jakarta: Economic Research Institute for ASEAN and East Asia.

Page, Sheila. 2000a. "Intensity Measures for Regional Groups." In *Regions and Development: Politics, Security, and Economics,* edited by Sheila Page, 67–89. London: Frank Cass.

Page, Sheila. 2000b. *Regionalism among Developing Countries.* London: MacMillan.

Page, Sheila, and Sanoussi Bilal. 2001. "Regional Integration in Western Africa: Report Prepared for and Financed by the Ministry of Foreign Affairs, the Netherlands." Overseas Development Institute, London.

Parsons, Craig. 2003. *A Certain Idea for Europe.* Ithaca: Cornell University Press.

Payne, Anthony. 1994. "The Politics of Regional Cooperation in the Caribbean: The Case of CARICOM." In *The Political Economy of Regional Cooperation: Comparative Case Studies,* edited by W. Andrew Axline, 72–104. Madison: Fairleigh Dickinson University Press.

Peck, Connie. 2001. "The Role of Regional Organizations in Preventing and Resolving Conflict." In *Turbulent Peace: The Challenges of Managing International Conflict,* edited by Chester A. Crocker, Fen Osler Hampson, and Pamela Aall, 561–83. Washington, DC: United States Institute of Peace Press.

Peou, Sorpong. 2002. "Realism and Constructivism in Southeast Asian Security Studies Today: A Review Essay." *Pacific Review* 15:119–58.

Peterson, Erik R. 1988. *The Gulf Cooperation Council: Search for Unity in a Dynamic Region.* Boulder: Westview.

Pevehouse, Jon C. 2005. *Democracy from Above: Regional Organizations and Democratization.* Cambridge: Cambridge University Press.

Pevehouse, Jon C., Timothy Nordstrom, and Kevin Warnke. 2004. "The Correlates of War 2 International Governmental Organizations Data Version 2.0." *Conflict Management and Peace Science* 21:101–19.

Pevehouse, Jon C., and Bruce Russett. 2006. "Democratic International Governmental Organizations Promote Peace." *International Organization* 60:969–1000.

Poast, Paul. 2010. "(Mis)Using Dyadic Data to Analyze Multilateral Events." *Political Analysis* 18:403–25.

Poku, Nana. 2001. *Regionalization and Security in Southern Africa.* Hampshire: Palgrave Macmillan.

Polachek, Solomon W. 1980. "Conflict and Trade." *Journal of Conflict Resolution* 24:55–78.

Polachek, Solomon W., and Jun Xiang. 2010. "How Opportunity Costs Decrease the Probability of War in an Incomplete Information Game." *International Organization* 64:133–44.

Pollins, Brian M. 1989. "Does Trade Still Follow the Flag?" *American Political Science Review* 83:465–80.

Pollins, Brian M. 1996. "Global Political Order, Economic Change, and Armed

Conflict: Coevolving Systems and the Use of Force." *American Political Science Review* 90:103–17.

Pondi, Jean-Emmanuel. 2000. "Compensation for Weak Asymmetry in the Mali–Burkina Faso Conflict, 1985–1986." In *Power and Negotiation,* edited by I. William Zartman and Jeffery Z. Rubin, 203–24. Ann Arbor: University of Michigan Press.

Posner, Eric, and John Yoo. 2005. "Judicial Independence in International Tribunals." *California Law Review* 93:1–74.

Powell, Robert. 2006. "War as a Commitment Problem." *International Organization* 60:169–203.

Press-Barnathan, Galia. 2009. *The Political Economy of Transitions to Peace: A Comparative Perspective.* Pittsburgh: University of Pittsburgh Press.

Princen, Thomas. 1992. *Intermediaries in International Conflict.* Princeton: Princeton University Press.

Rauchhaus, Robert. 2006. "Asymmetric Information, Mediation, and Conflict Management." *World Politics* 58:207–41.

Raustiala, Kal, and Anne Marie Slaughter. 2002. "International Law, International Relations, and Compliance." In *Handbook of International Relations,* edited by Walter Carlsnaes, Thomas Risse, and Beth A. Simmons, 538–58. London: Sage.

Ravenhill, John. 1995. "Economic Cooperation in Southeast Asia." *Asian Survey* 35:850–66.

Ravenhill, John. 2008. "Fighting Irrelevance: An Economic Community with ASEAN Characteristics." *Pacific Review* 21:469–88.

Redmond, John. 1996. "From 'European Community Summit' to 'European Council': The Development and Role of Summitry in the European Union." In *Diplomacy at the Highest Level: The Evolution of International Summitry,* edited by David H. Dunn, 53–66. New York: Macmillan.

Reiter, Dan. 2003. "Exploring the Bargaining Model of War." *Perspectives on Politics* 1:27–43.

Rieger, Hans Christoph. 1985. *ASEAN Co-operation and Intra-ASEAN Trade.* Research Notes and Discussion Papers 57. Singapore: Institute of Southeast Asian Studies.

Ripsman, Norrin M., and Jean-Marc F. Blanchard. 1996/97. "Commercial Liberalism under Fire: Evidence from 1914 and 1936." *Security Studies* 6:4–50.

Risse, Thomas. 2000. "'Let's Argue!': Communicative Action in World Politics." *International Organization* 54:1–39.

Robson, Peter. 1987. "The West African Economic Community." In *International Economic Integration,* edited by Ali M. El-Agraa, 190–219. London: Macmillan.

Ropivia, Marc-Louis. 1999. "Failing Institutions and Shattered Space: What Regional Integration in Central Africa?" In *Regionalisation in Africa: Integration and Disintegration,* edited by Daniel C. Bach, 125–27. Oxford: James Curry.

Rosecrance, Richard, and Peter Thompson. 2003. "Trade, Foreign Investment, and Security." *Annual Review of Political Science* 6:377–98.

Russett, Bruce, and John R. Oneal. 2001. *Triangulating Peace: Democracy, Interdependence, and International Organizations.* New York: Norton.

Russett, Bruce, John R. Oneal, and David R. Davis. 1998. "The Third Leg of the Kantian Tripod for Peace: International Organizations and Militarized Disputes, 1950–85." *International Organization* 52:441–67.

Rüland, Jürgen. 2003. "ASEAN Regionalism Five Years after the 1997/98 Financial Crisis: A Case of 'Co-operative Realism'?" In *Asia-Pacific Economic and Security Cooperation: New Regional Agendas,* edited by Christopher M. Dent, 53–71. New York: Palgrave Macmillan.

Sánchez Sánchez, Rafael A. 2009. *The Politics of Central American Integration.* New York: Routledge.

Sartori, Anne E. 2002. "The Might of the Pen: A Reputational Theory of Communication in International Disputes." *International Organization* 56:121–49.

Sartori, Anne E. 2005. *Deterrence by Diplomacy.* Princeton: Princeton University Press.

Savun, Burcu. 2008. "Information, Bias, and Mediation Success." *International Studies Quarterly* 52:25–47.

Schumpeter, Joseph A. 1951. *Imperialism and Social Classes.* New York: Augustus M. Kelley.

Schweller, Randall L. 2001. "The Problem of International Order Revisited." *International Security* 26:161–86.

Schweller, Randall L., and David Priess. 1997. "A Tale of Two Realisms: Expanding the Institutions Debate." *Mershon International Studies Review* 41:1–32.

Sequeira, Maricel, and Juan Ramon Duran. 1999. "Honduras-Nicaragua: Central America's Maritime Borders Heat Up." *Inter Press Services,* December 2.

Sesay, Amadu. 1990. "Obstacles to Intraunion Trade in the Mano River Union." In *West African Regional Cooperation and Development,* edited by Julius Emeka Okolo and Stephen Wright, 67–86. Boulder: Westview.

Severino, Rodolpho C. 2006. *Southeast Asia in Search of ASEAN Community: Insights from the Former ASEAN Secretary-General.* Singapore: Institute of Southeast Asian Studies.

Severino, Rodolpho C. 2007. "ASEAN beyond Forty: Towards Political and Economic Integration." *Contemporary Southeast Asia* 29:406–23.

Shannon, Megan. 2009. "Preventing War and Providing the Peace? International Organizations and the Management of Territorial Disputes." *Conflict Management and Peace Science* 26:144–63.

Signorino, Curtis S., and Jeffrey M. Ritter. 1999. "Tau-b or Not Tau-b: Measuring the Similarity of Foreign Policy Positions." *International Studies Quarterly* 43:115–44.

Simmons, Beth. 1998. "Compliance with International Agreements." *Annual Review of Political Science* 1:75–93.

Simmons, Beth. 1999. "See You in 'Court'? The Appeal to Quasi-Judicial Legal Processes in the Settlement of Territorial Disputes." In *A Road Map to War: Territorial Dimensions of International Conflict,* edited by Paul F. Diehl, 205–37. Nashville, TN: Vanderbilt University Press.

Simmons, Beth. 2003. "Pax Mercatoria and the Theory of the State." In *Economic In-*

terdependence and International Conflict: New Perspectives on an Enduring Debate, edited by Edward D. Mansfield and Brian M. Pollins, 31–43. Ann Arbor: University of Michigan Press.

Simmons, Beth. 2005a. "Forward-Looking Dispute Resolution: Ecuador, Peru, and the Border Issue." In *Peace versus Justice: Negotiating Forward- and Backward-Looking Outcomes,* edited by I. William Zartman and Victor Kremenyuk, 243–63. Lanham, MD: Rowman and Littlefield.

Simmons, Beth. 2005b. "Rules over Real Estate: Trade, Territorial Conflict, and International Borders as Institutions." *Journal of Conflict Resolution* 49:823–48.

Simmons, Beth. 2010. "Treaty Compliance and Violation." *Annual Review of Political Science* 13:273–96.

Simon, Sheldon W. 1982. *The ASEAN States and Regional Security.* Stanford: Hoover Institution Press.

Simon, Sheldon W. 1990. "ASEAN Security in the 1990s." In *ASEAN into the 1990s,* edited by Alison Broinowski, 111–37. London: Macmillan.

Singer, J. David, Stuart Bremer, and John Stuckey. 1972. "Capability, Distribution, Uncertainty, and Major Power War, 1820–1965." In *Peace, War, and Numbers,* edited by Bruce Russett, 19–48. Ann Arbor: University of Michigan Press.

Singer, J. David, and Michael Wallace. 1970. "Intergovernmental Organizations and the Preservation of Peace, 1816–1964: Some Bivariate Relationships." *International Organization* 24:520–47.

Smith, Alastair, and Allan Stam. 2003. "Mediation and Peacekeeping in a Random Walk Model of Civil and Inter-state War." *International Studies Review* 5:115–35.

Smith, James McCall. 2000. "The Politics of Dispute Settlement Design: Explaining Legalism in Regional Trade Pacts." *International Organization* 54:137–80.

Soesastro, Hadi. 2001. "ASEAN in 2030: The Long View." In *Reinventing ASEAN,* edited by Simon S. C. Tay, Jesus P. Estanislao, and Hadi Soesastro, 273–310. Singapore: Institute of Southeast Asian Studies.

Solidum, Estrella D. 1974. *Towards a Southeast Asian Community.* Quezon City: University of the Philippines Press.

Solingen, Etel. 1998. *Regional Orders at Century's Dawn: Global and Domestic Influences on Grand Strategy.* Princeton: Princeton University Press.

Solingen, Etel. 1999. "ASEAN, *Quo Vadis?* Domestic Coalitions and Regional Cooperation." *Contemporary Southeast Asia* 21:30–53.

Sopiee, Noordin. 1986. "ASEAN and Regional Security." In *Regional Security in the Third World: Case Studies from Southeast Asia and the Middle East,* edited by Mohammed Ayoob, 221–31. London: Croom Helm.

South China Morning Post. 1991. "ASEAN Fluidity Serves as Vital Regional Safety Valve." August 4.

Stein, Arthur A. 1993. "Governments, Economic Interdependence, and International Cooperation." In *Behavior, Society, and International Conflict,* edited by Philip Tetlock, Jo Husbands, Robert Jervis, Paul Stern, and Charles Tilly, 241–324. New York: Oxford University Press.

Stein, Arthur A. 2003. "Trade and Conflict: Uncertainty, Strategic Signaling, and Inter-state Disputes." In *Economic Interdependence and International Conflict: New Perspectives on an Enduring Debate,* edited by Edward D. Mansfield and Brian M. Pollins, 111–26. Ann Arbor: University of Michigan Press.

Stein, Arthur A., and Steven Lobell. 1997. "Geostructuralism and International Politics: The End of the Cold War and the Regionalization of International Security." In *Regional Orders: Building Security in a New World,* edited by David A. Lake and Patrick M. Morgan, 101–22. University Park: Pennsylvania State University Press.

Stinnett, Douglas M. 2007. "Depth, Compliance, and the Design of Regional Trade Institutions." Paper presented at the annual meeting of the Midwest Political Science Association, Chicago IL, April 12–15.

Stinnett, Douglas M., Jaroslav Tir, Philip Schafer, Paul F. Diehl, and Charles Gochman. 2002. "The Correlates of War Project Direct Contiguity Data, Version 3." *Conflict Management and Peace Science* 19:58–66.

Stone Sweet, Alec, and Wayne Sandholtz. 1998. "Integration, Supranational Governance, and the Institutionalization of the European Polity." In *European Integration and Supranational Governance,* edited by Wayne Sandholtz and Alec Stone Sweet, 1–26. New York: Oxford University Press.

Stubbs, Richard. 2000. "Signing on to Liberalization: AFTA and the Politics of Regional Economic Cooperation." *Pacific Review* 13:297–318.

Stulberg, Joseph B. 1987. *Taking Charge: Managing Conflict.* Lexington, MA: Lexington Books.

Sukma, Rizal. 2008. "Thai-Cambodia Row a Slap in the Face of ASEAN Charter." *Jakarta Post,* October 21.

Suriyamongkol, Marjorie L. 1988. *Politics of ASEAN Economic Co-operation: The Case of ASEAN Industrial Projects.* Singapore: Oxford University Press.

Swann, Dennis. 1996. *European Economic Integration: The Common Market, European Union, and Beyond.* Cheltenham: Edward Elgar.

Taccone, Juan J., and Uziel Nogueira. 2002. *CARICOM Report No. 1.* Buenos Aires: Institute for the Integration of Latin America and the Caribbean.

Takirambudde, Peter. 1999. "The Rival Strategies of SADC and PTA/COMESA in Southern Africa." In *Regionalisation in Africa: Integration and Disintegration,* edited by Daniel C. Bach, 151–58. Oxford: James Curry.

Tan, Andrew. 2000. *Intra-ASEAN Tensions.* London: Royal Institute of International Affairs.

Tan, Andrew. 2001. *Malaysia–Singapore Relations: Troubled Past and Uncertain Future?* Hull: Centre for South-East Asian Studies and Institute of Pacific Asia Studies, University of Hull.

Tarrow, Sidney. 1995. "Bridging the Quantitative-Qualitative Divide in Political Science." *American Political Science Review* 89:471–74.

Tay, Simon S. C. 2001. "Institutions and Processes: Dilemmas and Possibilities." In *Reinventing ASEAN,* edited by Simon S. C. Tay, Jesus P. Estanislao, and Hadi Soesastro, 243–72. Singapore: Institute of Southeast Asian Studies.

Thompson, Alexander. 2006. "Coercion through IOs: The Security Council and the Logic of Information Transmission." *International Organization* 61:1–34.

Thompson, Alexander. 2009. *Channels of Power: The UN Security Council and U.S. Statecraft in Iraq.* Ithaca: Cornell University Press.

Tollison, Robert D., and Thomas D. Willett. 1979. "An Economic Theory of Mutually Advantageous Issue Linkages in International Negotiations." *International Organization* 33:425–49.

Tongzon, Jose L. 1998. *The Economies of Southeast Asia: The Growth and Development of ASEAN Economics.* Cheltenham: Edward Elgar.

Touval, Saadia, and I. William Zartman. 2001. "International Mediation in the Post–Cold War Era." In *Turbulent Peace: The Challenges of Managing International Conflict,* edited by Chester A. Crocker, Fen Osler Hampson, and Pamela Aall, 427–43. Washington, DC: United States Institute of Peace Press.

Treib, Oliver. 2008. "Implementing and Complying with EU Governance Outputs." *Living Reviews in European Governance* 3:4–30.

Tuan, Hoang Anh. 1996. "ASEAN Dispute Management: Implications for Vietnam and an Expanded ASEAN." *Contemporary Southeast Asia* 18:61–80.

Union of International Associations. 2000. *Yearbook of International Organizations, 1999/2000.* 36th ed. Munich: K. G. Saur.

United Nations Conference on Trade and Development. 1996. *Handbook of Economic Integration and Cooperation Groupings of Developing Countries.* Vol. 1, *Regional and Subregional Economic Integration Groupings.* Geneva: United Nations.

United Nations Conference on Trade and Development. 2006. *Investment Provisions in Economic Integration Agreements.* New York: United Nations.

Underdal, Arild. 1998. "Explaining Compliance and Defection: Three Models." *European Journal of International Relations* 4:5–30.

Urpelainen Johannes. 2011. "The Enforcement-Exploitation Tradeoff in International Cooperation between Weak and Powerful States." *European Journal of International Relations* 17 (4): 631–53.

Vatikiotis, Michael. 2008. "The Faltering Asean Way." *Straits Time* (Singapore), October 28.

Vatikiotis, Michael. 2009. "Managing Armed Conflict in Southeast Asia: The Role of Mediation." *Southeast Asian Affairs* 36:28–35.

Väyrynen, Raimo. 2003. "Regionalism: Old and New." *International Studies Review* 5:25–51.

Victor, David G., Kal Raustiala, and Eugene Skolnikoff. 1998. "Introduction and Overview." In *The Implementation and Effectiveness of International Environmental Commitments,* edited by David G. Victor, Kal Raustiala, and Eugene Skolnikoff, 1–46. Cambridge, MA: MIT Press.

Visser, Dean. 1997. "Singapore-Malaysia Row an ASEAN Acid Test?" *Deutsche Presse-Agentur,* June 9.

Waltz, Kenneth N. 1970. "The Myth of National Interdependence." In *The International Corporation,* edited by Charles Kindleberger, 205–23. Cambridge, MA: MIT Press.

Waltz, Kenneth N. 1979. *Theory of International Politics.* New York: McGraw-Hill.

Wæver, Ole. 1998. "Integration as Security: Constructing a Europe at Peace." In *Atlantic Security: Contending Visions,* edited by Charles A. Kupchan, 45–63. New York: Council on Foreign Relations.

Wallander, Celeste A., and Robert O. Keohane. 1999. "Risk, Threat, and Security Institutions." In *Imperfect Unions: Security Institutions over Time and Space,* edited by Helga Haftendorn, Robert O. Keohane, and Celeste Wallander, 21–47. Oxford: Oxford University Press.

Weatherbee, Donald E. 1995. "The Foreign Policy Dimensions of Subregional Economic Zones." *Contemporary Southeast Asia* 16:421–32.

Webber, Douglas. 2003. "Two Funerals and a Wedding? The Ups and Downs of Regionalism in East Asia and Asia-Pacific after the Asian Crisis." In *Comparative Regional Integration: Theoretical Perspectives,* edited by Finn Laursen, 125–57. Aldershot: Ashgate.

Weilemann, Peter R. 2000. "The Summit Meeting: The Role and Agenda of Diplomacy at Its Highest Level." *NIRA Review* 7, no. 2:16–20.

Wendt, Alexander. 1999. *Social Theory of International Politics.* Cambridge: Cambridge University Press.

World Bank. 2000. *Trade Blocs: A World Bank Policy Research Report.* New York: Oxford University Press.

Yarbrough, Beth, and Robert Yarbrough. 1992. *Cooperation and Governance in International Trade: The Strategic Organizational Approach.* Princeton: Princeton University Press.

Yarbrough, Beth, and Robert Yarbrough. 1997. "Dispute Settlement in International Trade: Regionalism and Procedural Coordination." In *The Political Economy of Regionalism,* edited by Edward D. Mansfield and Helen V. Milner, 134–63. New York: Columbia University Press.

Yew, Lee Kuan. 2000. *From Third World to First: The Singapore Story, 1965–2000.* New York: HarperCollins.

Yoshimatsu, Hidetaka. 2006. "Collective Action Problems and Regional Integration in ASEAN." *Contemporary Southeast Asia* 28:115–40.

Young, Oran R. 1967. *Intermediaries: Third Parties in International Crises.* Princeton: Princeton University Press.

INDEX

Note: Page numbers in italics indicate tables and figures.

Acharya, Amitav, 49, 51, 57, 93, 172–73
ad hoc versus serial regional conferences,
34–38, 213n20. *See also* high-level officials
variable theorization
Adler, Emanuel, 51
AEC (ASEAN Economic Community), 175.
See also ASEAN (Association of Southeast
Asian Nations)
affinity alliances variable, 103, 136, 148, 201,
217n14, 219n14
affinity UN variable, 103, 106, 111, 136, 148,
219n14
Afghanistan, *61*, 94
Africa: African Development Bank and, 69,
77, 78, 79, 80; Central, 94, 102–3, 135; design features and relationships of REOs in,
87, 88; East African Community and, 26;
institutional independence of REOs and,
88; monetary integration and macroeconomic coordination indicators in, 70;
power concentration in regions and, 2; regional institutionalization research design
and, 94; regional institutionalization variation assessment in, 85, 86, 216nn29–30;
South, 2; sub-Saharan, 1, 65, 94, 98–99;
West, 102–3. *See also specific countries; and
specific REOs*
AFTA (ASEAN Free Trade Area), 170–73,
175–76, 190. *See also* ASEAN (Association
of Southeast Asian Nations)
Algeria, 34, *61*, 94
AMM (annual ministerial meeting), 165. *See
also* ASEAN (Association of Southeast
Asian Nations)
AMU (Arab Maghreb Union), 25, 34, *61*, 72,
74, 83–84, 124, 138
ANCOM (Andean Community): coding and

data set for comparison of REOs and, 78;
corporate bureaucracy and, 74; customs
unions and, 68; (non)effect of militarized
disputes on high-level officials variable
and, 138–39; future benefits in scope of
economic activity and, 25; independent regional bureaucracies and, 42; large-*N* qualitative analysis and, *113*, 114, 115–16, 118,
197; movement of services and, 69; organization of, 4; overview of, *61*; regional bureaucracy as pacifying and, 41; regional institutionalization variation assessment in,
83; sectoral harmonization and cooperation indicators and, 70; trade liberalization
indicators and, 68; vulnerability interdependence in scope of economic activity
and, 28
Andean region: Andean Court of Justice and,
45, 46; interdependence and constraint of
violent conflicts in, 212n10; vulnerability
interdependence in scope of economic activity in, 212n10
annual ministerial meeting (AMM), 165. *See
also* ASEAN (Association of Southeast
Asian Nations)
APEC (Asia-Pacific Economic Cooperation),
60, 215n11. *See also* ASEAN (Association of
Southeast Asian Nations)
Arab Maghreb Union (AMU), 25, 34, *61*, 72,
74, 83–84, 124, 138
areas and indicators: bargaining power indicators and, *63*, 71; capital and investment
movement indicators and, *63*, 65–67, 69,
80; customs unions indicators and, *63*, 68;
labor movement indicators and, *63*, 69;
monetary integration and macroeconomic
coordination indicators and, *63*, 70, 214n8;

ECO (Economic Cooperation Organization):
coding and data set for comparison of
REOs and, 78; dependent variable in regional institutionalization research design
and, 98, *98;* large-*N* qualitative analysis
and, 117; organization of, 4; overview of,
61; regional institutionalization research
design and, 94; regional institutionalization
variation assessment and, 86; scope of economic activity of, 25; sectoral harmonization and cooperation indicators and, 70
Economic Commission for Africa, 78, 86
economic interdependence: ASEAN and,
198–99; control variables and, 133, 135;
overview of, 23; pacifying effects and,
22–24, 56, 194, 212n5; regional, 1, 9–10, 17,
100; regional institutionalization and,
135–36, 144; regional institutionalization
research design results and, 108–10, 194;
REOs and, 106; trade share variable and,
100
economic scope. *See* scope of economic activity
ECOWAS (Economic Community of West
African States): dependent variable in regional institutionalization research design
and, 97; design and scope of economic activity, 89; design features and relationships
in, 89; high-level officials variable in relation to REO variation, 72; institutional independence, 129; labor and cross-border
movement of workers, 69; large-*N* qualitative analysis, 117; monetary integration
and macroeconomic coordination indicators and, 70; overview of, *62;* regional bureaucracy as pacifying and, 40–42; regional
institutionalization variation assessment
and, 83, 86; REOs defined and, 1, 59–60;
scope of economic activity, 129
ECSC (European Coal and Steel Community), 7, 12, 21–22, 212n4
Ecuador, 25, 55, *61,* 94, 115, 139, 218n24
EFTA (European Free Trade Association), 4,
61, 71, 88, 98, *98,* 116, 216n29
Eilstrup-Sangiovanni, Mette, 21–22, 212n4
El Salvador, *61,* 114
endogeneity: demand-side views and, 52,
56–57, 117; institutional design analysis
and, 151, 152–53; international institutions
(non)effects on violent conflicts hypothesis
[H0] and, *19,* 54; overview of, 18–19, 52,

195; regional institutionalization variation
assessment and, 200–201; regional institutions' peace promotion and, 7, 9, 11–12;
Southeast Asian REOs' effects on conflicts
and, 54, 156, 186–87; supply-side views
and, 52, 53–57, 117, 214n31. *See also* regional institutional design and conflict effects theorization
Eritrea, *62,* 94, 216n5
estimation technique, 95–96, 216nn1–3. *See
also* independent variables in research design
Ethiopia, *62,* 94, 216n5
EU (European Union): ad hoc versus serial
regional conferences in, 36–37; bargaining
power indicators in, 71; capital and investment movement in, 69; customs unions
and, 68; dependent variable in regional institutionalization research design and, 99;
design features and relationships of REOs
in, 129; DSMs' nonpacifying effect in, 46;
future benefits in scope of economic activity in, 25; implemented scope and, 214n3;
institutional studies and, 13; issue linkage
with scope of economic activity in, 26; labor movement in, 69; large-*N* qualitative
analysis and, 116–17; mitigation of frictions between members and, 3; overview
of, *61;* regional bureaucracy as pacifying in,
41; regional institutionalization research
design and, 93, 94; regional institutionalization research design results and, 107–8;
regional institutionalization variation assessment in, 84, 85, 216n29; REOs defined
and, 1; scope of economic activity and social opportunity costs in, 29; sectoral harmonization and cooperation indicators in,
70; socialization mechanism and, 50–51;
supply-side views for endogeneity of regional institutionalization and, 53–54. *See
also* European region and Western Europe
European Free Trade Association (EFTA), 4,
61, 71, 88, 98, *98,* 116, 216n29
European region and Western Europe: European Court of Justice and, 46; interdependence and constraint of violent conflicts in,
212n10; monetary integration and macroeconomic coordination indicators in, 70;
regional institutionalization research design and, 94; security communities and, 51;
socialization mechanism and, 51; vulnera-

Printed and bound by CPI Group (UK) Ltd, Croydon, CR0 4YY

16/04/2025

14658542-0004